The
Mystery
of the
Princes

By the same author:

Thomas Paine: His Life, Work and Times
Wilkes: 'A Friend to Liberty'
Artists and Writers in Revolt: the Pre-Raphaelites
Bernard Shaw : Man and Writer
etc.

The Mystery
of the
Princes

An Investigation
into a
Supposed Murder

Audrey Williamson

Academy
Chicago
Publishers

Copyright © Audrey Williamson 1978

First published 1978
This edition first published in the U.S.A. 1986
  Academy Chicago Publishers
  425 North Michigan Avenue
  Chicago, IL. 60611

ISBN 0 89733 208 3

Printed in Great Britain

Contents

Illustrations

"History will tell lies, as usual."

General John Burgoyne in
The Devil's Disciple by
G. Bernard Shaw.

Prologue
The Building of a Legend:
A Critical Study of Sources

History is made, and is being made all the time; but it is not recorded with anything like the same degree of accuracy. It becomes subject to the shifting patterns of human thought and memory, and of social and moral attitudes; to the dictates of its own time in propaganda and interpretation, and in later periods to gaps in documentation or the proliferation of conflicting material.

Chronicles and accounts will vary, often quite widely, even if written at the time or within living memory of the events. Those of us whose memories go back half a century — say to the age of fifteen when the mind is quite mature enough to grasp certain political and social backgrounds — know that reports of those times by younger people who were not present can be often surprisingly inaccurate, and not only in minor details. Without reference back, our own memories too can be faulty. World War II is already a battleground of literary controversy, both inside Germany and among the Allies; the Crossman Diaries, one man's account of Cabinet meetings he attended, are far from being accepted as totally accurate by others also present; and who killed President Kennedy, or what body of dissidents planned his assassination, may well prove as long a matter for argument as who murdered the Princes in the Tower or if, indeed, they were murder - ed at all. Not even modern recording methods of film and television have eliminated inaccuracy and discussion; for it is well known that the camera can lie, and editing, selection and accompanying narrative may be used to alter the picture and limit breadth of vision. The slant can still be that of the director or writer, while state documents even in our time are not all released within generations.

If difference of opinion on historical fact and analysis, both during and after the event, can be highly subjective in periods of war, it is even more so in the case of civil war, when ideologies tend to rouse the most passionate partisanship, and clashes of personality. It was so during the civil war and brief commonwealth of the seventeenth century, and it was so during almost all the last century of the middle ages, when the succession to the English throne became a fluctuating contest between Lancastrian and Yorkist claimants, which was not really ended by the new dynasty of the Tudors. The last serious Yorkist descendant, the old Countess of Salisbury, daughter of "false, fleeting, perjur'd Clarence" of three reigns before, was executed in the reign of Henry VIII. And it has not without perception been pointed out that the seeds of the destruction of the Stuarts were sown by Henry VII, who to establish his Tudor-Lancastrian dynasty "by right of conquest", against continued Yorkist revolt, resorted to means of strengthening the monarchy which ended in the "Divine Right of Kings", the extinction of the Tudor and Stuart line, and the only English bloodless "revolution", that of 1688.

If history can be distorted by partisanship in times of civil war, truth is likely to be even more suppressed when a new dynasty, at the end of it, is established "by right of conquest". What happened to the reputation of King Richard III after the enthronement of his conqueror, King Henry VII, can arguably be compared with what might have happened to those of Sir Winston Churchill and his government supporters, as well as English historical records of the period, had Hitler and his Nazi régime triumphed in World War II, and established a Quisling-style cabinet after a German occupation. Yet in this case the obliteration of records would have been far more difficult, for we live in an age of swift world communication, the press, radio and television. A monarch at the end of the fifteenth century had an easier task; there were no press or news media, few if any political pamphlets (printing had only very recently reached this country), and the common people literally could not read, and largely had little idea of what was happening in the corridors of power. The close followers of Richard III had been killed at Bosworth, executed, or fled abroad, and the rolls and acts of parliament, and local public records, which give a very much more liberal picture of his character and reign, were not available for public reading and only gradually re-discovered after the end of the Tudor régime.

This process of clarification is still proceeding, and remains the only totally reliable factual record. What survived at the time of Henry's reign were a few chronicles written directly after Henry took the throne, or during the reign of his son, when to tell anything like the whole truth could mean death if discovered, and when the rumours implanted by the new dynasty were well-established.

Yet partisanship in this case still runs surprisingly high, and although most historians now admit there are flaws in the traditional characterisation of Richard and his reign, their general view still seems to be moulded by the "chronicles", with all their personal animosities and points of view, their actual proven errors and their conflicting details. In part this 'traditional' attitude has been fostered by a kind of ingrained academic trade unionism, making for positive schizophrenia when the historian, as James Gairdner in his *History of the Life and Reign of Richard the Third* (revised edition 1898), is forced to admit a great deal of contrary evidence while clinging desperately to his view of a tyrant and a murderer, on the grounds of the infallibility of "tradition" in history ("I cannot but think the sceptical spirit a most fatal one in history"). [1]

Partly, too, it arises from curious historical "double standards", which fail to note that the "acts of tyranny" of which Richard is accused were actually practised on a far larger scale by his successor and others who followed or preceded him (the number of his executions is moderate when compared with those executed by Henry VII after revolts in the north and Cornwall, nor was he the only king to execute without trial, in a few cases of armed treason). Unfortunately, it is the "winning side" which calls the tune in the records of history; and the propaganda nature of their style is overlooked even by many historians.

It must be confessed that admirers of Richard III this century (such as Sir Clements R. Markham, K.C.B., and Philip Lindsay, both of whom took the firm and, on the evidence, equally untenable view that Henry VII murdered the two young princes) have romanticized Richard to an opposite extreme, no less presenting supposition and theory as fact (although Markham's was the more original and scholarly work, which Lindsay mainly repeated, nearly thirty years later, for popular consumption). By far the longest (over 1,000 pages in two volumes), most detailed and fully referenced life of Richard III, that of Caroline Halsted (1844), is slightingly mentioned by Gairdner and Kendall but seems never to have been read, studied or annotated by these or any major biographer of Richard; and she alone, while largely revising the traditional estimate of his character and government, has given so many details from contemporary and other sources, including Appendices of original documents to the number of over eighty, that subsequent biographers have suffered to some degree through not consulting her book and its references. She used not only the Harleian MSS, until then scarcely investigated, but also the Croyland and other chronicles, the Cotton and similar collected MSS, rolls of parliament, contemporary letters and local histories and records still often overlooked. She could not use material discovered and analysed since her time, but her vindication of Richard was based on considerable documentary evidence and did not include evading the open issue of the murder of the princes, or a necessary allowance for the ruthlessness of the times, and its effect on Richard's own character. She did not "romanticize", certainly not against factual evidence; but she seriously questioned, and her material, even allowing for Victorian expansiveness and moralizing, is still the most extensive brought together in one work on Richard.

She had been anticipated in her more tolerant estimate of Richard, as she knew, early in the seventeenth century by Sir George Buck, descendant of an official of Richard III's household and by Horace Walpole, an astute writer and antiquary experienced in the higher ranks of politics (his father was Sir Robert Walpole, a notable Prime Minister). As he wrote in a later supplement to his book, "whoever has seen anything of factions at all, will not form his opinion of a cause from the behaviour of the most illustrious persons on either side".[2] Of this by birth and experience Walpole was particularly qualified to judge. His *Historic Doubts on the Reign of Richard III*, published in 1768, was so popular (its notable readers included the Earl of Bolingbroke[3] and King Louis XVI, who translated it into French[4]) that on 2 February Walpole was writing in a letter to Lord Hailes: "I can attribute to nothing but the curiosity of the subject the great demand for it; for though it was sold publicly but yesterday and twelve hundred and fifty copies were printed, Dodsley has been with me this morning to tell me he must prepare another edition directly.''

Buck was the first to use the Croyland Chronicle, not then printed; and although he does not publish all his sources, his work is of interest not only for its vindication of Richard, but for some new material whose reliability seems far from dubious. Professor A.R. Myers, in his Introduction to a 1973 reprinting, comes to the conclusion that in spite of some occasional errors it is ''a work of scholarship, founded on a good deal of research into public records, at the Tower and at the House of Converts in Chancery Lane (on the site of the Public Record Office), and into works in private libraries like those of Sir Robert Cotton and the Earl of Arundel''.[5]

Certainly Buck wrote when living persons might remember great-grandparents who were alive at the time. His work was not published in his lifetime (he died in 1622) and eventually a great-nephew of the same name published a badly corrupted and shortened version of it (1646) as his own. As the original MS was severely damaged by fire later, the work of transcribing it is extremely difficult, but it has been undertaken by Dr Arthur Kincaid.

Walpole used Buck and other sources, and although these were not extensive by modern standards, and a few of his points have since been proved not to be valid, his most challenging questions have still not been answered. His book remains, in fact, a shrewd assessment of the case for Richard. He later published a Supplement of wit and unrepentant iconoclasm, as well as answers to two of his critics: after which he resigned from the Society of Antiquaries.

Paul Murray Kendall's work (1955), the last substantial biography of Richard (although Dr. Charles Ross is engaged on a new one), did re-open many questions and used evidence, such as Mancini and the medical analysis of the bones found in the Tower, not available to Halsted; but although at one point it seemed he was seriously considering the Duke of Buckingham as murderer of the princes (as, indeed, tentatively, have other commentators from Philip de Commines and the Dutch Divisie Chronicle onwards), he finally seems to have taken the traditional view of Richard as the boys' murderer, mainly on the rather dubious evidence of the bones. In many respects his work stands as the most modern and scholastic reassessment of Richard's life and reign, highly readable and historically interesting although sometimes its assumptions border on the fictional.

How, then, did the black legend of Richard arise? Its main propagandist (perhaps unintentionally) was Sir Thomas More, whose *History of the Reign of Richard III,* written in English and Latin and never completed, was published in various corrupt forms after his death, until the more credited publication by his nephew, William Rastell, in 1557. Its picture of a "crook-backed" monster (there is no contemporary evidence at all that Richard was thus deformed), complete with extensive and witty dialogue which provided Shakespeare with almost ready-made material, was far too long taken as strictly accurate by historians, although not only its fictionalised construction but its occasional questioning of its own material, as "old wives' tales", should have warned of its unreliability. Historians developed an unfortunate habit of repeating the stories and omitting More's own doubts and alternative suggestions, according to other stories he had heard from less hostile informants. It is now obvious it was an exercise in the new "humanist" idea of dramatising history, following classical models. (Its modern equivalent to some degree is "faction", a recently-coined word for freely dramatised documentary or history as presented in the media.)

More was, in fact, no special admirer of Henry VII: in the Parliament of Spring, 1504, he had opposed the Bill demanding aid of 3/15th on the plea of the marriage of the King's eldest daughter Margaret to the King of Scotland, using "such arguments and reasons there against that the King's demands were thereby clean overthrown".[6] But his book on Richard (on modern estimates) was written soon after 1514 (there is mention of Thomas Howard, "after Earl of Surrey", which suggests at least this year) and More had already hailed the coronation of the new young king, Henry VIII, in one of his English poems, in terms of unparalleled hope: "This day is the limit of our slavery, the beginning our freedom ..."* It was no moment to suggest any slur on the dynasty that bred

* This (p.130) and other More poems, including translations of the Latin ones, are included in the paperback edition of More's *History of King Richard III* edited by Richard S. Sylvester (Yale University Press, 1976). This book was on sale at the Sir Thomas More Exhibition at the National Portrait Gallery, 1977-8, commemorating the 500th anniversary of his birth, and I have therefore used it for reference, as the edition most easily available to the modern reader.

this hopeful young prince.

Paradoxically, More's hatred of tyranny, expressed in many of his poems, as well as his theoretic republicanism, incited his inflation of Richard III into horror-comic proportions, as a moral example, not a human portrait. This was the humanist style. One of his main informants (although he obviously had others) was almost certainly Richard's most virulent and persistent enemy, John Morton, Bishop of Ely and later (under King Henry VII, in whose elevation to the throne he was a major factor) both Chancellor and Archbishop of Canterbury. It was into Morton's household that More was put as a child and youth, in the manner of the times. It was long suggested that Morton, in fact, wrote More's MS: as early as 1596 Sir John Harrington (*Metamorphosis of Ajax*) claimed he had heard Morton was the author.[7] The theory is no longer seriously held and indeed much of More's text goes against it. It is more interesting to conjecture why More abandoned the history, leaving gaps for names and unaltered errors in these and other details. It was certainly not (as suggested by Sylvester and others) because of pressure of his civic duties, as immediately on abandoning it he must have begun work on his *Utopia*,[8] a description of a republican state which was enormously to influence lines of political thought in the future. Some of its ideas are still potent (in the agrarian society of Cuba, for instance, which under the Castro régime has a number of points of contact with More's Utopia).

Did More begin to sense he was finding out too much *contrary* to the Tudor legend (some of his informants obviously suggested doubts, which he repeated, about the murder of the princes), and therefore, under a Tudor dynasty which was still not without Yorkist dissidents, running into danger? More's attempt as long as possible to reconcile his conscience with the state, and keep his head, we all know, and it is not without significance that he so shaped *Utopia* that this communist state of No-Place, where there are equal shares for all, no religious persecution and no money, is described in his book by a traveller who has visited it. More himself in the dialogue is diplomatically cast as the occasional questioner of its virtues. He might well have begun to feel there was another side to Richard's story too, and this developed into a war between his integrity and his sense of safety and commitment to the Tudor monarchy, through the young, still idealised King, Henry VIII. His advice to Erasmus two years later was not to be hasty to publish, and carefully to avoid all occasions of giving offence.[9]

Historians patronised by King Henry VII and Henry VIII, such as Bernard André or Andreas and Polydore Vergil, were obviously obliged to support the new dynasty by blackening the man from whom Henry Tudor had taken the throne. It was reported of Vergil that many of his details were evidently founded upon authentic documents which have not survived the lapse of time, or which he may have wilfully destroyed — "a practice imputed to this foreigner".[10] More and more fictional details were added until Shakespeare, who automatically took as sources the later Tudor historical writers, Hall and Holinshed, cast Richard into the iron mould of the greatest tyrant and royal murderer in our history.

"The Lancastrian partialities of Shakespeare and a certain knack at embodying them have turned history upside down, or rather inside out", wrote Sir Walter Scott in *Rob Roy*. And as Surtees, in his *History of Durham,* put it: "the magic powers of Shakespeare have struck more terror to the soul of Richard, than fifty Mores or Bacons armed in proof." More's literary panache, wit and irony inevitably had admirers disinclined to question the material historically: Swift, not surprisingly, was particularly impressed by the irony.

Francis Bacon wrote his *Life of Henry VII* just outside Tudor times (in the reign of James I, who nevertheless gained the throne through his Tudor descent from Henry VII's daughter Margaret). Bacon was a distinguished lawyer and therefore quick and honest enough to note Richard was "a prince in military honour approved, jealous of the honour of the English nation; and likewise a good law-maker for the ease and solace of the common people".[11] Though Bacon subscribed to the legend of murderer, there was at last a flicker of doubt about the nature of Richard's reign and character. It had long ago flickered, too, in two works by Richard's contemporary, John Rous, "the monk of Warwick", who in a roll on the Earls of Warwick, known as the Rous Roll and not meant for publication or even Richard's own eyes, had given enthusiastic and extravagant testimony to King Richard and his beneficent reign. Yet Rous later produced his *Historiae Regum Angliae* which, being dedicated to Henry VII and needing his patronage, reversed the verdict with much genuine malice. It was Rous, having seen Richard during his lifetime at Warwick and not commented on any deformity, except "uneven shoulders, the left being lower than the right", who now made a remarkable contribution to biological research by ascertaining that Richard lay two years in his mother's womb, and was born with all his teeth and hair to his shoulders. This was later repeated, with a wry indication of uncertainty, by the ironic Sir Thomas More.

In our own time, 1936, C.A.J. Armstrong's discovery in the Lille archives of a MS entitled *The Usurpation of Richard III* (as he translated it), by an Italian-born visitor to this country from France, the Latin scholar Dominico Mancini, greatly revived the legend. For Mancini in his Preface makes clear he wrote his account in December, 1483, following a few months' period in England up to early July, 1483, when Richard had accepted the throne and had just been, or was about to be, crowned. It partly covered events of Edward IV's reign, some of which are garbled, and seems largely based on gossip, in many cases by Lancastrian sympathisers, including a repetition of the rumour that the boy King Edward V was in danger. "I have seen many men burst forth into tears and lamentations when mention was made of him after his removal from men's sight; and already there was a suspicion that he had been done away with. Whether, however, he has been done away with, and by what manner of death, so far I have not at all discovered." [12]

Notwithstanding Mancini's use of the word "suspicion", historians have pounced on this as *fact,* and confirmation of Richard's guilt. Actually, there was no doubt that at the time Mancini left England the princes were still alive, in the Royal apartments of the Tower. But his narrative is interesting because although it has some illuminating differences, and is by one close to the scene at the time, it is curiously similar to More's (written thirty years later) in some details and indeed also to the Third Continuation of the Croyland Chronicle (written at the monastery community of Croyland apparently early in 1486, some months after Henry VII took the throne).

Mancini's work has, however, been far too little questioned as a source, and indeed accepted as total fact on the murder and many other happenings by at least one recent "traditionalist" historian (Alison Hanham: *Richard III and his early historians, 1483-1535,* published 1975). This seems to me quite astonishing, if only because Mancini prefaces his report with a protest to his patron,

Angelo Cato, Archbishop of Vienne, who had asked for it, that "As a result of my solicitude for your requirements I shall undoubtedly expose myself in writing to the criticism of my readers. Wherefore you should not expect from me the names of individual men and places, nor that this account should be complete in all details".[13] He earlier emphasised this: "I had not sufficiently ascertained the names of those to be described, the intervals of time, and the secret designs of men in this whole affair."

In fact he is far from reliable where he can be checked, and his gossip often reveals a suspect and Lancastrian point of view. He never names his sources, perhaps for this reason (and another I shall discuss later). Like More he had humanist associations, and certainly fictionalised some details, even although he rarely resorts to dialogue. And it seems to me that the credentials of his patron, at whose urgent request this report was written, have been far too little scrutinised. Cato seems to have sent him to England on a spying mission of some kind: exactly what, is not clear, but it was certainly not complimentary to the English government as a whole. This mission could hardly have directly concerned Richard, as Mancini appears to have arrived in the last months of Edward IV's life, if not before, and the king's sudden death at the age of forty (More in his opening paragraph gets his age wrong by thirteen years!) was anticipated by no one.

Nevertheless, Cato, a physician and astrologer to Louis XI, was a close friend in Paris of Gui de Rochefort;[14] and it was immediately after Mancini's report was given to Cato that the Chancellor of France, Guillaume de Rochfort (Gui's brother, according to C.A.J. Armstrong, editor of Mancini's account)* made his famous speech against the English, accusing Richard III (for the first time openly), of murdering the two princes. Rumour at last became a "fact", but significantly in a speech aimed directly to discredit the English nation and their ways, and give comfort to Henry Tudor and the Lancastrian-Woodville exiles not far away. The fact that Richard III was believed by some to be aiming to renew the French wars may also have been a factor. His attitude at

---

* I nevertheless wonder if "Gui" was, in fact, really a contraction of "Guillaume", and it was actually the Chancellor whom Cato knew in Paris. In any case, the association cannot be without significance, politically.

the Treaty of Pecquiny, in 1475, when he openly resented his brother's acceptance of an annual pension from Louis XI as a bribe for taking his army back to England [15], had not endeared him to either the French king or his subjects, and a more warlike confrontation may well have been anticipated by the French now Richard had become king. The French, I suggest, later supported Henry Tudor because in his need for their aid in his invasion they knew he would be willing to call off the wars with France, which had wracked both countries for generations, when he became king. Much of Cato's use of Mancini suggests an Intelligence Service report of our own time.

As for Mancini himself, "it must be assumed", writes Armstrong, "that Mancini did not readily understand English, perhaps not at all" [16]. This in itself is extraordinary, considering the detailed and circumstantial narrative of "inside" politics and events that (in spite of his protests of inadequacy) he eventually gives. Some of it is not only similar to More and Croyland, it is also close to Vergil. One inevitably wonders if for some of it, at least, Mancini did not have a *written* source (presumably in Latin) to copy; and a common source has been tentatively suggested in respect of several chronicles. There are indications of the humanist style in all and it is worth noting that Mancini's close friend, the French humanist Robert Gaguin, was a patron of Erasmus and Gaguin's work was praised by Thomas More, Erasmus' great friend. The links between the humanist writers (and more are discussed later) may be tenuous, but they are there. In all cases the general attitude is Lancastrian, and once again Morton springs to mind.

Morton is strikingly praised by Mancini. "Now these men [Rotherham, Ely, Hastings] being in age mature, and instructed by long experience of public affairs, helped more than other councillors to form the King's [Edward IV's] policy, and besides carried it out" [17] ... "As for the bishop of Ely, he was of great resource and daring, for he had been trained in party intrigue since King Henry's time." If the last line seems slightly equivocal, the reader may remember it in references to Morton under another King Henry (the VII) later in this book.

It may be worth noting here that the Belgian-born medieval historian, Philip de Commines, also dedicated his Memoirs to Cato, Archbishop of Vienne, and he conspicuously takes the

Lancastrian line on English affairs. His work was written between 1488 and 1503. Another link with Cato's French spy ring seems indicated, especially as Commines mentions meeting and talking with Henry Tudor.[18] Commines was a politician closely attached to King Louis XI and is extraordinarily interesting on European affairs, described at first hand, but his comments on English national events are frequently inaccurate and based on gossip.

Whether Morton was in France at the time Mancini wrote is questionable. At the time of his escape during the Buckingham rebellion he "lyvyd in Flanders" (in Vergil's words) [19] and his biographer, R.I. Woodhouse (1895), does not make clear if and when he left later for Brittany or France, although he obviously helped Henry's cause and was in frequent touch with him. A MS life of Morton of 1610 is equally inexplicit. He could well have been an informant when Mancini was in London; it was very soon afterwards that Richard accused Morton, as one of his Council, of betraying its secrets to Henry Tudor. [20] The recognisable Morton "tone" can be discerned in Mancini as it can, indeed, in so many other works.

Among these I include the Third Continuation of the Croyland Chronicle.* Attempts have been made to ascribe this wholly to John Russell, Bishop of Lincoln. This I contest, and not only on the grounds that Russell was Richard III's Chancellor throughout his reign, obviously (from Richard's letters to him) trusted and valued by him, and highly unlikely even under the new régime to write so venomously of the "disgraceful" events and Parliament of the reign of the king he served, and for whose policies he must certainly take some responsibility. In fact Russell delivered the opening oration at Richard's Parliament, and there is another in MS which he proposed to give at an earlier convocation.

This slender and (on internal evidence) incredible hypothesis rests on a marginal note (not provably in the original MS which is not extant) made in Fulman's first published edition. This claims the anonymous Third Continuator was a doctor of canon law and a member of the King's Council (Morton, too, was a member of the Councils of Edward IV, Richard III and Henry VII, and a doctor

---

*The writer is usually (from Fulman's translation, 1684) described as the Second Continuator, but Third seems more correct and is labelled thus in the edition and translation I have used (see p.24)

of canon law). The marginal note also has been read to suggest that this same person was sent by the King as envoy to the Duke of Burgundy in 1471. In fact, Morton himself was the leader of a far more important and conspicuous mission to the Duke of Burgundy in 1474, and was also involved in earlier ones. It is true that Russell visited Croyland Abbey for a month in the period of ten days in 1486 in which the Third Continuator claims he wrote; but it was to officiate at a long and involved dispute on monastery lands which appears in full, written by or in the name of Russell, in the work of the succeeding (Fourth) Continuator, who claims he does not know the identity of the Third Croyland Continuator from whom he took up the tale. This legal document, drawn up by or for Russell, is in a complex and repetitive style far removed from the concise and condensed narrative of the Third Continuator. It has been suggested that only a person actually present could have narrated many of the council and political events of the reigns of Edward IV and Richard III described; but this would seem to be true at times of all the chronicles (*vide* Sidney Lee on Thomas More's *History* in the Dictionary of National Biography: "The tone is strongly Lancastrian, and often implies that the writer was a contemporary witness of some of the events described.")

Whole passages of the Croyland Third Continuator make use of Woodville and Lancastrian secret activities, in the south-west of England particularly, at which there is no probability that Russell, Richard's Chancellor, could have been present; and many of the criticisms (such as of Richard's wasting of King Edward IV's "treasure", said by Mancini and others have been largely spirited away by the Woodvilles) are not only inaccurate information but derogatory, as I said, to any high official of Richard's court and government. When eye-witnessing is involved (to a certain extent undeniable in all the near-contemporary chronicles), it is eye-witnessing frequently from a Lancastrian viewpoint, and passage after passage can be quoted to show this. *If* Russell was responsible, I agree with Dr. Pamela Tudor-Craig (Richard III Exhibition Catalogue, National Portrait Gallery, 1973) that Russell, in the position of Chancellor, which was the nearest medieval equivalent to Prime Minister, emerges as a highly unlikeable character. There is no historical evidence for this, or such a despicable *volte face:* unless, of course, Russell was throughout the reign a double agent, which seems to me hardly credible in his case. I have discussed this 'identification' further in the text.

It does seem possible that Russell wrote some information about the reigns of Edward IV and Richard III, in both of which he was officially involved, while staying at Croyland, and the Croyland writer embellished this from other sources. Morton and Margaret Beaufort, Henry VII's mother, both had local associations. Some years earlier Morton, always an active character, had as Bishop of Ely been responsible for a scheme to drain the fens and the cutting of a canal known as Morton's Leame between Peterborough and Wisbech: "the banks on the north of the river Nene and also that of the south of Morton's Leame were raised by the monks of the neighbourhood of S. Peter's, Crowland, Thorney, and Ely"[21]

As for Margaret Beaufort, the Third Continuator makes quite clear the need to propitiate her:

> "The second question was the one which concerned the people of Depying. Although these people, with a sort of innate frenzy, are always struggling to preserve their boundaries, still, what with the patience displayed by the said abbat Edmund and his monks, and the prudent counsel of the most illustrious mother of our lord the king, to whom the manor of Depying is well known to belong, the question has hitherto received such treatment, that, through God's protection, the monastery seems likely neither to lose its rights nor to incur the resentment of those more powerful persons, with whom it cannot place itself upon an equality." [22]

It is presumably to this that one owes the Croyland Continuator's unlikely depiction of Henry Tudor as "the glorious conqueror", receiving "the praises of all, as though he had been an angel sent down from heaven, through whom God had deigned to visit His people, and to deliver it from the evils with which it had hitherto, beyond measure, been afflicted". [23]

It is noticeable that the Croyland Chronicle also states of the Battle of Bosworth that "the earl of Richmond, together with his knights, made straight for king Richard".[24] It was, in fact, notorious that Henry took no part in the fighting, and it was Richard and his followers who lost their lives in making straight for *him*. It sounds to me like a mother's inflated account of her son's mythical heroic exploits: certainly not like that of one of Richard's principal ministers.

On the matter of the curious sense of *déja vu* one sometimes gets from reading the near-contemporary chronicles, I would only, as a writer, instance (Croyland): "Oh God! why should we any longer dwell on this subject, multiplying our recital of things so distasteful .... and so pernicious in their example"[25], and (More): "Oh good God, the blindness of our mortal nature!"[26] The moral posture, and the rhythm (including in Mancini, translated from the Latin), carry a recognisable echo. Moralizing is, of course, a feature of humanist historical writing. More was commenting on Hastings' blithe spirits and imperviousness to prophecies of doom on the day of his execution. It is one of the anomalies of his *History* that he should so emphasise superstitious portents. He may have merely been repeating classical precedents; but one cannot help remembering that Mancini's earlier account bears resemblances to More's, and it was written at the instigation of an astrologer to Louis XI. (There was to be a later connection between astrology and spying: it was from the device used by John Dee, Queen Elizabeth's Astrologer Royal, in signing his secret agent reports to Walsingham, that Ian Fleming took James Bond's "007".)

More's Latin poetry shows a conspicuously more sceptical outlook, including with regard to astrology. It makes nonsense of some of his supposed history of Richard III, although his basic preference for a republic to a monarchy (on the ground that a king cannot be curbed in tyranny, while in a senate there are always other senators to restrain) is symbolically implied in his emphasis on the wickedness and depredations of this particular king. One wonders how much, in prison and on the scaffold, his mind reverted to these early republican sentiments. Circumspection in politics had led More into strange paths. Long ago, when his son-in-law William Roper had remarked on the King's affection for him, More had shrewdly expressed his disillusion with Henry VIII with the words: "I may tell thee I have no cause to be proud thereof, for if my head could win him a castle in France, it should not fail to go."[27]

This preliminary analysis of the growth of the Richard III legend, and the often suspect nature or inter-dependence of the sources, seems to me necessary for any clear understanding of what follows. Some of the speculations are individual to myself. The sources will become plain in this investigation into a supposed murder, and they are listed at the end of the book. I should point out that I have used, not the Fulman edition of the Croyland Chronicle, but *Ingulph's History of the Abbey of Croyland* edited by Henry T. Riley (1854), which has different paging and translation, and which I could keep beside me while writing. The two volumes of the *Memoirs* of Philip de Commines, long in my possession, are also a nineteenth century edition, with a short biography and notes by Andrew R. Scoble (1855).

I have had access to a large amount of material (not only books but published and unpublished articles and lectures) in the library of the Richard III Society, whose quarterly journal, *The Ricardian,* edited by Peter Hammond, the Society's official researcher, is a thoroughly documented and valuable source of direct and peripheral material, unearthed by professional historians and amateur researchers. Some of this material has not, as far as I know, been used elsewhere.

In addition I am grateful to the Guilles-Allès Library of Guernsey for a copy of La Societé Guernesiaise Report and Transactions for the year 1956, Vol. XVI, Part II, which contains an important article on Sir Edward Brampton by Cecil Roth, D.Phil., F.R. Hist.S., a lifelong researcher into this subject; and to Mrs. Kathleen Margaret Drewe, who following an article of mine in the Sunday Times Magazine (11 March 1973), first drew my attention to the tradition in the Tyrell family which was repeated to her personally by her mother and grandmother, who lived at the Tyrell family home, Gipping Hall in Suffolk (Mrs. Drewe is directly descended from one of three French boys, refugees from the Revolution, adopted as sons and given the Tyrell name by a descendant of James Tyrell in the eighteenth century. Mrs. Drewe's grandmother obtained the story not only from her husband, but also from his mother, the daughter of the original French adopted son. It was said to be already a tradition of long standing in the family.)

This tradition, it seems to me, may well be very significant: at least it must now be given serious consideration among so many others. It directed me towards research into Tyrell wills and papers, kindly listed and provided by the Suffolk County Record Office, Ipswich branch. These seem not to have been studied before and a portion of Sir James Tyrell's will, with his signature, is published here for the first time.

It was after I had written my comments on the Mancini report in this chapter that I learned of, and was put in touch with, an ex-Foreign Office diplomat who had been working and lecturing along the same lines, but with the benefit of long experience of international statecraft and the style of Intelligence reports. I am particularly grateful therefore for the generous co-operation of J.A. Speares, whose study of Mancini and political aspects of Richard's reign valuably reinforce and supplement my own conclusions. Mr. Speares' own planned book on the subject "as an exercise in statecraft" should add to our knowledge and understanding.

I would like, too, to thank Isolde Wigram for much interesting correspondence, and Peter and Carolyn Hammond, of the Richard III Society, for assistance in reading the Tyrell wills and the generous loan of books and papers from the library. Miss M.M. Condon, of the Search Department, Public Record Office, has also been helpful on the subject of preservation of wills, as well as on bequests and possessions as they concern attainted traitors.

There is still more to be gleaned on this highly ambivalent subject, including, as Walpole suggested long ago, a thorough examination of Burgundian papers which might throw more light on the enigmatic character of Margaret, Duchess of Burgundy, and her relationship with her family, including her brother Richard III, Yorkists in exile and that still mysterious and not totally explained figure, Perkin Warbeck. The Harleian MSS 433, many of which have proved of such value on this period, are even now being transcribed and examined in full, and further revelations can be expected from them, as they may be from other MS discoveries in the future. It is hardly credible that only the Pastons, Stonors and Plumptons wrote letters that survived, among ordinary families. Other letters have been discovered and more doubtless will be. The apparent destruction of documents by interested parties is something that bedevils this case, and I have suggested that the appointment of Robert Morton as Master of the Rolls (in which John Morton had served before him) may not be unsignificant. Nevertheless, the Act of Richard's Parliament, Titulus Regius, finally escaped his successor's methodical efforts to destroy it and all records of it. Truth, as one of my predecessors on this subject wrote, is still "the daughter of time".

In the meantime, this book is a first full-length attempt, outside biographies of Richard where the space for it is limited, and

Josephine Tey's expert and popular but inevitably out-dated detective story, *The Daughter of Time* (which based its material on Markham's 1906 biography of Richard III), to correlate the extensive material on the period now available, some of it very recent, and discuss it from new angles as well as old.

This is still an unsolved murder mystery: but from so much accumulated material, new and old, a sounder and more detailed picture of Richard III, the central mystery of his reign, and the nature of his government should emerge. How much of the legend survives the proliferation of facts and suggestive details now uncovered I have left it open for the reader to decide.

NOTES & REFERENCES
Prologue
The Building of a Legend

1 Gairdner, p.x.

2 Complete Works, Vol. 5, p.206.

3 Walpole: *Reply to Dr. Milles:* Complete Works, p.221.

4 Louis' translation was sold at Sotheby's in 1949. Audrey Williamson: *Thomas Paine: His Life, Work and Times,* p.185.

5 *The History of the Life and Reigne of Richard III*, p.vii.

6. Sidney Lee: *Dictionary of National Biography.* Thomas More.

7 Ibid.

8 R.W. Chambers: *Thomas More.* pp.115-6. A.F. Pollard also points this out.

9 A.F. Pollard: *The Making of Sir Thomas More's Richard III.* p.238.

10 Plumpton Correspondence, p.xxiii.

11 Bacon, p.2. Halsted: *Richard III*, i.364.

12 *The Usurpation of Richard III* (1969 ed., C.A.J. Armstrong), p.93.

13 Ibid, p.57.

14 Ibid, Intro. by Armstrong, p.23.

15 Philip de Commines: *Memoirs*, i.277.

16 Mancini: *Usurpation*. Intro. by Armstong, pp.15-6.

17 Ibid. p.69.

18 Commines: *Memoirs*, i.396-7.

19 Vergil, pp. 205-7. *England Under the Yorkists*, p.133.

20 Buck, p.35.

21 R.I. Woodhouse: *The Life of John Morton*, pp.106-7.

22 Croyland Third Continuator, pp.507-8.

23 Ibid, pp.504-5.

24 Ibid, p.503.

25 Ibid, p.498.

26 More: *History of King Richard III* (ed. Sylvester), p.53.

27 Sylvester: Introduction, More's *History*, p.xvi.

I
Sons and Brothers

King Edward V, like his uncle and reputed murderer, Richard III, was born under an unlucky star. His father, King Edward IV, had at the time been forced into exile in Flanders, by the restoration of the gentle and mentally unstable King Henry VI by the Earl of Warwick ("the Kingmaker"). Warwick had formed an alliance with his old enemy, Henry's Queen, Margaret of Anjou, "an heroine virago of her time".[1] Warwick's defection from Edward, whom he had helped to place on the throne, had, whatever its causes (and they are not all psychologically clear), been supported by the temporary alienation from his family of the Duke of Clarence, second brother to Edward and the husband of Warwick's elder daughter, Isabel Neville. There is small doubt Clarence had his eye on the succession, and so had Warwick, through his daughter (he had no son). Although Margaret of Anjou fought like a tigress for her son, the young Prince Edward of Wales, as heir to the throne, his paternity by the saint-like Henry (who on his birth is said to have breathed a pious conviction that he was the son of the Holy Ghost) was questioned by at least some English subjects. The hatred between Warwick and Margaret had been, it seemed possible, only temporarily suppressed for a common purpose.

The family of York was a conspicuously united one, Clarence apart; and King Edward's younger brother, Richard, Duke of Gloucester, scarcely eighteen years old, had loyally chosen to share his exile with him. With them had gone Anthony, Lord Rivers, an ambitious, magnificent and scholarly brother of Edward's Queen, Elizabeth Woodville, who remained in England in sanctuary at

Richard, Duke of York (L) and Edward, Prince of Wales (later
Edward V)

The Burial of the Princes: from a print by Boydell.

Westminster. And there, on 2 November 1470, her son and heir, named Edward after his absent father, was born.

The Woodville marriage was to prove the treacherous rock on which the Yorkist succession finally foundered. The Queen, a young widow whose husband, Sir John Grey, had been killed on the Lancastrian side, had captivated Edward, then a youth of under twenty and some years her junior, and he had married her secretly when it seemed the only way to entice this cool and lovely widow, of the "gilt" hair, into his bed. Although her mother, Jacqueline, Countess of Bedford, had European royal connections, the match was considered beneath Edward's status as founder of a new dynasty, which his father, Richard, Duke of York, of royal descent, had missed achieving by only three months. The Duke of York was highly regarded for probity and capability, and when made Protector had indeed been moderate enough to waive his claim to the throne while Henry VI lived. He had been forced to reassert it by Margaret of Anjou's resumption of war, on behalf of her husband and son. He had been killed at the Battle of Wakefield in 1460, with his seventeen-year-old son Edmund, and his head placed on the walls of York, with a mockery crown of paper (or reeds). After defeating the Lancastrians at Towton, his son Edward had therefore ascended the throne which his father had so narrowly missed.

The son's fair personal beauty was much commented upon, and Edward, as dazzling as his emblem, the "Sun of York", responded with fervour to the women this handsome aspect attracted. He was over six feet tall (unlike his father whom dark, small, compact Richard of Gloucester was said to resemble) and only after years of over-indulgence ran to the corpulence which later sapped both his looks and his energy as a ruler. But his marriage, and his Queen's tireless exertions on behalf of her ambitious relatives, tarnished the gold of his natural popularity. Although constantly unfaithful to her, he yielded to her pressures in this, and with his easygoing nature (except when his throne and authority were challenged) carelessly built up resentments and jealousies around him which were to prove ominous in the future.

When, ten years after he ascended the throne, the Lancastrian winds of change blew him across the North Sea into temporary exile, in a state of dire poverty, the Queen had given him only daughters: the eldest of whom, Elizabeth of York, was herself to become a pawn in the chess-game of history. When he returned, with a handful of followers but immense panache and magnetic impact, it was, he said, only to reclaim his inheritance of York: a ruse adopted by Henry Bolingbroke, heir to Lancaster, when he returned from exile less than a century before and displaced the ill-starred Richard II as King Henry IV. Edward was no less capable of dissimulation, a lesson which some will say his young brother Richard, ten years his junior, may have quickly absorbed. On 11 April 1471 Edward entered London, master of his kingdom and the art of surprise. It was six months to the day since he had landed, a bedraggled exile, with his small band of followers near the Hague.

London was a principal jewel in his crown; and another awaited him at Westminster, his five-month old son and heir whom he now saw for the first time. He placed him and the Queen with his mother, Cecily, Duchess of York, in her house by the Thames, Baynard's Castle:[2] and set about the urgent business of finally assuring the safety of his kingdom. London had not resisted him, as the Common Council put it, because he "was hastening towards the city with a powerful army", and the inhabitants "were not sufficiently versed in the use of arms to withstand so large a force".[3] Edward was also popular there as a person, and in particular for his encouragement of trade and commerce: a raising of the merchants into prominence which was to bring about the eventual dissolution of the feudal baronage and elevation of the rich middle class into new importance in British history. To some of these merchants he already owed money, and their anticipation of repaid loans as well as (it was said) the entreaties of their ladies were no doubt also responsible for the warmth of Edward's reception.[4]

Warwick, however, though by-passed, was not defeated. His indolence always fired and transformed by necessity, Edward tarried not even for Easter in departing from the city with an army of some 9,000 men. With him went Richard of Gloucester and Anthony, Lord Rivers; and on Easter Sunday at the Battle of Barnet Warwick was slain, a kingmaker defeated by the man he had set on the throne, and betrayed.

The wavering Clarence had already been won back, uncertainly, to the Yorkist side. On 2 April he had met with Edward's army surging south towards London; and there Gloucester "and other

lords ... past often formally betweene the brothers, and urged them
in all respects, both religious and politicke,to prevent a quarrell so
ruinous and so scandalous to both''.[5] Richard's position as
mediator in reuniting the family had already been buttressed by
letters to Clarence from, among others, his mother and his sister,
Margaret of Burgundy, whose favourite brother Clarence was said
to be.[6] The perhaps home-sick Margaret's indomitable loyalty was
to play a not inconsiderable part in future Yorkist and even Tudor
history.

Edward IV, with Warwick dead and Clarence reconciled, was
still not in command of his kingdom. Queen Margaret had landed
at Weymouth with her son, Edward, Prince of Wales, on the day
that Warwick was killed.[7] Expecting to be greeted with the
Kingmaker's victory, the 'virago' reeled only momentarily from
this supremely ironic coincidence. Within no time at all she and her
son emerged from the sanctuary into which they had fled, and
joined a swelling army of Lancastrian supporters near Tewkesbury.

The young prince, seventeen years old (hardly a year younger
than Richard of Gloucester) took command of his father's army
and personally addressed the soldiers on his behalf.[8] It was a
moment of brief glory that was to turn, for his mother, to bitter
pain; for in the battle that followed not only were the Lancastrians
decisively defeated, but the prince on whom, after the unstable
Henry, all their hopes rested was slain.

Long after the event, and the supposed killing of his brother
Edward's sons, this death was to become the first dark murder
ascribed to Richard of Gloucester. Contemporary accounts make
no such accusation. The prince was, wrote the contemporary
Yorkist chronicler, "taken fleeing the townwards, and slain in the
field."[9] Warkworth, a Lancastrian authority of the time, also
claims "and there was slain in the field Prince Edward, which cried
for succour to his brother-in-law the Duke of Clarence" (p.18).
There is no hint even of this anti-Yorkist embroidery in the
contemporary account of Robert Cole, Canon of Llanthony. His
Rental of all the Houses in Gloucester, 1455, added in Appendix a
history of the Kings of England, 1478-9 and 1481-2, and his last
entry (p.125) on Henricus Sextus Rex Angliae reads:

"This Kyng tooke to his wyfe Margarete the Kyngus douztur of
Cicile, whit wham he had his sone Edward, Pryns of Wales, *that
aftur that he come from Fraunce with his moder with a gret ost*

*was sley at the Batel by syde Tewkesbur, the yere of Oure Lord
MCCCCLXXII.*

Although the date given is wrong, the section italicised was
written in Cole's hand but in a different ink. It was obviously
added after 1471: [10]

When Warwick defected to Queen Margaret, the pact had been
sealed by the betrothal of the prince to his younger daughter, Anne.
It would seem, partly from Queen Margaret's prudence while the
kingdom's future still hung in the balance, and distrust of
Warwick, and partly because both parties to the contract were so
young, the marriage was not consummated, although Anne had
been given much honour in France. Whether Clarence was actually
concerned in the young prince's death is unlikely, in view of the
contemporary account. Fabyan, a Lancastrian and prominent
City draper who wrote his London Chronicle in Henry VII's time,
but who was in London during Richard III's reign, began the
embroidery by stating the prince was taken to the King's tent and
"by the king's servants incontinently slain". [11] Sir George Buck
quotes from a Cotton MS to the effect that Richard was present but
merely stood by and did not intervene, because of his "attachment
to Anne". [12] If the tent story is not total legend, this is an
interesting sidelight on the knowledge that Richard was already in
love with Anne Neville (or her potential as an heiress of Warwick):
it could have been added to a fictional account from a more reliable
knowledge of Richard's attachment. Richard certainly received his
original knightly training in Warwick's household (an account
exists paying Warwick for his expenses on his behalf), and both he
and Anne were present as children at a banquet when the Earl's
brother, George Neville, Archbishop of York, visited the castle.

An Italian letter, at least, gives a sour picture of the character of
the slain prince, Edward. Writing three years before, the Milanese
ambassador had described how Edward "though only thirteen
years of age, already talks of nothing else but of cutting off heads
or making war". [13] Doubtless the 'virago's' training and influence
had been ferocious enough, although whether the prince retained
this character as he grew into young adulthood we cannot tell. On
Anne's actual feeling for him, if any, history is silent. Assuming
(and there is some reason for it) Richard's genuine devotion to
Anne Neville, it is indicative of his disciplined emotions and
steadfastness to his brother Edward that he resisted the temptation,

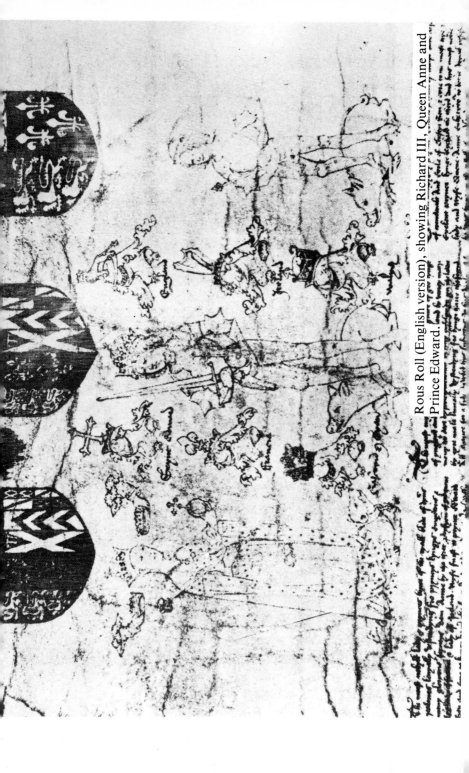

Rous Roll (English version), showing Richard III, Queen Anne and Prince Edward.

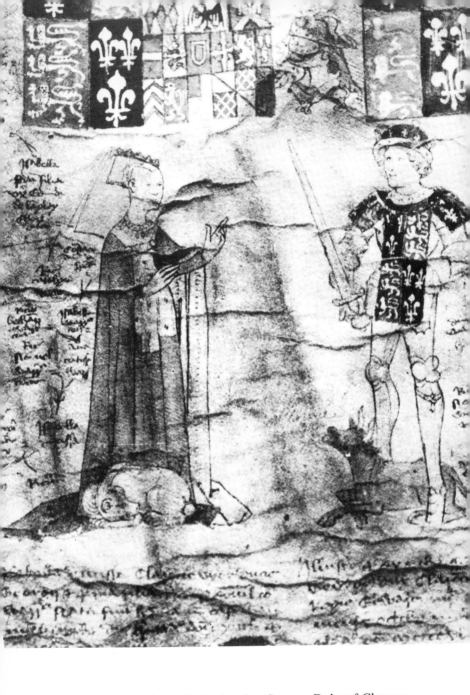

Rous Roll (later Latin version), showing George, Duke of Clarence and his wife Isabel.

unlike Clarence, to side with Warwick, even though this might have meant alliance with Anne, and a share in her inheritance (Warwick had made his two daughters his co-heirs). Clarence had been rewarded with the hand of her elder sister, and Warwick would probably have been eager enough to ensure his hold on the succession with a second line of defence. Both girls proved short-lived, and were probably known to tbe frail.

Breaking his word to the Abbot to spare those who had taken refuge in Tewkesbury Abbey, King Edward had them seized when he heard his bitter enemy, the Duke of Somerset, was within. Somerset and about a dozen others were tried before Richard, as Constable of England, and the Duke of Norfolk, Lord Marshal. [14] The Lancastrian leaders were immediately beheaded. Richard, at eighteen, was learning the swift and ruthless rules governing the punishment of treason. But he learned something else too, which was to influence his own reign later. Although merciless to the upper ranks, Edward, as was always his custom, spared the common soldiers of the other side, as well as some prominent lawyers and civilians (including the former Chief Justice John Fortescue, who had been a Chancellor of Henry VI in exile). [15]

Queen Margaret, with the equally wretched Anne, still hardly more than a child, were quickly discovered and taken. Margaret, her hopes dead with her son, was handed over to Edward at Coventry by Sir William Stanley (she was eventually allowed to leave the kingdom), while Anne was given into the charge of her brother-in-law, Clarence, and her sister. Quite soon, she was to become the silent victim of a parliamentary quarrel between Clarence and Gloucester. There was no doubt Clarence, greedy for the whole of the Warwick lands, resented his young brother's eagerness to marry the younger sister, and he appears to have tried to circumvent this by hiding Anne in a London hostelry, disguised as a kitchenmaid. Here Richard, apparently in desperate search, found the girl and "caused her to be placed in the sanctuary of St. Martin." [16] Richard then successfully pressed his suit with the king and parliament. In fact, there was an attainder still on Warwick's lands and Richard could not have been sure Anne would be granted her inheritance at the time. Edward as king had himself a right to these lands, lost by attainder, and he might have chosen to assert this right. Strictly speaking, they had come to Warwick, a Neville closely related to Richard's mother by birth, through his wife, the

Countess of Warwick. In the main, Anne's share was eventually granted to Richard, perhaps because Edward realised only too well the need to curb Clarence's growing power.

The Countess, Anne's mother, had remained in sanctuary at Beaulieu ever since the Battle of Tewkesbury. Soon after his marriage to her daughter, Richard seems to have made an appeal to Edward and the Countess was escorted north by Sir James Tyrell. Much has been made of her deprivation of her lands, through her husband's attainder, but there seems no reason to suppose that her removal from Beaulieu, which can only have been by her consent, was not in the nature of a kindly intervention by Richard on behalf of his wife, and that she did not thereafter live with or near them, enjoying at least some of the amenities of her property without the legal and other troubles attached to their upkeep. Widows of attainted traitors under many régimes fared worse.[17]

In the meantime, the Lancastrian cause was lost but Edward's command of the kingdom was still not total. Early in May a Lancastrian adherent, Thomas, known as the Bastard of Fauconberg, had attempted to seize London with a body of rebels from Kent, Calais and the Cinque Ports. They had been stoutly resisted, but had ravaged the area of the Thames with their ships. With the advent of some of Edward's army the rebels fled, but Fauconberg, whose aim had been to release King Henry VI from the Tower, only retired as far as Canterbury, ominously ready to spring again.

This was the situation when Edward, on 21 May, triumphantly re-entered London; and it apparently signed the hapless Henry's death warrant. Although it was officially given out that he had died of "pure displeasure and melancholy",[18] and grief for his son could certainly be a cause of the melancholy, the death was really too timely for credibility in King Edward's current situation, knowing of Fauconberg's objective. The ex-King's body was shown to the populace, as customary, on 23 May, but a slightly crushed skull, at the back of the dead man's head, would not have been noticeable. It was said to be found when Henry VI's dismembered skeleton was examined by W.H. St. John Hope in 1910. The skull was thin, but the report of Dr. Macalister in fact gives no indication of a blow on the head. The state of the bones were too "unsatisfactory". Henry's death is, however, suspect.[19]

It was another murder later to be confidently ascribed to Richard. It is certain King Edward, his brother and followers were in the Tower (the Royal apartments there were often used for Court gatherings and Council meetings) on 21 May, the date most chroniclers give for Henry's death, and on 23 May Edward left for Canterbury. Richard went ahead to Sandwich, where he arrived on 26 May. There is a slight uncertainty of date in that Tower accounts regarding Henry's upkeep only ended on 23 May. What seems certain is that Henry VI could only have been assassinated on Edward's order, probably after consultation with his Council at the Tower, and it is highly unlikely that the King would have arranged for the order to have been personally carried out by his eighteen-year-old brother, even although he was officially Constable of England. No contemporary account makes this accusation, although Philip de Commines confidently states that the Duke of Gloucester "slew this poor King Henry with his own hand, or caused him to be carried into some private place, and stood by while he was killed." [20] But Commines, vivid and informative on those episodes of French history in which he was personally concerned, was often grossly inaccurate on affairs across the Channel, particularly in view of his master King Louis XI's fear of English invasion and the proximity of Henry Tudor and the Lancastrian exiles. When Commines wrote this, the Richard III black legend was beginning to be well established with Tudor historians.

The general agreement among modern historians (and even Hume, no Richard partisan, in the eighteenth century) is that Richard can be absolved from this crime, of which there is no contemporary evidence whatever. Indeed, when in 1499 (Henry VII's reign) a convocation of English clergy sent a Petition to Pope Alexander VI, praying that Henry VI's remains might be removed to Westminster Abbey, they stated: "He had yielded to a pitiable death, by the order of Edward, who was then king of England." [21] No attempt was made to throw any suspicion on Richard, the King who had, in fact, been responsible for the removal of Henry's body, with all honour, from Chertsey Abbey to Windsor.

Nevertheless, it must be borne in mind, when assessing his future character as king, that even if not party to the act he must have had suspicions of his brother's decision, if not actual knowledge. He acquiesced, at least tacitly, and continued to remain loyal and devoted to Edward. His experience of the ruthlessness attached, in medieval times, to the acquisition and retention of a throne was growing; and the effect of this on his precocious, highly intelligent and rapidly maturing mind cannot have been negligible. If there was ever, in later years, a deep psychological conflict between his natural probity of spirit, liberality as a ruler and religious nature, and the ambition and consciousness of power inherent in the proud houses of York and Neville, it must have stirred for the first time at this moment of an old King's timely death, which so conveniently stabilised his brother's throne and restored a long and fruitful peace to a kingdom torn by civil dissension.

When Richard and his wife Anne departed for the north, this stability in the country seemed likely to be lasting. They themselves were bound together by obvious common experiences. Childhood memories, attainder, exile, poverty and loss of possessions; both these young people, before the age of twenty, had known them all. Richard voluntarily resigned the office of Great Chamberlain when he left London, and allowed it to pass to Clarence. [22] (Did this in Gloucester seem ambitious? Ambition should be made of sterner stuff.) He had, nevertheless, been heaped with honours and lands by his grateful elder brother, and as Governor in the north he was second in the kingdom. There were some early complaints of failure to cope with the administrative problems of maintaining his more widely-scattered forests and lands, partly because of a drain on funds through his attempt to ensure increased fees and allowances for Glamorgan officials: a reform measure arising from "a genuine concern for the welfare of its inhabitants", who had suffered under ill-paid and therefore negligent bureaucrats. [23] He soon settled in to his duties with such conspicuous regard for justice and the common weal that the loyalty of the northerners was to remain with him throughout the vicissitudes of his later reign. In Yorkshire, the expression "a good Dick" remained for centuries, and derived from memories of Richard's rule. "It is plain", wrote Drake in his York records, *Eboracum,* "that Richard, represented as a monster of mankind by most, was not so esteemed in his lifetime in these northern parts" [24] Indeed to his love for Yorkshire and his estates there (in particular the Castle of Middleham where his son and heir, Edward, was born and mainly lived) can be ascribed some of the later distrust of the Lancastrian-dominated peoples of the south, who in fact had rarely or never seen him.

He came back to London infrequently, and the fact that he was apparently there when Clarence at last went too far, and met an obscure death for treason, meant that yet one more opportunity presented itself to his enemies, long after his death, to pin on him the urging of the murder of his brother. George of Clarence, for all his charm, on which many contemporaries commented, had a high-reaching ambition that could never long be controlled. Edward had forgiven much; but this time it seems his Council and Parliament both pressed him to action. The reasoning was clear enough: could family nepotism be allowed, once again, to shield Clarence when others, in the same position, would be, and indeed had been, executed for treason?

"The circumstances that happened in the ensuing Parliament" caused the Croyland chronicler to shudder, witnessing the "sad strife carried on before these two brothers of such high estate. For not a single person uttered a word against the duke, except the king; not one individual made answer to the king except the duke." [25]

Clarence seems this time to have flashed danger signs that even Edward could not ignore. Just what those danger signs might have been only later began to emerge, at least as a possibility. At any rate Edward's qualms were overcome, though not to the extent of publicly executing his brother. There was a conspicuous delay before the Commons speaker, William Allington, demanded in the House of Lords that the verdict of death be implemented. [26] It suggests Edward was still hesitating. The story that Clarence was drowned in a butt of malmsey, even though spread among foreigners like Mancini, throwing up their hands (yet again) in horror at the barbaric English, is surely pure "old wives' tale", although surprisingly Dr Charles Ross gives it credence. Perhaps it was a sardonic contemporary quip about the duke's known drinking habits. "In consequence of this", wrote the Croyland chronicler after referring to the Speaker's intervention, "in a few days after, the execution, whatever its nature may have been, took place (and would that it had ended these troubles!) in the Tower of London, it being the year of our Lord, 1478, and the eighteenth of the reign of King Edward." [27]

In other words, it was a secret execution of undisclosed nature, to veil family disunity and conceal any sense of dissension in the Yorkist ranks. The Duke of Buckingham had passed sentence of death as Seneschal of England. His own ambitions as one of the royal line may already have been stirring. An interesting corollary, as will appear later, was the imprisonment of Robert Stillington, Bishop of Bath and Wells and Edward's former Chancellor, at the time of the execution of Clarence, of whom he was a close associate.

There is nothing to connect Richard with his brother's death. Even some Tudor chroniclers such as Hall, Holinshed and Stow actually state he denounced the sentence, and Fabyan and Vergil simply do not mention him. The legend of his responsibility for his brother's death grew later, perhaps because as husband of Anne Neville he was eventually granted Clarence's share of the Warwick estates (Clarence's wife, Isabel Neville, had already died, provoking an extraordinary reaction from the unstable Clarence, who had taken the authority into his own hands of accusing her servant, Ankaret Twynho, of poisoning her and executing her without any legal procedure whatsoever. It gives some indication of what Edward had to deal with in his brother's megalomania and contempt for the king's authority). Nevertheless, Richard's gain by Clarence's death could by no means have been assured, as once again Edward, as King, had prior right to lands forfeited by an attainder. In view of his constant need for money to support his state projects and luxurious tastes, Edward's generosity to his younger, faithful brother Richard seems marked. He did keep some of Clarence's lands and property for himself, but the Warwick ones are likely to have been by far the most extensive and valuable, as Clarence's struggle not to have to share them with Richard had shown.

Years before, the magnificent elder brother, Edward, had visited both younger boys, George and Richard, "every day" when, still children, they had been placed for safety in the house of Sir John Paston; [28] but both then and during their childhood exile in Utrecht the smaller boys can be expected to have been closer to each other. Richard, the youngest, seems likely to have been attached to Clarence by childhood memories, not shared by the older Edward. His earlier successful attempt to win Clarence back from Warwick also suggests this.

Three days after Clarence was executed, Richard secured a licence to found two colleges, one at Barnard Castle (not to be confused with his mother's home, Baynard's Castle, in London) and one at Middleham. Their purpose was to house priests and choristers who would pray for the King and Queen, for Richard and Anne and their little son, and for the souls of the King's deceased brothers and sisters, of whom Clarence was now one. [29] On the 'hypocrisy' theory later built around every good action of Richard's, this can be taken to suggest the salving of a guilty conscience. In the manner of the times, it was far more probably a gesture seeking expiation for his brother Edward's responsibility, or more simply of sorrow for his ill-fated other brother.

Even Mancini, six years or so later, wrote that Richard "was so overcome with grief for his brother, that he could not dissimulate so well, but that he was overheard to say that he would one day avenge his brother's death. Thenceforth he came very rarely to court. He kept himself within his own lands and set out to acquire the loyalty of his people through favours and justice. The good reputation of his private life and public activities powerfully attracted the esteem of strangers." Mancini, as a French agent sent by Cato, had no reason to lie about what he heard; and if later rumours from different informants contradicted this earlier estimate of Richard's character he simply faithfully recorded the gossip he listened to. It is part of a spy's business to give information of another, potentially dangerous, country as accurately as he is able. He recorded Richard's supposed murder of, or intention to murder, the princes as a rumour only, and stated clearly (in December, 1483), that he had been unable to verify it in any way. This unfortunately has not prevented some writers on the subject from treating his work, like others, as factual evidence of the princes' death at Richard's hands.

Clarence died in 1478. By 1473 Edward IV already had another son, Richard, Duke of York. "This Yeare the Duke of Yorke was borne in the Blacke frears within the towne of Shrewsbury" records an old chronicle there (Taylor's MS). It thus corrects an earlier assumption that the date was 17 August, 1472 — in fact an impossibility, as Elizabeth Woodville's biographer points out, as the boy's sister, Princess Margaret, was born on 19th April that year. [31] It may be worth noting that this second son was named after King Edward's favourite and most loyal brother, Richard, Duke of Gloucester, then himself only twenty years of age. When, on 15 January 1477, the infant Prince Richard was married to Anne Mowbray, the daughter and heir of the last Mowbray, Duke of Norfolk, his namesake Richard of Gloucester came to London to be present: "and then there was great number of gold and silver cast among the common people, brought in basins of gold, cast by the high and mighty prince the Duke of Gloucester .... and from St. Stephen's Chapel the Duke of Gloucester led the bride on the right hand and the Duke of Buckingham on the left." [32]

Did Gloucester cast the gold and silver among the common people on his own suggestion? It would not be out of character with the laws for "the ease and solace of the common people" a few years later in his own reign. The little Anne Mowbray suffered a fate as early and tragic as her three-year-old husband was reputed to have done. She died on 19 November 1481, at not quite ten years old. Her coffin was found during excavations at the Minories in London in 1965. [33] Her bones, like those claimed to be of her husband, also play their part in the obscure fate of the princes. They have been claimed to show possible consanguinity.

Elizabeth, the Queen, and her rapacious family are believed with more credibility to have been concerned with Clarence's execution, and to have urged it on Edward. One reason for Elizabeth's animosity or fear will be discussed later. It is certain that her eldest son, the Marquess of Dorset, lucratively benfited from Clarence's death, and so did her brother, Lord Rivers. [34] It is equally certain that Richard did not, as stated by Gairdner, receive the grant of the lordship of Barnard Castle (held by Clarence) at this time. As Kendal notes, such a grant does not exist, and Richard's ownership through his wife dates from the division of the Countess of Warwick's property four years earlier, in 1474. [35]

It seems, in fact, probable that Richard's resentment of the Woodvilles (if it existed in any measure before their attempt to control the throne under a boy king) dated from their share in his brother's fate. He returned to London only twice more, on the first occasion in 1480 when his sister Margaret, now Dowager Duchess of Burgundy owing to the death of Duke Charles, paid a brief visit to England (Richard's long journey south to see her shows that the strength of family unity still held). On the second, in 1481, it was partly to report on Scottish affairs.

It was a year later that, as recently appointed lieutenant-general, Richard laid siege to Berwick, the gateway to Scotland, with an army reputed to be 23,000 strong. Edward ballasted this new attempt to hammer the always-threatening Scots by sending his treasurer, Sir John Elrington, and his own physician to attend on Richard.

Richard was always a general of quick military decision and

surprise tactics (he had helped win the Battle of Barnet, the first in which he took part, by a surprise manoeuvre). He left the siege, which seemed likely to be prolonged, in the hands of Lord Stanley, and before King James could anticipate his next move promptly marched direct to Edinburgh. He was well received by the Council, in control of an artistic-minded king, and having burned and destroyed the country on the way made amends, as far as amends could be said to be made, by totally sparing the city. It was a characteristic of Richard never to use brutality except as a necessity; but the brutality, by our own standards (although not always our military or aerial standards), was certainly there.

Having made a peace which was (nevertheless) likely to be as impermanent as all arrangements with the marauding Scots, Richard returned to Berwick where he briskly ended the siege. The town, torn historically between its Scottish and English border heritage, had been in Scottish hands for twenty-one years. King Edward's rejoicing was tempered only by a sudden acute awareness of the cost of the enterprise.

Richard's prestige had never stood higher. North of the kingdom, he had almost unlimited power. But when his brother died suddenly (his magnificent physique perhaps weakened by his excesses; perhaps also, it was rumoured in France, because of melancholy over an unexpected reverse in his French policy) he was totally unprepared. Edward was only forty; and although it is believed his Will named his brother as Protector, it is not extant. [36] One is recorded in *Excerpta Historica,* but there appears to have been a later one naming Richard, according to Dr. Ducarel, found in the registers at Lambeth, but apparently destroyed. [37]

Richard was not the only one caught unawares. The Woodvilles immediately realised their danger and the preciousness of their charge. For ever since 1473, except for brief visits of a ceremonial nature to London, the young king, Edward V, had been at Ludlow Castle (the stronghold of his grandfather, Richard, Duke of York), under the exclusive care and tutelage of his mother's relatives and adherents, in particular the splendid, erudite and grasping Anthony, Lord Rivers. Elizabeth had been with the prince there in 1473, for a time, but as in many cases among the English nobility (then and now) a boy of very tender years was taken away from his parents for tuition and experience. It was the younger son, and his sisters, that Elizabeth had in her direct care. And these had been born at various places on royal progresses.

Elizabeth's power to fascinate Edward had never waned, in spite of his infidelities, which she was far too cool-minded, and shrewd, to resent. Her tolerance appears to have been extended especially to Elizabeth Shore, whom history has incorrectly named "Jane" (unless the City mercer's wife used "Jane" after becoming the royal mistress, much as actresses often change their name for public purposes. It could, perhaps, also have been to avoid confusion with Edward's queen, or even out of delicacy in the circumstances.) The amiable Jane Shore was very soon to transfer her affections to the Queen's eldest son, the Marquess of Dorset, whose protection was perforce to prove fairly brief.

At Edward's death Queen Elizabeth was by his side in London, and the whole Woodville clan closed ranks in alarm. A great power struggle for control of the young king was about to begin.

NOTES AND REFERENCES
I — *Sons and Brothers*

1 Budden's MS life of Morton (1610)

2 *History of Arrivall of Edward IV in England* (Camden Society — Harl. MSS). Halsted, i.176. Kendall, p.92.

3 Scofield: *The Life and Reign of Edward the Fourth,* I.575. Ross: *Edward IV,* p.166.

4 Commines: *Memoirs,* i.200.

5 Habington: *Life of Edward IV.* p.77. Halsted, i.173.

6 *England Under the Yorkists,* p.67, extract from *Arrivall.*

7 Warkworth Chronicle, p.17: Halsted, i.182.

8 Harl. MSS, 543. Halsted, i.184.

9 *Arrivall,* p.30.

10 *Ricardian,* IV, 56. March 1977, p.23.

11 Fabyan, p.662.

12 Buck: *The Life and Reigne of Richard III,* p.81.

13 Cal. Milan Papers, I, 117-8. Kendall, p.106.

14 Kendall: *Richard III,* p.103.

15 Warkworth: p.19. Ross: p.172.

16 Croyland Third Continuator, p.469. Croyland suggests Richard through 'craftiness' disguised Anne himself; but it hardly makes sense that he then took her away to sanctuary, and Clarence's responsibility for trying to hide her is generally agreed.

17 Kendall, p.111

18 *Arrivall,* p.38.

19 *Archaeologia,* LXII, 533-42. Mary Clive: *This Sun of York,* pp. 174-5.

20 Commines: I.201.

21 *Wilk. Concil.* iii p.635. Halsted, ii.355n.

22 Rymer, Add. MSS, fo.4614, art. 70.

23 T.B. Pugh : *The Marcher Lords of Glamorgan and Morgannwg,* 1317-1485, (Glam. County History, Vol. III, The Middle Ages ed. Pugh, Cardiff, 1971) pp.202-3.

24 Eboracum, p.123.

25 Croyland Third Continuator, p.479.

26 Ibid, p.480. Ross, p.243.

27 Croyland Third Continuator, p.480.

28 Paston Letters, i.199 Halsted; i.76.

29 Cal. Pat. Rolls, 1476-85, p.67. Kendall, p.127.

30 Mancini, pp.63, 65.

31 David MacGibbon: *Elizabeth Woodville,* p.117, n.2.

32 Sandford: *Genealogical History,* Book v., p.393. Halsted, i.451. Kendall, p.126.

33 Ross, p.248.

34 *Foedera,* vol. xii, p.95. Halsted, i.324n.

35 Kendall, p.455. Gairdner, pp.36-7.

36 Bernard André, p.23. Vergil, p.539.

37 Halsted, ii.17n.

II
The Way to a Throne

"Edward", writes Charles Ross with hindsight but also perception, "had created a real risk to the future political peace of his realm in allowing his heir to be surrounded by Woodvilles from infancy, educated under their guidance, and necessarily under their influence."[1]

Rivers, on 9 April 1483, the day of Edward's death, was in a new position of authority and potential menace. His powers in Wales had been greatly enlarged in February. He was in a position to raise an army, having on 8 March sent to London for a copy of his letters patent giving him this authority. Apart from Richard Grey, the Queen's younger son by her first marriage, who was with Rivers and the young king in Wales, the principal other Woodvilles were all in London and in powerful positions. Thomas, Marquess of Dorset, the Queen's eldest son, was deputy-constable of the Tower, where he had a certain control of Edward IV's treasure.[2] It was, wrote even Mancini, "immense" and "was kept in the hands of the queen and her people." Sir Edward Woodville, the Queen's brother, was soon appointed by the Council in London commander of the king's fleet of twenty ships, and although this step was apparently taken because of a threat of French piracy in the English Channel, it put yet another threatening weapon in Woodville hands. In the event, Sir Edward was to put to sea at approximately the same day the Queen fled to sanctuary, and much of the king's treasure, "which had taken such years and such pains to gather, was divided between the queen, the marquess and Edward [Woodville]", or so Mancini reported as common belief.[3] Almost certainly Woodville took some of it to sea with him, and possibly the Marquess, when eventually forced into sanctuary and later exile, took more with him from the Tower.

This is worth mentioning here because of the Lancastrian-orientated Croyland Third Continuator's deliberate accusation that to Richard III was owed "the waste, in a short time, of those most ample treasures which King Edward supposed he should leave behind him for a quite different purpose". [4] It is a reiterated accusation of this Croyland Continuator, as will appear later, and if he was, as is now sometimes claimed, John Russell, Bishop of Lincoln, Richard's Chancellor, it is among many things for which he could not himself totally avoid responsibility, and the identification is highly suspect for this reason. Only the Woodvilles (and possibly Henry Tudor to whom they eventually fled), would, in the circumstances, be so anxious to explain away the rapid diminution of Edward IV's treasure. Their sifting of it away themselves would explain at least some of the financial difficulties Richard had to face in his short and, on the evidence, by no means extravagant reign. On the Woodville reputation for avarice, it was totally in character. Mancini had no need to shelter or whitewash the English Woodvilles, and indeed he does not do so.

These events, however, took place immediately after the Woodville realisation that their plot to take control of the king, and through him the government, had been circumvented. At the time of King Edward's death their position of power was considerable, and realising time was short they struck as quickly as they could. As relatives of the Dowager Queen they had no automatic right to govern in the new king's name. The young king's coronation was fixed by the Council for the obviously "rushed" date of Sunday, 4 May; and Rivers, Grey and their young charge left Ludlow on 24 April, waiting only to celebrate St. George's Day. [5]

They had reckoned both without Richard and the London Privy Council, which was not without second thoughts and fears. Richard's first reaction had been grief for his brother, and doubtless an element of shock. The news reached him, most authorities agree, at Middleham Castle, where a chaplain was immediately instructed to say requiem masses for the dead king's soul and mourning black was quickly assumed. [6] Richard seems early to have realised he was expected to become Protector during his nephew's minority. But his movements were not at this stage over-hurried. According to Croyland, he wrote "most soothing letters in order to console the queen, with ... assurances of all duty, fealty, and due obedience to his king and lord Edward the fifth", and proceeded to York with a retinue of knights in mourning, where "he performed a solemn funeral service for the king, the same being accompanied with plenteous tears. Constraining all the nobility of those parts to take the oath of fealty to the late king's son, he himself was the first of all to take the oath." [7]

It would seem from this that Richard at this point was certainly not planning to depose his nephew, or he would surely not have weakened his possible later support by ensuring that the nobles and knights present swore an oath of loyalty to the young king. It was a superstitious age, and the risk that they might consider this oath binding would be, for an intended usurper, too great, setting aside his own involvement. "Loyeaultè me liè" (Loyalty Binds Me) was his chosen motto; and that he set great value on loyalty is shown by his own to his brother, his persuasion of Clarence to return to his allegiance, and his fury at betrayal by his own supposed friends on two future occasions. It was not in Richard's natural character to disregard this quality in political alliances, and whatever pressures he may have worked under later, no disregard of this could have come easily to him. He had already himself sworn an earlier oath of fealty to the then one-year-old Prince of Wales on 3 July 1471.[8]

Although there is no actual evidence in letters, it has been assumed Richard learned of Rivers' advance with the young king towards London either from a messenger of the Earl himself, or from the Duke of Buckingham, who joined Richard on what had, until then, seemed a not very expeditious journey south.[9] The intentions of the Woodville faction to seize power, excuding the very able Richard himself, were considered probable enough in London for the "more prudent members of the Council" to warn firmly that "the guardianship of so youthful a person, until he should reach the years of maturity, ought to be utterly forbidden to his uncles and brothers by the mother's side". Supported by Lord Hastings, Captain of Calais and a close friend and fellow reveller of the late king, they urged that the escort of the new king from Ludlow should be restricted to "a moderate number of horse", and the queen, quickly realising the signs of disturbance, "wrote to her son, requesting him, on his road to London not to exceed an escort of two thousand men." [10] It is noticeable that the narrator here, the anonymous Croyland Third Continuator, writes "son", because it would be more natural in such circumstances for the queen to write to her *brother,* Lord Rivers, the actual governor of the young king. A state official as experienced as Russell would surely have known that Rivers, not the young Richard Grey, led the expedition.

Richard of Gloucester, by the time he reached Northampton on 29 April, and either sought or was given a rendezvous with the king's escort, was on the alert. It was here that he was joined by the Duke of Buckingham, who was married to the ex-Queen's sister and may well through her have gleaned news of what was toward, among the Woodvilles. A meeting with Rivers, Grey and others of the king's party was arranged. But at this meeting the young king himself was conspicuously absent. He had been sent ahead by his relatives to Stony Stratford.

Perhaps it was at this moment that Richard became seriously alarmed. He acted with his customary swift decision in a crisis. The following morning Rivers, Grey and Sir Thomas Vaughan were arrested and judiciously parted. Rivers went north to Richard's fine country stronghold at Sheriff Hutton; Grey to another of his castles, his favourite home of Middleham. Although well-guarded and separated, a first vital rift in the Woodville faction, they were not imprisoned in the ordinary sense and it would seem that at this stage at least Richard was merely taking precautionary measures against a Woodville *coup d'état.* The arrests were so unexpected and sudden that it appears the 2,000 men with Rivers, robbed of their leader and without any authority of their own, quickly accepted the inevitable and continued with Richard's and Buckingham's smaller force to London.

The situation was explained to the young king at Stony Stratford, only fifty miles from London, and although chronicles agree that Richard greeted him with affection and respect, kneeling to him as king in fact, it must be taken as inevitable that the boy would not be mollified. He had been brought up under the prime charge of his mother's family and was doubtless attached to them. How much he yet realised of the true nature of Richard's reasons is difficult to judge. At twelve years old he was not far off maturity, as it was reckoned in medieval royalty. He had been carefully educated and tutored in full knowledge of his future rank and the statecraft he must understand in order successfully to inherit. Nevertheless, in accounts that have come down to us there is a general impression that he was rather of a literary, not greatly assertive, bent. Suddenly, he had been pitched into the maëlstrom of politics, ahead of his time. His uncle Richard he had met, probably, only a few times, and then when much younger than now. King Edward would have impressed on him his brother's loyalty; but he had seen his father (or indeed his mother, who stayed and travelled closely by the king) little too, and his malleable young mind had been directed mainly to the magnificence and capabilities of his mother's relatives.

Nevertheless, he was not a child, at least not totally to the political mind of his times.[11] Within a very short time indeed he would be released from the control even of a Protector. That thought, too, must have been uppermost in Richard of Gloucester's mind. Of what use was this sudden leap to power if the young king, by natural predilection, would be able to reverse it before the governance of the state was fully and irrevocably re-established in his paternal family's hands? And Richard, like many of the Council, must have had a very shrewd idea of to whom Edward would hand the reins of power once he was of an age to assume control. The mighty Woodvilles would be, as the British Empire was hopefully prophesied to become in later days, mightier yet. Richard and the moderates on the Privy Council could then expect short shrift.

The dangers of rule when a minor was king were written into English history. The young, and eventually inept, King Henry VI, a king at nine months old, was still fresh in the memories of the old: so was the fate of his uncle and Protector, Duke Humphrey of Gloucester, reputedly murdered when others gained control of the young king's mind. Richard, and possibly Hastings and Buckingham, would not be the only ones thinking along these lines.

The reception of the Duke of Gloucester in London, therefore, was less wary than thankful. Mancini, his ear to the ground, records a letter setting out his honourable intentions which Richard had written to the Council, and states that this letter "had a great effect on the minds of the people, who, as they previously favoured the duke in their hearts from a belief in his probity, now began to support him openly and aloud: so that it was commonly said by all that the duke deserved the government".[12] This letter is, quite probably, the same that the Croyland Continuator suggests was written to the queen: on the whole, Mancini's information seems the more likely. At any rate Richard entered London without opposition, treating the young king with honour, and four wagons of weapons with the Woodville arms were shown in public. It was said they had been seized near London and had been intended to enforce Woodville control. But by now Mancini's informants on the opposition side were in full spate ... "The arms in question had been placed there long before the late king's death for an altogether different purpose, when war was being waged against the Scots."[13] It was not a probable explanation, for it had been Richard himself, from the north, who had conducted the last successful Scottish enterprise; it was most unlikely that arms ready for that brief "war" were still lying for the taking in the environs of London. A Woodville *coup* seems strongly indicated. That Mancini, the neutral observer for France, recorded indiscriminately gossip from different factions is apparent throughout his text.

It is, I think, questionable how much Richard was yet, if indeed at all, influenced in his actions by "deep-revolving, witty Buckingham" — a Shakespearean description which perhaps owes more to Sir Thomas More's buoyant, ironically-humorous dialogue than to authentic characterisation. The intention was still to have the young king crowned. But Elizabeth Woodville, hearing ot the arrest of her brother and son, realised their schemes had failed and fled into sanctuary at Westminster, taking with her not only her daughters and nine-year-old second son, Richard, Duke of York, but according to More a considerable amount of property. The Archbishop of York, then Chancellor, came to her, according to More, and found about her "much heaviness, rumble, haste and business, carriage and conveyance of her stuff into sanctuary — chests, coffers, packs, fardelles, trusses, all on men's backs ... some going, some discharging, some coming for more, some breaking down the walls ...".[14]

In spite of the obvious fictional element in the ensuing dialogue, this scene of bustle has the ring of journalistic truth. It is the kind of chaos that ensues from an urgent sense of danger, and of Woodville rapacity too. If the story of the Queen's letter of warning to her son (or brother) is true, she had already been aware of the danger and even seems, by her suggestion of moderation in the escort to London, to have tried to advise against too open a bid for power. We have no reason to believe Elizabeth a totally willing party to the plot. She knew only too well, in London, some of the feeling against her family, and that opposition to their thrust towards control of the king would be strong.

It was perhaps because they knew it too that Rivers and Grey may have decided that quick action, even if dangerous, was necessary. Once out of their control, the king, under age, would not be able to prevent possible huge losses of office, status and income. It seemed widely accepted that Richard would become Protector, and, long in the north, he had no special commitment to the Woodvilles even if, until now, no specific antagonism towards them.

It is probably not without reason, nevertheless, that Mancini noted that the queen's family were afraid, too, that Richard would blame them for Clarence's death, by which Lord Rivers and Dorset had been greatly enriched and the queen, as will appear, quite possibly released from another, more urgent, fear. The fact that Mancini heard this, from whatever source, is another contemporary indication that Richard, so far from wishing, had actively opposed and resented Clarence's execution.[15]

The Chronicles of London, written much later, confuse Lord Rivers with the Marquess of Dorset; but they are clear that Gloucester and Buckingham took charge of the king at Stony Stratford: "And so from thens brought hym unto London; and the iiijth day of May he cam thrugh the Cite, ffet and met by the Mayr and Citezeins of the Cite at Harnsey [Hornsey] park, the kyng Ridying in blew velvet, and the Duke of Glowcetir in blak cloth, like a mourner; and so he was conveid to the Bysshoppys palaes in London, and there logid."[16]

Oaths of fealty to the young king were now sworn at St. Paul's and the coronation was fixed for 22 June. Richard, meantime, went to live with his mother, the Duchess of York, at Baynard's Castle, and the king seems, from the documents he signed in conjunction with Richard, to have moved between the Bishop's palace, Westminster and the Tower, according to where his Council met. Richard conspicuously usually signed these documents with his motto, "Loyeaultè me liè". After a time, perhaps for reasons of the coming coronation, to which all English monarchs proceeded from the Tower, and perhaps also to facilitate the ordering of and measuring for coronation robes (the Wardrobe Accounts of the Tower contain details of these[17]), young Edward moved permanently to the Tower royal apartments.

The crisis seems to have begun soon after 8 June, the date of a meeting of the Council of State at which Richard appears not to have been present. Certainly on this day Richard wrote to the Mayor and Aldermen of the City of York on a matter of no urgent moment; in fact regarding York's lack of repayment for its losses sustained in the war against the Scots:

"We let you wot, that for such great matters and businesses as we now have to do, for the weal and usefulness of the realm, we as yet ne can have convenient leisure to acomplish this your business, but be assured that for your loving and kind disposition to us at all times shewed, which we never can forget, we in all goodly haste shall so endeavour for your ease in this behalf ..." [18]

If Richard was staving off a repayment appeal which he obviously felt was just, and merited an early reply and reassurance, it may have been partly because he well knew the matter of the royal treasure was still a cause for anxiety. Sir Edward Woodville, while the queen fled to sanctuary, remained in dangerous command of the fleet. Edward Brampton, a converted Portuguese Jewish merchant who had notably served Edward IV, his Christian godfather whose name he had taken, was sent to sea with two others, and "ships to take Sir Edward Woodville". An offer of the king's pardon was conveyed to lure the sailors from Woodville. Some of them were Italian commanders who had innocently enough accompanied Woodville with their Genoese ships. The lure worked, and all but two of the fleet deserted Woodville and hoist sail for London. Woodville escaped with two ships only to Brittany, where the young exiled Lancastrian, Henry Tudor, was lurking with a minor but persistent claim to the English throne. It is a reasonable assumption that a portion of Edward IV's treasure went with Sir Edward. The Marquess of Dorset was to follow him within a few months, possibly conveying more as has been said. [19]

It was on 10 June that Richard, in another letter to York, first indicated his need for help.

"Right trusty and well-beloved, we greet you well. And as you love the weal of us and the weal and surety of your own self, we heartily pray you to come unto us to London in all diligence ye can possible, after the sight hereof, with as many as ye can make defensibly arrayed, there to aid and assist us against the queen, her bloody adherents and affinity, which have intended and daily doth intend to murder and utterly destroy us and our cousin the

Duke of Buckingham and the old royal blood of this realm..." [20]

The change of tone was startling, and in only two days. What had happened?

Two things, either almost simultaneously, or one growing out of the other. Richard had discovered the conspiracy of Lord Hastings and John Morton, Bishop of Ely, to challenge his authority; and Robert Stillington, Bishop of Bath and Wells, and long-serving Chancellor of Edward IV, had made a startling revelation (possibly at the 8 June Council meeting Richard had not attended) that opened up the way for the Protector to take the throne.

Protector was one thing: a man in supreme power was quite another. If Hastings' unexpected rebellion had been provoked by Stillington's revelation, and his sense of thwarted ambitions of his own had thrown him into the enemy camp, there is small doubt that Morton, Lancastrian to the bone and a time-server not completely trusted by Edward IV when he first turned Yorkist, had simply been awaiting his opportunity. Not, surely, for nothing was Richard to accuse him later of giving, as a Privy Councillor, "secret advert to the Earle of Richmond [Henry Tudor] of what passed in the secret Councells of the King." [21] In the web of spying and counter-spying that stretched intricately across the Channel, between France, Brittany and England, Morton seems to have been a far from negligible thread. King Louis XI of France was known as "the Spider", but on the English side too there were indefatigable spinners of intrigue.

It is not certain at what date Stillington released his bombshell; but one of the early June Council meetings seems indicated, and most probably that of 8 June as I have suggested. His revelation was as follows and it entirely altered the succession. Edward IV, whose predilection for any pretty face was well-known, had before his marriage to Elizabeth Woodville (which was itself secret) allowed himself to become contracted clandestinely to marry Dame Eleanor Butler, a daughter of the famous Talbot, Earl of Shrewsbury, and widow of Sir Thomas Butler. This contract had been solemnly entered into at a ceremony at which Robert Stillington, he himself claimed, had officiated, and under medieval law (which we will discuss later) it was a fully binding marriage. Edward's subsequent marriage to Elizabeth Woodville was therefore bigamous, and his sons and daughters by that marriage illegitimate. Edward V, therefore, was not the lawful king of

England, only legitimate sons being recognised heirs to the throne.

Now partly because Henry Tudor, on his succession, and wishing to marry the princes' sister Elizabeth to strengthen his claim, had the details of this revelation, and the law that embodied it, suppressed, and partly because the chroniclers, with one exception, therefore ignored it or gave only a garbled incorrect version, it was long assumed that this Stillington story was simply a far-fetched device by which Richard, the next legitimate heir after the princes, assumed the throne. Modern scholarship and study of similar cases in law has, however, given a very different picture. It was not simply casuistry; if true, it made the bastardizing of the princes inevitable, under medieval law.

More's version of what happened was so unbelievable that it gave the impression (probably deliberately on the part of his informers) that this was a totally incredible device to open the way to the throne to Richard. More gave the name of Elizabeth Lucy as the lady of the pre-contract. Elizabeth Lucy, it was well-known, was one of Edward's courtesans, not of specially high birth and in fact mother of his illegitimate son, Arthur Plantagenet, whom he acknowledged. The liaison was widely known and there had been no question of marital contract. Eleanor Butler, by birth, was a totally different and more serious proposition, and any contract made with her was likely to have been binding. According to Stillington, a full contract of marriage had been entered into, and this contract *was* legally binding.

Historians anxious to decry it have not apparently been aware of the widespread nature of these pre-contracts, their establishment at the time as equivalent of marriage, and *the other cases of legal inheritance extant,* based on similar double alliances. It was only after Buck's discovery of the Croyland Chronicle, and its correct account of the claim, naming Eleanor Butler, that it was realised this story had some possible substance; and the Act of Titulus Regius in Richard's Parliament of January 1484, which set forth the matter of Edward's bigamous marriage and the illegitimacy of the princes in full, but which was suppressed by order of Henry VII, was only discovered (one copy having escaped destruction) thereafter.

What proofs Stillington gave to the Council are not known; but Richard's power as Protector not then being absolute (and indeed still challengeable, as the rebellion of Hastings and Morton was to show), it is difficult to imagine by what force the Council could have been made to accept this story, and allow Richard's claim to the throne, if some serious evidence at least had not been produced by Stillington. From Edward IV's known character, it was only too likely, as the Council must have been fully aware. Perhaps this fact did help to sway their judgment a little.

The fact that such a pre-contract would invalidate a subsequent marriage has recently been more fully established by a scholarly article by Mary O'Regan in *The Ricardian,* in 1976. [22] From this, certain contemporary legalities and accepted practices emerge. Marriage was from the twelfth century the exclusive province of the church: it was one of the sacraments and not a civil contract. Canon law, in fact, regulated marriage, and "by these rules a valid marriage could be formed by the simple exchange of consents. Parties making this avowall — 'I do marry you' — became validly man and wife, even if the full sacramental rites prescribed by the Church had not been carried out."

The writer goes on to point out that there are "several medieval cases in which the ecclesiastical courts (the proper forum) decided against a later, solemnly performed marriage ceremony, followed by consummation in favour of a prior, informal unconsummated marriage *per verba de praesenti.*" She cites the case of Richard of Annesley (c.1150-62), and quotes J. Jackson (*The Formation and Annulment of Marriage,* 2nd ed. 1969, p.11), L. Shelford (*Law of Marriage and Divorce,* 1841, pp.27-8) and S. Cretney (*Family Law,* 1974, p.34). If intercourse took place this had the effect of validating the marriage, and complaints that a later solemn marriage ceremony between two parties, B and C, would be invalidated by previous "indiscreet and quickly forgotten words breathed under the influence of passion" by B and A, were a frequent ground for petitions of nullity of marriage brought during the Middle Ages. "If a marriage was found to be null and void, it was void for all time; no valid marriage had ever existed between the parties. Hence any children of the union were illegitimate."

If it could be proved one of the parties in a second, invalid marriage "had acted in good faith", the Church allowed that the children of such a putative marriage were legitimate, even though the marriage was void. And marriage in public would be accounted valid in the absence of a decision to the contrary by an ecclesiastical court. The objections made in 1483 to the marriage of Edward IV and Elizabeth Woodville were as follows.

(1) The contract at Grafton Regis was made "privaly and secretly without edition of bannes, in a private chambre a prophane place and nat openly in the face of the church aftre the lawe of Goddes churche..."

(This was undoubtedly true of his marriage to Elizabeth Woodville at Grafton Regis, which Edward kept secret on the assumption that it would arouse the hostility of Warwick.)

(2)"at the time of contract of the same pretensed marriage and bifore and longe tyme after, the seid King Edward was and stode married and trouthplight to oone Dame Elianor Butteler..."

The void marriage of Edward and Elizabeth "could only have become a valid one if Edward and Elizabeth *exchanged vows again after Eleanor's death* ... There is no evidence, or any suggestion, that this was ever done."

Horace Walpole made a similar point in his *Short Observations on The Remarks of the Rev. Mr. Masters:* "If lady Eleanor Butler was Edward's lawful wife, lady Gray could not become his lawful wife by a marriage performed during lady Eleanor's life. To make her his lawful wife, he must have married her again on Eleanor's death, or the pope must at least have legitimated her children." [23]

The fact that Elizabeth Woodville acted in good faith and ignorance did not apply; for this could only legalize the marriage if the ceremony were incontestably open and not clandestine.

Further even later cases can be cited of disputed inheritance through such invalid marriages, for instance the case of Pride v. The Earl of Bath in 1694, when Chief Justice Holt ruled that if a marriage was void then the child could be bastardized after the death of one or both parents, "but if he had had the reputation of heir at his father's death and before, then the rule would give him an 'unimpeachable right and title to the land' in spite of the void marriage of his parents."

One view might therefore be (but on this much later Court ruling) that as Edward, Prince of Wales, was acknowledged heir during Edward IV's lifetime, he had a right to succeed on his death, irrespective of the validity or otherwise of his parents' marriage. But the Crown is not a mere title of honours, it carries its powers and rights with it. "We must conclude that the Crown is neither

Richard III

Horace Walpole: author of *Historic Doubts*.

real property nor a peerage, but *sui generis* — unique — and that its
descent need not follow the rules customary in either of these
things''.

"If the Eleanor Butler story was true", Mary O'Regan
concludes, "then Richard was right to call the later 'marriage'
void, but the matter should properly have gone before a spiritual
court for decision''.

On the other hand, Parliament being a court of final appeal, had
a right to decide the issue, which was "passed over in its Act of
Titulus Regius without argument". The Act of Richard's
Parliament settling the Crown on him and his heirs was, therefore,
"just as effective in removing any taint of usurpation as were
similar Acts of Henry IV, Mary I and Elizabeth I.''

Richard's "usurpation" of the crown is thus legally now proved
a myth, which could validly be maintained only as long as the true
facts were concealed and the Act of Titulus Regius destroyed, as
Henry Tudor must have known.

The only point at issue in Richard's succession is not, therefore,
any longer a matter of his legal right in the circumstances put
forward; it can only be the question as to whether these
circumstances, i.e. of Edward's prior contract, were true.

This is, of course, more difficult to maintain in the absence of
the evidence. That it was likely, no one who has studied Edward's
character when young would deny. What of Stillington himself?
And did Richard have prior knowledge of his revelation?

From Eleanor Butler herself we can look for no evidence. She
died on 30 June 1468. [24] In any case, this was within a very few
years of Edward's marriage, valid or invalid, to Elizabeth
Woodville: but it is surely pertinent to surmise that perhaps the
very secrecy of this marriage stemmed in part from the young
king's knowledge of his prior contract, as well as of Warwick's
disapproval. It has long been accepted that his wedding to
Elizabeth had been made under pressure, for this young
Lancastrian widow of the enticing "gilt hair", who had come to
plead with him for restoration of her husband's lands, had refused
his ardent advances until the offer of marriage was made. (It is
possible he had had to meet the same difficulty with Eleanor
Butler.) Elizabeth Woodville, or her close relatives, undoubtedly
had an eye to the main chance; and her belief in her power to sway
the king was not misplaced, for in spite of his notoriously roving

eye she retained the ability to influence him until his death. Calculating though she might be, Elizabeth had genuine beauty and genuine sexual attractions, which survived the inroads of time quite remarkably when one remembers that she was some years Edward's senior. It is perhaps worth noting that the young Edward's predilection for older, experienced women make the Eleanor Butler story, too, not out of character.

Commines, a foreign observer, Mancini, another, and Croyland all show clear knowledge of the prior contract, although Mancini and Commines do not give Eleanor Butler's name and Mancini with his often garbled details refers to "another wife to whom the [earl] of Warwick had joined him". [25]   None attempts to claim it was a fabricated story. Croyland specifically states it was "set forth . . . in an address in a certain roll of parchment", and Richard "was entreated, at the end of the said roll, on part of the lords and commons of the realm, to assume his lawful rights". [26] Commines names the Bishop of Bath, and states he "discovered this matter to the Duke of Gloucester"on the urging of "the beautiful young lady's" family. [27] Sir George Buck quotes Commines, and further states that the Bishop dared not approach Edward IV on the matter but "rather wisht thay would apply it to the Duke of Gloucester, as the man most inward with the king." [28]

This rather suggests Richard was told the story by Stillington long before 1483. It may have been true: certainly Richard would have been too young to have known anything about his elder brother's youthful marriages at the time. Yet his actions until June, 1483, give no indication that he knew this old story or was prepared to make use of it. Everything points to his genuine intention of crowning the young king. But on 10 June his letter to York suggests an entirely new crisis, and although this could have been a prior hint of the Hastings conspiracy, it also might have been a sudden decision to make use, in the dangerous circumstances in which he was beginning to find himself, of a revelation about his nephew's legitimacy which was quite new to him.

What were Stillington's own credentials? He had taken the degree of Doctor of Laws at Oxford with high distinction, and had a great name there. Edward IV made him successively Archdeacon of Taunton, Bishop of Bath and Wells, Keeper of the Privy Seal, and finally Lord Chancellor. He was no longer, by the end of the reign, a young man, and in fact he had resigned the chancellorship because of ill health as early as 8 June 1473, although he resumed it a short time later, until 1475. He was likely to be no more, and no less, prone to deep religious principles than other prelates of the age who were primarily statesmen and court officials, but who received their church livings by way of emoluments. Their great advantage to the kings, in fact, in both medieval and Tudor times was their ability to give unpaid service in the great offices of state. The bishoprics and archbishoprics were given in lieu of salary, as happened with Morton under the grateful King Henry VII.

On the other hand, there is nothing to suggest Stillington would receive any particular advantage from making up such a story; his major active career was past, and on assuming the throne Richard gave the Chancellorship to John Russell, Bishop of Lincoln. There seems nothing against Stillington's general character. Documents regarding his Chancellorship, including in 1473 his settling of a foreign merchant's legal rights in the Court of Star Chamber, give no indication of graft or unreasonableness, and in 1484, during Richard's reign, a private Act of Parliament gave an account of his founding of a Grammar School at Acaster, near his family's estates: "all the seid iii masters and informatours to teache the seid iii faculties [i.e. grammar, music and writing] severally, openly and freely, without exaction of money or other thyngs of any of their suche scholers and disciples."[29] He may quite well have felt a sense of conscience over the matter of Eleanor Butler and her betrayal, which would not have been of urgent political import in King Edward's own reign. Two marriages or not, Edward IV's title to the throne was unaffected and indisputable. But now, with the state in need of a strong ruler and all the dangers of a king's minority looming, he may well have decided it was time to speak, and give Richard his chance.

One episode in Stillington's background may not have been unsignificant. At the time of Clarence's imprisonment and death, accused so conspicuously but unspecifically by his brother the king of treasonable activities, Stillington himself was imprisoned. Clarence was executed on 18 February 1478, and on 6 March the same year Elizabeth Stonor wrote a letter to her husband to the effect that "the Bishop of Bath is brought into the Tower since you departed".[30] On 20 June Stillington, after paying a heavy fine, received a royal pardon. His offence was stated to be uttering words prejudicial to the king and his state.[31]

Stillington's closeness to Clarence was undeniable; his diocese was in the Duke's lands, and he had been among those — Cecily, Duchess of York, Margaret of Burgundy, Richard himself — who had pleaded with him to desert Warwick. Obviously he had some influence with the Duke. Could he have told Clarence of the Butler marriage, and had Clarence let this slip in his quarrel with his brother? Had Clarence even suggested that, in the circumstances, he himself was Edward's true heir? It was a dangerous indiscretion of which the vacillating and ambitious Clarence seems to have been more than capable. Edward IV's sudden ruthlessness, as compared with considerable earlier tolerance towards his brother's disloyalties, has always seemed surprising, and his motive in the execution certainly never fully explained.

Elizabeth Woodville's animosity, and that of her relatives, would, of course, in this case be fully understandable: they were fighting for the inheritance of her son and heir. The Marquess of Dorset had, after Clarence's death, been given control of Clarence's own son and heir, the child Edward, Earl of Warwick, and also of his estates. He still kept the boy in safe custody, in the Tower.

We can really only guess here, but the imprisonment of Clarence and Stillington at the same time, on unspecified charges, cannot but seem a strange coincidence. On the other hand, Clarence never proclaimed his knowledge, as far as we know, even when Warwick was supporting him as a possible royal son-in-law. Most historians agree that he did throw out hints of his elder brother's own illegitimacy (Edward was born in Rouen, where Cecily of York had joined her husband and presumably was supposed, in Clarence's tale, to have had a lover). The story was to reappear again just before Richard took the throne. It was in any case unlikely, as Cecily regularly followed her husband in England and abroad, as is shown by the birthplaces of her children. Her marriage would appear to have been one of genuine attachment.

Now Edward IV was dead, the matter became a vital issue, or so Stillington may have thought. Whether Richard already knew or, perhaps more likely, suddenly became aware of the weapon thrust into his hands, it would seem he was ready to wield it, and quickly. This would be all the more so if he had also become aware of the movement of a jealous faction, headed by Morton and

Hastings, against himself. The Protectorate was open to seizure, especially after a king's crowning, as the case of Humphrey, Duke of Gloucester, had proved. He was used to taking decisions in both battle and government. And he was highly conscious of his family's royal claim and the need for a strong basis of undisputed power.

The knowledge of a flaw in the Yorkist succession could dangerously raise Tudor hopes. It was Stillington himself, according to Buck, who had been sent by Edward IV to treat for the extradition of Henry Tudor, Earl of Richmond,*from Brittany, as indeed he had been sent on a number of foreign missions. Henry's claim to the throne through his mother and the Lancastrian line, although slenderly based on the illegitimate (as far as the succession was concerned) issue of Edward III's son John of Gaunt, was still the only Lancastrian one of value once Henry VI and his son had been removed. There was nothing new in this threat; and with the illegitimizing of the princes, Edward IV's sons, it was bound to revive. Henry, a grown man with English dissidents behind him and obviously with spies and secret adherents operating in England (not to count potential French aid if it so proved to suit French foreign policy) was far more dangerous to Richard than the young princes, now officially at least out of the succession. This must always be borne in mind in assessing subsequent events. To Henry, even if he used the unjust treatment of the princes as a psychological weapon, they were in fact more dangerous than to Richard.

---

* In fact, Henry Tudor did not legally hold this title, which had been taken away from Edmund Tudor through attainder. Officially, it now belonged to the holder of the English crown. Hence English state descriptions of Henry as "calling himself Earl of Richmond".[32]

NOTES AND REFERENCES
II — *The Way to a Throne*

1 *Edward IV,* p.103.

2 Ibid, p.424.

3 *Usurpation of Richard III* (ed. Armstrong), p.81.

4 Croyland Third Continuator, p.495.

5 Halsted: *Richard III*, ii.16.

6 Kendall, *Richard III*, p.162.

7 Croyland, p.486. Halsted, ii.6. Drake: *Eboracum,* p.111.

8 Halsted, i.228.

9 Gairdner: *The Life and Reign of Richard III*, p.49.

10 Croyland, p.485.

11 Hanham: *Richard III and his early historians,* p.4.

12 Mancini, p.73.

13 Ibid, p.83.

14 More: *The History of King Richard III*, p.22.

15 Mancini, p.71.

17 *Chronicles of London* (ed. Kingsford), p.190.

17 *Archaeologia,* vol. i, p.361.

18 Drake, p.111. Halsted, ii.518.

19 Kendall, p.188.

20 Gairdner, p.59-60.

21 Buck, p.36.

22 *The Pre-Contract and its Effect on the Succession in 1483: Ricardian,* IV, No. 54, Sept. 1976. pp.2-7.

23 Complete Works, Vol. 5, p.247.

24 Halsted, ii.91n, gives 30 July 1466, and states she was buried in the Carmelites' church at Norwich.

25 Mancini, p.97.

26 Croyland, p.489.

27 Commines, *Memoirs,* i.395.

28 Buck, p.122.

29 *England Under the Yorkists,* p.172 and p.249.

30 *Stonor Letters,* II, p.42. Kendall, p.217.

31 *Foedera,* XII, p.66.

32 Rot. Parl., vol. vi, p.227. Markham, *Richard III*, p.38.

III
Hastings: The First Flaw

Already two factions were operating in London. When Richard's wife Anne Neville joined him from the north, he moved from his mother's house to Crosby Place in Bishopsgate Street, a new and fine residence built by Alderman Sir John Crosby and now leased to Richard by Sir John's widow. Meetings, highly charged one would guess, took place either there or once again at Baynard's Castle, which suggested Richard's mother, Cecily of York, fully supported her son. Elsewhere, another faction of intrigue seemed to be operating, with Hastings and Morton as its leading lights. On 9 June a meeting of the Lords Spiritual and Temporal had taken place in the Council Chamber at Westminster,[1] at which it would appear Stillington's bombshell was discussed: according even to the hostile Grafton (ed. and continuation of More) the Bishop "brought in instruments, authentic doctors, proctors, and notaries of the law, with depositions of divers witnesses".

Morton, already acting as a spy in the Council for Henry Tudor, must have instantly realised the importance to Lancastrian claims of this flaw in the Yorkist inheritance. How he carried Hastings, hitherto a staunch Yorkist who owed his wealth and elevation to Edward IV, into his schemes is not totally explainable as no papers between the two exist. William Hastings was not without ambition, and may have been led to see himself in the rôle of Protector. If Morton was an agent operating on behalf of France or Henry Tudor (or both), it has been widely overlooked that Hastings, too, was the recipient of a French annual pension, acquired alongside that of Edward IV in the famous affair at Pecquiny. Commines (who was certainly in a position to know) mentions this pension of

2000 crowns a year, and although he maintains Hastings prudently gave no receipt for it, he certainly did so in respect of a pension granted him by Burgundy in 1471. Morton, too, "who is at present Chancellor of England and Archbishop of Canterbury", is specifically mentioned by Commines as being present in the 1475 Pecquiny negotiations. [2]

Hastings had never been close to Richard (long in the north) as he had to his brother, and in temperament the two were clearly opposites. The general opinion was that Hastings more than shared Edward IV's more luxurious excesses, and indeed helped provide the king with mistresses; and not only was Richard in his laws and letters to show a rather sharp puritanical outlook, with which he may already have irritated Hastings, he was also soon to make a genuine effort, as king, to return to the more just and liberal style of government which Edward IV had early practised, but partly abandoned in the self-indulgence and laxity of his later years. Already Richard may have made Hastings aware that he blamed Edward's associates in this respect; and, if so, Hastings may have begun to wonder about his future. The move from Protector to King would make Hastings and his like even more vulnerable to Richard's disapproval. It was Hastings who had tasted the sweets of power and new-found wealth in London, and, an older and, he may have felt, more experienced statesman, he would not be prepared to lose this rich and intoxicating confectionery without a struggle, to the death if need be.

It would be understandable, in many ways, if his resentment of Richard, twenty years or so younger and little known in London, suddenly leaping to power over his head, carried an echo of Cassius' of Brutus:

I am a soldier, I,
Older in practice, abler than yourself
To make conditions.

And there was no deeper personal bond, as with the two Romans, to bridge the rift as Cassius tries stumblingly to bridge it with his

I said, an elder soldier, not a better:
Did I say, better?

Morton, whose shrewd grasp of intrigue has never been disputed, would have sensed or known much of this and easily gauged his man, quite apart from reminding him of the French pension. He may even have dangled before Hasting's dazzled eyes the gratitude and rewards that would be heaped on him by Henry Tudor, should his aid help establish him on the English throne. Hastings may have accepted as legally irreversible the bastardizing of the princes and been made to realise it was now either Richard or Henry as king. If Morton also managed to insinuate that the next step after disinheritance might well be the murder of the princes, old loyalties would support present treason. Although there was no question of any disappearance of the boys at this time — Edward V was in the royal apartments in the Tower, Richard, Duke of York, the younger boy, in sanctuary with his mother or only just released — this rumour was certainly put out to support Henry Tudor's invasion a few months later, at the time of the Duke of Buckingham's rebellion, also partly manoeuvred by Morton.

The traditional assumption that fear for the princes alone, especially at such an early stage in the proceedings, could have motivated Hastings seems to me to show a starry-eyed misapprehension of the complexities of late medieval statesmanship and the power struggle, especially where characters like Hastings and Morton were concerned. In effect, it would mean that Hastings was hazarding his life and career on the *possibility* that an uncle, hitherto known for probity and a sense of justice, *might* at some unspecified future date get rid of the child nephews whose claim to the throne had just been legally nullified. A far more tangible and self-aggrandizing objective must surely have induced Hastings to take such risks. The argument that in fact Hastings and Morton were totally innocent, and that Richard made up the whole thing in order to get rid of them (but why, if innocent?), hardly merits intelligent consideration; although Morton seems at times to have tried to convey this senseless impression (perhaps understandably, if he did not want his secret connection with Henry Tudor known), and the Croyland Third Continuator's reference to the execution of Rivers and Grey (after Hastings' own death) as "the second innocent blood which was shed on the occasion of this sudden change"[3] appears to try to support it. (Once again, how could such a sentiment, showing such Woodville-Hastings-Morton bias, be expressed by John Russell, the man who as Chancellor was to open Richard's 1484 Parliament with a plea against "rebellion or commotion against the prince", and reference to the "fall and righteous punishment" of Buckingham? "... the kingdom has been led into darkness by those who recently rebelled against their king, an act contrary to the commandments of God Himself. This darkness can be remedied only if the people of England employ the light of reason for 'the advancing of the common weal' ''.)[4]

One traces the same unlikely claim of the innocence of Morton and Hastings in Mancini (Russell had been stringent on Mancini's masters the faithless French — "our old new-reconciled enemies" — who had broken oaths and treaties). "At first", writes Mancini, "the ignorant crowd believed, although the real truth was on the lips of many, namely that the plot had been feigned by the duke so as to escape the odium of such a crime".[5] "The crime", in fact, of executing a friend totally without cause! How can anyone believe Mancini's informants were unbiassed after such a passage, and that some of the same partisans did not influence whoever wrote the Croyland accounts? The assumption of innocence on Morton's part is, in fact, palpably contrary to his actions throughout his later career, dedicated as it was to the elevation of Henry Tudor to the throne. It was not without shrewdness that Edward IV had at first distrusted the turn-coat nature of his temporary conversion from the Lancastrian to the Yorkist cause. Morton was ambitious, able and worth using; but Edward's initial uneasiness proved fully justified.

More's statement of Richard that he loved Hastings well "and loath was to have lost him"[6] gives a very different impression and may be partly true. Richard may not have realised the effect of some of his remarks on Hastings, still Lord Chamberlain, or indeed intended anything that Hastings may have feared. What emerges clearly is the anger and decisive action Richard always showed at unexpected disloyalty in those he had trusted.

This decisive action was taken, of course, at the celebrated Tower meeting immortalised by Shakespeare and More, quite obviously on the version he had heard from Morton or from others, perhaps older than himself, in Morton's household or state employment. Those, like Alison Hanham, who deride More's having been influenced by Morton owing to his youth, overlook not only Morton's special interest in the young More's intelligence (he was responsible for sending him to university) but also the fact that many besides More, older as well as younger, passed through Morton's household and More would naturally be acquainted with them and talk to them. And as Morton did not die until 1500, his influence would stretch on, through others, well into the sixteenth century.

The accretions of witchcraft accusations and Richard's "wither'd arm" (which he viciously accused Jane Shore and the Queen of causing) are purely fictional devices in this story of the Tower arrest of Hastings and Morton. It is well established on contemporary evidence that the only "deformity" ever attributed to Richard, even by his bitter later enemies such as Rous (writing to seek the patronage of Henry VII) was that one shoulder was slightly higher than the other: this is suggested in the nearest contemporary portrait (based, it is generally agreed, on an original) and the hump that appeared on some versions of it later has been proved, by modern infra-red photography, as Dr. Pamela Tudor-Craig the art historian has recorded, to be a deliberate "fake" painted on the original, in Tudor times. Richard's prowess in battle was in no way affected. More, we must remember, was writing a humanist "morality" on the theme of tyranny, for which the Tudor portrait of the defeated enemy, Richard III, provided the ideal central figure. It was capable of being extended to monster size for dramatic purposes. There is no doubt that the theatre-minded More's intentions were dramatized semi-fiction. As A.F. Pollard has pointed out: "If More's Richard III is primarily dramatic, the question of its fidelity to historical fact hardly arises".[7]

It is possible that in between the first Council meeting, from which it is claimed Richard disappeared for an hour, and his return, the Protector did discover by some means a plot against his authority and some treasonable activity in respect of Henry Tudor. (That he himself had spies in]Brittany later we know, and some report from there may well have reached him.) It may be (we have only Morton's description of the two appearances to go on) he really appeared only once, having made his discovery overnight, or at least before the meeting began. In view of his letter to York on 10 June he could indeed have been accumulating evidence of the intended revolt for at least three days. In any case, the accusation of treason against Hastings, Morton and Lord Stanley (present husband of Henry Tudor's mother) was apparently made, and with armed support the revolt was suppressed before it had time to come to a head.

More controversial, is the question of the date of Hastings' death. According to More he was executed without trial, on the spot, and the date was Friday, 13 June. A week later, Friday, 20 June, has been argued, curiously enough, by both a rigid traditionalist (Alison Hanham) and some revisionists of the more romantic kind (Markham, Lindsay, Josephine Tey), for totally different reasons: one derogatory to, one highly sympathetic to, Richard. Hanham dates the whole Tower meeting as well as execution a week later in order, it becomes clear, to post-date the obtaining of the young Richard, Duke of York, from sanctuary, given by Croyland as Monday, 16 June. The Hastings-Morton plot is thereby made to spring directly from this event and their supposed fears for the lives of both princes now they were in Richard's power. The revisionists, on the other hand, maintain the date of Friday, 13 June for the Tower meeting and Richard's arrest of Hastings, but claim he was not executed until after a due pause for investigation and trial, on the following Friday, 20 June.

It must be added that J.A. Speares also thinks 20 June the more likely date for Hastings' execution, his study and experience of statecraft and English law convincing him that in fact Richard could not possibly have ordered and carried out this execution in the way described: it was a totally unconstitutional action which no monarch, with his Privy Council present, let alone a Protector, could take, or even believe he could take. And there is no question that there were many others present, who not only would protest and prevent but whose support Richard would be dependent on later. Only a handful of the full Council present were conspirators. From time immemorial there had been certain restraints on this kind of action and a king was always subject to a Council in some degree. *And the Council in this case was present,* and Richard was not even king.

One argument for the date of 13 June for Hastings' execution has always been the *Inquisitio Post Mortem,* "the usual official inquiry into the estates of a deceased tenant of the crown". This was, accordingly to A.R. Myers, "made by Richard's own officials; and it stated that Hastings died on June 13th."[8] Mr. Speares denies that this is conclusive evidence, on the ground that the entry would have been made later and dates given in these cases were often mis-remembered and incorrect. Alison Hanham in any case ignores the Post Mortem, and bases her conjecture (which she thereafter treats as fact) that both the Tower meeting and execution took place a week later, on 20 June, on an entry in the London

Mercers Company minutes of Sunday, 15 June. This shows, she maintains, that Morton (arrested at the same time as Hastings) was still at liberty. "The mercers' meeting had been called to discuss a reported conversation between Hastings, Morton and Russell, and there is no suggestion whatever that Hastings was now dead". She adds the admittedly ambiguous letter from Simon Stallworth to Sir William Stonor, on 21 June, in which he gives the date of Hastings' execution as "Friday last". [9]

Apart from arguments that "Friday last" in this case, and medieval usage, could mean not "Friday, yesterday" but the Friday of the previous week, Mrs. Hanham's contentions have been challenged by Dr. B.P. Wolffe, on the grounds that the entry in the Mercers' book belongs more probably to the year 1482 or 1479, and the accounts of the controller of Calais (of which Hastings was Constable until his death) gave this date 13 June, in addition to the Post Mortem.[10] J.A. Speares on this maintains his objection of late entries and faulty dates, and the controversy remains unresolved. Mrs. Hanham's contention that Mancini and the early Tudor chroniclers place Hastings' execution after the delivery of the Duke of York is true, but, as in her own case, one feels this is done mainly because it logically follows the assumption of Richard's guilt, and that he would have to have the child in his power before moving against Hastings. This seems to me partisanship to a theory rather than a genuine regard for the evidence, equivalent to Lingard's bold and revealing assumption of Richard's murder of the princes in order to justify another improbability: "the man who could shed the blood of two nephews to procure the crown would not refuse to allow the character of his mother to be slandered for the same purpose".[11] This is chop logic, and not historical investigation.

What no one has pointed out is the extreme oddity of the fact that in this case of the execution of a peer of considerable authority, Lord Chamberlain of England in fact, not a single *official* record appears to exist, and we are totally dependent on the story of one of the alleged conspirators, Morton. No one else present has left a record. This lack of documentation of a Council meeting, with such a dramatic and unusual climax, must be rare in English history, and I strongly suggest that it may not be coincidental that John Morton's nephew, Robert Morton, always very close to him, became Master of the Rolls in the Tower under

King Henry VII. It would explain the missing official documents more damningly than the rumours that the Tudor-patronised Polydore Vergil also destroyed some documents.

We must, I feel, in the circumstances leave the question of the date of Hastings' execution open. Whether Richard acted arbitrarily, or followed a due course of law in allowing an interval for trial or production of his proofs to the Council, Hastings died, Morton and (it would seem) Lord Stanley were accused and put in custody, and one John Foster, who had entered Hastings' service in 1481, was arrested at the same time, and released from the Tower only on 10 March the following year. He was associated by marriage with John Morton's nephew Robert and his fate was mentioned anxiously by Stallworth to one of Foster's relatives, Sir William Stonor. The Stonors were Lancastrian in sympathy and for holders of the theory that John Russell, Bishop of Lincoln, in spite of being Richard's Chancellor, was responsible for the antagonistic and pro-Lancastrian passages in the Third Continuation of the Croyland Chronicle, it may be worth noting that Stallworth was prebendary of Lincoln and therefore a servant to Russell. If Russell were a double agent, only ostensibly serving the crown, it would explain the Croyland malice; but it seems a rather far-fetched notion in this case, as there are no other evidences of Russell's dissent and associations, as so notably with Morton. It was Morton, not Russell, who was awarded the Chancellorship and other high offices under Henry VII. Russell retired to his diocese.

There are conflicting accounts in chronicles even that Lord Stanley was present or arrested. If he was, he would appear to have been suspect mainly because of his wife, Margaret Beaufort, for he must certainly have been released quickly: he witnessed the delivery of the great seal to John Russell on 27 June,[12] and he took a prominent part in Richard's coronation on 6 July. He may well have felt less antagonistic to Richard than his wife, and no special bond of loyalty to her long-absent son. His ambivalence indeed remained marked even up to the last minute at Bosworth Field.

A point worth considering is Hastings' "formidable body of indentured retainers, men of substance with hosts of followers behind them, who had contracted to serve him in peace and war."[13] This powerful build-up of what might be termed almost a private army, in the feudal tradition, must have constituted a threat, and it is difficult to believe Richard was not aware of it, and perhaps of an imminent move to use it. S.B. Chrimes also suggests Hastings may have been killed accidentally while others were being arrested, although the fact that such a theory could be put forward by a noted historian of the period shows something of the obscurity of the actual proceedings. Memoranda by a wool merchant, George Cely, on the rumours buzzing round London use, of Hastings, the words "deceased in trouble",[14] and the Calais entry is also inexplicit.

If Richard at the same time accused the ex-Queen and Jane Shore of complicity, as More maintains, the connecting link here would be Shore, for Hastings originally appears to have had no love for the Woodvilles and his influence on Edward IV is said to have been resented by them. Although Jane Shore is often given as Hastings' mistress (including by More), she was more certainly that of the Marquess of Dorset, the Queen's son, and came under Hastings' protection (not necessarily in the sexual sense) only on Dorset's flight into sanctuary. Many historians, including More, have thought her association with the Queen, as the King's former mistress, impossible ("yet would she, of all folk, least make Shore's wife of counsel, whom of all women she most hated"[15]); but this is Victorian or humanist morality, not that of the medieval Court, or even of the Edwardian (Queen Alexandra so liked Edward VII's last mistress, Mrs. Alice Keppel, that she arranged for her to see him on his death-bed). Jane Shore's character by reputation (even with More) was disarmingly amiable and generous.

Richard seems to have caused her to do public penance following this affair, "going before the cross in procession upon a Sunday, with a taper in her hand";[16] but it was a mild enough rebuke if conspiracy were involved. More is only partly right that Richard "spoiled her of all that ever she had — and sent her body to prison", and he was provably wrong in the required religious "morality" climax of her death in old age and penury. In fact, when Richard was king his solicitor-general, Thomas Lynom, desired to marry Jane, and the King's letter to "the Right Rev. Father in God the Bishop of Lincoln our Chancellor", although expressing doubts on the desirability of such a match, was a model of tolerance:

"BY THE KING.

"Right Reverend Father in God, &c, signifying unto you that

it is showed unto us, that our servant and solicitor, Thos. Lynom, marvellously blinded and abused with the late wife of William Shore, now being in Ludgate by our commandment, hath made contract of matrimony with her, as it is said, and intendeth, to our full great marvel, to proceed to effect the same. We, for many causes, would be sorry that he so should be disposed, pray you therefore to send for him, and in that ye godly may exhort and stir him to the contrary. And if ye find him utterly set for to marry her, and none otherwise would be advertised, then, if it may stand with the law of the church, we be content (the time of marriage being deferred to our coming next to London), that upon sufficient surety found of her good abearing ye do send for her keeper and discharge him of our commandment by warrant of these, committing her to the rule and guiding of her father or any other, by your discretion, in the mean season." [17]

Richard's "full great marvel", which seems unfeigned, rather amusingly indicates his own imperviousness to Jane's physical attractions, which captivated so many, and perhaps less a puritanical than an a-sexual nature. It is usually affirmed that the bedazzled Thomas did, in fact, heed the King's advice, but this is not so. In the Will of her father (1487) "Elizabeth Lineham" is described as "my daughter". As wife of a solicitor-general (Lineham did not die until 1518) she would certainly not have lived and died in poverty; and her father, William Lambert, was himself three times Warden of the Mercers Company, and therefore a City man of substantial means. William Schore, her first husband, was either dead or the marriage annulled. A Papal letter of 1476, long before, appointed a commission of bishops to hear her petition for the annulment of her marriage to Schore (described as a Mercer and not as a Goldsmith, the traditional description) on the ground of impotence. [18]

In letters to York Richard certainly accused the ex-Queen and her adherents of conspiracy; yet this, too, assorts oddly with his urging of the Queen, through his intermediary Thomas Bourchier, Archbishop of Canterbury, to give up her son Richard to join his brother.* This she did on Monday, 16 June, apparently without

* It is another of More's notable errors that he gives Rotherham, Archbishop of York (a known Woodville adherent also detained for a time after the Hastings conspiracy), as this intermediary.

realising she was being personally accused in any way, although she was still too afraid, it seems, to leave sanctuary herself. The suggestion that "threats" were used seems hardly viable, though More and others claim the Council itself had suggested the presence of the child in sanctuary (and his possible escape) was a danger to the state and if he were not yielded up force might be necessary. This seems like an "explanation" of Elizabeth Woodville's behaviour diplomatically concocted in Tudor times, to excuse the mother of Henry VII's queen who was also the grandmother of Henry VIII. The main plea with her to release the child seems to have been that the elder boy, alone in the Tower, would welcome his brother's company, especially in view of his coming coronation, fixed for 22 June. The elaborate dialogue and lamentations dreamt up by Sir Thomas More in his drama can certainly be discounted, although it may contain some elements of truth, including the interesting plea of Elizabeth that the younger boy had been ill. It is difficult to believe that, had she refused, Richard, overriding the Archbishop whose support he needed to retain, would have used force, or that Bourchier, an aged and respected cleric, would have passed on such a message. Sanctuary was sanctuary, and Elizabeth would have been in her rights to refuse to release her son.

The sanctuary was guarded, not unnaturally, for there was either a rumour or an assumption that an attempt might be made for the escape of the Queen's daughters, and doubtless the boy too. It is a not uninteresting rumour in view of later ones concerning the princes. Whatever her distrust of Richard (and news of Stillington's revelations may not have reached her, as King Edward V's coronation had not yet been cancelled), it is necessary to point out that at the date she released her small son no attempt had been made to execute her brother, Lord Rivers, and her other son, Sir Richard Grey.

That this came, on 25 June, seems to have been an inevitable result of the Hastings-Morton conspiracy. Already in custody in Yorkshire, it is difficult to see how either Woodville could have been *directly* concerned; yet Richard's accusation of Woodville involvement was clear, unless in his letter to York of 10 June he was referring to a quite different plot. If so, this has not come to light. If Hastings was executed on 13 June, there was still an unexplained delay, even allowing for Rous' statement that Rivers and Grey were executed only after trial by the Duke of Northumberland.

Northumberland or others (Richard's close adherent, Richard Ratcliffe, has been named) could have travelled north in the five days from 20 June. The delay after 13 June could possibly have been caused by the gathering of full evidence of Woodville complicity. At any rate both men, and the elderly Sir Thomas Vaughan, were executed at Pontefract, Rivers having made a Will at Sheriff Hutton on 23 June, requesting "my Lord of Gloucester, in the worship of Christ's passion and for the merit and weal of his soul, to comfort, help, and assist, as supervisor (for very trust) of this testament, that mine executors may with his pleasure fulfill this my last will".[19]

A scholar of learning and a courtier of florid display, he was not by nature a man of action; the Woodvilles had played for high stakes, and lost, and in the manner of the time accepted the penalty (Caxton, whose first printed book had been Rivers' *Dictes or Sayings of Philosophers,* took his death less philosophically than Rivers himself had done, lamenting the untimely demise of so learned a man). Richard ordered his widow to receive payment of all duties accruing from the estates which had been settled on her as her jointure, and to Hastings' widow he acted with even more generosity, allowing her the wardship and marriage of her son, and the sole charge of her husband's vast estates, from which he removed the attainder.[20] It was by no means a usual royal gesture: in such cases the king had the right to take all, and often did, in order to divide the spoils between himself and his more loyal followers. Such wardships had once been given to the Woodvilles after attainders, as when Dorset was granted the rich pickings yielded by the wardship of Clarence's son. But Richard's concern for women was always conspicuous; an odd characteristic, some might say, in one who is supposed to have had no concern at all for the lives of small children. Kindness to women and children often go together.

On the whole, there was a minimum of executions, and at least two Woodvilles, Lionel, Bishop of Salisbury, Queen Elizabeth's brother, and Viscount Lisle, her brother-in-law, came over to Richard's side. Stallworth again is one informant on this. Hastings' earlier boast that Richard's triumph over the Woodvilles had been "effected without any slaughter, or indeed causing as much blood to be shed as would be produced by a cut finger",[21] had recoiled ironically upon himself. But others went free, and were soon taking part, Lancastrians and Yorkists alike, at Richard's coronation. Ruthlessness had been used, but it was not prolonged. The Duke of Northumberland was coming south again with the requested troops from Yorkshire, but when they came they gave little indication of the strength and fierceness the south popularly attributed to them in anticipation, and to the "wild North" in general. They appeared "in their best jackes and rusty salettes", wrote Fabyan (who was there) contemptuously, "with a few in white harness not burnished to the sale". [22] By the time they arrived, in any case, the capital was calm, after the usual plethora of rumours, and fears of retaliations. The wool merchant George Cely left on the spare leaf of his memorandum curious evidence of the confused reports that circulated. "Chamberlain is deceased in trouble ... The Bishop of Ely is dead." [23]

But John Morton, Bishop of Ely, unlike the Chamberlain, was not dead. With deference to his cloth (which would in any case prevent his execution, except with papal sanction on a matter of heresy), and in response to a plea on his behalf, assuring Richard of their own loyalty, by Oxford University, Richard had merely placed him in the Duke of Buckingham's protective custody. He was to be the Nemesis that pursued Richard to his death at Bosworth Field, and beyond.

1 Letter from Simon Stallworth to Sir William Stonor (*Excerpta Historica,* p.16)

2 Commines, i.267: 262.

3 Croyland Third Continuator, p.489.

4 Cotton MSS, Vitel. E.x.p.139. Halsted, ii.288n. Kendall, p.281.

5 Mancini, p.91.

6 More, p.46.

7 A.F. Pollard: *The Making of Sir Thomas More's Richard III.* p. 231.

8 *The Character of Richard III: History Today,* Vol. IV, No. 8, August 1954, p. 519n.

9 Stonor Letters, No. 331. Hanham, p.24.

10 EHR LXXXIX (1974) 835-44. See also Isolde Wigram, *The Ricardian*, III, 50, Sept. 1975, pp.27-29, and J.A.F. Thomson, BIHR. No. 117, Vol. 48, 1975, pp.22-30.

11 John Lingard: *History of England,* Vol. IV, p.114n.

12 Rymer, *Foedera,* XII, 189. Hanham, p.113.

13 S.B. Chrimes: *Lancastrians, Yorkists and Henry VII*, p.131.

14 Hanham, p.41.

15 More, p.49.

16 Ibid, p.55.

17 Halsted, ii.343.

18 *Ricardian,* No. 39, Dec. 1972, p.13.

19 *Excerpta Hist.* p.248.

20 Harl. MSS. 433, fol. 166 and 27.

21 Croyland, p.488.

22 Fabyan, p.516. Halsted, ii.125.

23 P.R.O. S.C.1 53/19. Hanham, p.41.

IV
Rumours of Murder and Invasion

The throne was now Richard's for the taking, but there were still formalities to be observed. The date for Edward V's coronation was cancelled. Instead, a Sunday discourse was given at St. Paul's Cross, a customary place for ecclesiastical and political announcements, by Dr. Ralph Shaa, brother of the Lord Mayor of London, Edmund Shaa. This "showed openly that the children of King Edward IV were not legitimate, nor rightful inheritors of the crown", and concluded by pointing out the greater title of the Lord Protector and urging his immediate election as king. [1]

Fabyan's chronicle, quoted above, was written years later but he was a citizen of the time and possibly present, being an alderman of the City and a prominent member of the Drapers Company. He makes no mention of Shaa's stating, as subsequent chronicles claim, that Edward IV himself was illegitimate and indeed it is difficult to conceive Richard allowing this reflection on his mother, with whom he had been recently living and whose house he still used for meetings. Neither the Croyland Third Continuator nor the malicious Rous mention Shaa's sermon, and although More does, and states the use of this old story, he notes it was "rather signified than fully explained" and Richard had no hand in it (it is obvious More, who was no fool, realised the story he had heard was highly improbable if Richard were involved). Even later Tudor chroniclers such as Hall claim the over-zealous doctor angered Richard by using it. Though some historians accept it, I suggest myself that the story was not used by Shaa at all, as the Fabyan account suggests, and confusion with a claim of Clarence's about his elder brother's being a "bastard" gave rise to it.

Parliament had been summoned on 13 May in the name of Edward V, but in rather mysterious circumstances the order for it had been countermanded — whether by Richard himself, or by his enemies, remains a matter of historians' dispute. The Assembly that now gathered at Westminster on 25 June was not legally a true Parliament, but it was very fully attended, comprising Lords and Commons. The Duke of Buckingham the day before had addressed the chief citizens, Mayor and Aldermen of the City at Guildhall, on the subject of Richard's accession, with an eloquence remarked on by Fabyan, and some of these chief citizens formed a delegation in the less attended Commons section.[2] A roll of parchment endorsed Richard's title, the Woodvilles and the evils they had brought on the state were castigated, and the matter of the late king's illegal marriage was reiterated. It was resolved to present the roll to Richard at his mother's house, Baynard's Castle, the following day.

This was done by an impressive assembly, and in the circumstances it seems clear that Cecily, Duchess of York, fully approved of her son's assuming the crown. A number of sources suggest (in highly dramatised fashion) that she in fact knew of the prior contract and had remonstrated with Edward IV on his marriage to Elizabeth Woodville. Of this there is no proof. But Richard's election to the throne was, from the point of view of medieval statesmanship, preferable to the rule of a minor, and Cecily was not a Neville by birth for nothing. Richard had shown himself an able administrator and general, impeccably loyal to his brother throughout his reign. In the political morality of the times it was not an unwise decision, nor a generally unpopular one. He seems to have shown some reluctance, which Tudor chronicles naturally claim to have been hypocrisy; but by this stage his refusal would have been unthinkable. There was no alternative candidate.

His reign officially commenced on that day, 26 June, and "upon thursday after", according to the *Chronicles of London,* "the said Duke of Glowcestir wt a greate company of lordes and Gentilmen wt also the Mayr and the Craftes, went vnto Westmynster, and there toke possession of the Regalite sitting in Westmynster halle; wher vpon his right hand satte the Duke of Northfolk, and vpon that other hand the Duke of Suffolk.

"And he, there so sittyng, called byfore hym alle the Juges of the

Temporall lawe, gyuyng theym straitely in Commaundement to execute his lawes Justly and indifferently to euerych persone aswell to powre as Riche. And aftir departed in to the kynges palays, and ther was loged. And the said Duke was with quene Anne his wif at and in Westmynster Chirch crowned wt greate solempnyte of many states and gentilmen, the vjth day of July."[3]

Richard's Coronation was, in fact, splendidly attended by the nobility, great care having been taken to divide the honours between known Lancastrians and Yorkists, neither taking precedence. Henry Tudor's mother, Margaret Beaufort, bore the Queen's train, and her husband, Lord Stanley, whose last-minute treachery with his brother at Bosworth was to cost Richard his kingdom and his life, carried the mace.

"These be the dukes, earls, lords and knights that were at the coronation of our sovereign lord King Richard III and Queen Anne, the first year of his noble reign, the 6th day of July, 1483" is written in an ancient MS roll. [4] The list of over one hundred given includes three Dukes, nine Earls, two Viscounts, twenty-one Lords and innumerable knights, as well as seventeen who were made Knights of the Bath for the occasion. Apart from the Stanleys and others of rank, one notes the Lancastrian receiver of so many letters, Sir William Stonor, and a name to play an important part in Richard's history, Sir James Tyrell, in addition to a Sir Thomas Bulleyn, a surname which was destined to reverberate ominously two reigns hence.

The attempt at reconciliation and peace was so marked that it seems totally irrational to suppose that Richard, having achieved his object by legal means, now intended inevitably to shatter this peace, and the binding together of the white rose and the red, by a wanton act of murder: that of his officially displaced nephews. Nothing that Richard ever did was irrational or unintelligent: the irrationality is surely in the supposition.

Where were the princes? They were still in the Tower apartments, and there has even been speculation that Edward V attended his uncle's coronation. The Tower Wardrobe accounts give elaborate details of clothes apparently prepared for the boy's coronation, but they are inserted among the later coronation accounts with the wearer styled "lord Edward, son to late king Edward the fourth", which certainly suggests the account was written up, at least, after Edward V had officially been degraded to "the Lord Bastard".

This title was given him after he lost the kingship, because he was allowed to retain the earldoms of March and Pembroke conferred on him by his father. Horace Walpole was convinced that these robes were intended for the ex-king to attend Richard's coronation, and reiterated this belief when challenged in his *Reply to the Observations of the Rev. Dr. Milies,* Dean of Exeter and President of the Society of Antiquaries, on the Wardobe Account of 1483, published by the Society of Antiquaries of London. [5] The robe account could, of course, have been entered up later, as has been suggested already of other records of events, and the general view is that they were clothes intended for the young king's own coronation, if not some other ceremony. It would surely have been needlessly embittering for the boy to be made to attend the coronation of his supplanter, nor would Richard be likely to remind those who took part, unduly, of the means by which he had succeeded.

But disaffection does not vanish with the pomp and circumstance of a royal occasion. Regal power breeds jealousy, and a new enemy to Richard was scheming with an old one. At the Coronation, Buckingham had headed the list of peers and bore the king's train, holding the white staff of office as seneschal or hereditary lord high steward of England. He had appeared (and I use this word deliberately) not only to support and even press for Richard's elevation to the throne, but also to stand aside from the Morton-Hastings plot to thwart this design. Nevertheless, we hear nothing from the records of his reaction to this plot, only the fact that Richard gave Morton *into his custody.* The details of this are certainly obscure, and it is often overlooked that one account, that of the hostile Rous, maintains that this was done at *Buckingham's own request.* Rous lets slips, perhaps inadvertently, that Richard imprisoned the Archbishop of York and the Bishop of Ely in separate places, strongly encouraged in these things by Henry, Duke of Buckingham. [6]

In view of the apparently swift *volte face* that followed, I suggest this request, if true, may not be without serious significance. There is also some question as to when and where exactly this custody took place. Certainly Morton and Buckingham finally discussed schemes for eliminating Richard at the Duke's principal home at Brecknock in Wales; but they (or at least the Duke) certainly did not go there right away. The Hastings affair was shattered by

Richard and his supporters on 13 June (or 20 June at the latest); but Richard was still then only Protector, and I have already pointed out, a view emphasised by the ex-Foreign Office diplomat J.A. Speares, that the very fact that Richard was only Protector, not even presumptive king, makes the More story of his arbitrary action, without legal trial or warrant, in this matter highly unlikely, unless he were already backed by the loyal members of the Council present. (It is not normally pointed out that Morton and Hastings were at the Tower as members of the Council, and obviously the other Council members were present. No other explanation of their presence at the Tower than a Council meeting is feasible.) It was subsequent to this, in any case, that Richard was formally offered the throne, and indeed it may have been that the Council's fears were aroused enough by the discovery of this plot to make the necessity for a grown man as King seem to them the more urgent. The shadow of renewed civil war cannot have been far from men's thoughts. The Hastings/Morton conspiracy showed the dangers that were looming, with the situation obviously fertile for a power struggle.

Buckingham, at least, was not at Brecknock; he was in London openly supporting the idea that Richard should become king. Probably in the circumstances the councillors and prominent officials in the City needed little persuasion, and Buckingham's contribution to their attitude has been greatly exaggerated. We are told only a few citizens at the back of the hall cried out for Richard to be king, in particular the apprentices;[7] but the English apprentices and journeymen have always been a more potent force in English politics than most historians allow for, and in this case their masters, the master craftsmen and merchants who provided them with employment in the City of London, were obviously also deeply involved in the move for Richard's election. The English workman of the better class and skills has always shared a certain amount of snobbery with the middle classes, and been suspicious of the "new rich" thrown up by wars and political upheavals. Edward IV was highly popular in the City, and the jumped-up Woodvilles with their avarice would be infinitely less preferable as rulers, in City eyes, than Edward's own brother, known to be closely loyal to him and a capable administrator.

Hastings, too, was something of a *parvenu**, known to have been

---

*It is curious that Alison Hanham accepts that he disliked the Woodvilles because of

enriched by Edward but also a panderer to his vices; and the more staid men of the City, with their solid virtues and an anxious eye on their wives and daughters, again would have felt Richard, Edward's brother of more sober disposition, a safer figure to control the government. More's picture of Mayor and Aldermen as credulous cretins (entertainingly dramatised by Shakespeare) does not fit in with the facts of City life and aspirations, although it is certainly the picture that Morton, the failed plotter, would try to present. What was the real nature of his involvement with the Mercers Company, one wonders, and why were Hastings and John Russell, Bishop of Lincoln, noted as being concerned? It is perhaps the only suspicious connection of Russell's name with plotters against Richard, although there is no proof that what concerned the Mercers Company at their proposed meeting was in any way political. It is certainly, however, worth noting that Jane Shore's father was a prominent Mercer, and Jane Shore seems almost indisputably to have been implicated in the Hastings conspiracy. Could the Mercers Company have been used, or intended to be used, as a "cover" for something more sinister than an ordinary tradesmen's meeting?

How much, in fact, was Buckingham disaffected already? The ambiguity of his character has been so marked that both More and the later chroniclers, as well as Shakespeare, have been forced back on to the totally invalid suggestion that he became disaffected mainly because Richard refused him certain marks of gratitude for his support, most notably the Bohun estates. But it has long had to be acknowledged even by traditionalist historians that in fact this is a total red herring: so far from being refused these lucrative estates, Buckingham in fact had been granted livery of all these lands, which he claimed by right of descent as cousin and heir of Humfrey de Bohun, Earl of Hereford, on 13 July (within a week of Richard's coronation); and with them two days later also went the office which had been held by Hereford himself, Constable of England. [9] Whatever Buckingham considered he lacked under Richard, it was certainly not the Bohun inheritance, or wealth, power and high office.

---

their "base blood". In fact, his fortunes had been equally dependent on Edward's patronage (*vide* More, comparing Buckingham and Hastings: "both men of honor and of great power, the one by long succession from his ancestry, the other by his office and the king's favour."[8])

One of the factors always overlooked is that Henry Stafford, Duke of Buckingham, was married in 1466 to Elizabeth Woodville's sister Catherine.[10] Historians have occasionally assumed that he was resentful of this youthful "forced" marriage into the despised Woodville family, but there is absolutely no direct evidence for this, outside Mancini's statement that for this reason "he detested the queen's kin", which would appear to be based on gossip.[11] There is no reason to suppose that seventeen years later the marriage had not become a reasonably close and satisfactory one, as aristocratic marriages go. Certainly by 1483 there was a growing son and heir to help bind husband and wife together. It is surely reasonable to assume that it was through his wife that Buckingham learned of the journey towards London of Lord Rivers and the young king, and Woodville intentions or hopes to seize power. Perhaps he was sitting on the fence even at this stage, but keeping an eye to the main chance open in case his wife's family succeeded. That Catherine, Duchess of Buckingham, was still close to her sister will appear later.

It is necessary at this point to follow the situation as it developed in the Westminster sanctuary, where a totally new and dazzling proposition had been secretly made to the ex-Queen, who in spite of the vigilance of Richard's trusted adherent, John Nesfield, was certainly not completely sealed off from outside contacts. In fact, she had early been approached by Margaret Beaufort, wife of Lord Stanley and mother of that Henry Tudor who lurked in exile in faraway Brittany. It was through this mother that Henry derived a claim to the throne of England. Although the Beauforts from whom he inherited the claim were originally illegitimate, John of Gaunt's children by his liaison (later marriage) to Katherine Swynford had subsequently been legitimized, under the name De Beaufort, but with the parliamentary proviso that legitimization did not include any hereditary right to the throne.[12] (Gaunt was the fourth son of King Edward III, and uncle to the ill-starred Richard II. Edward IV claimed his royal descent through a female line descended from Edward III's third son, Lionel, Duke of Clarence, but it was ballasted by direct male descent from Edward III's fifth son, Edmund, Duke of York;[13] and there was no bar sinister in this Yorkist descent.) As Gaunt was Duke of Lancaster his descendants represented the Lancastrian claim. But with the deaths of King Henry VI and his son, Edward, Prince of

Wales, the Lancastrian line was extinct apart from those who held such slender claims as descendants of Edward III; and the obscure young Welshman, Henry Tudor, whose grandfather, the "commoner" Owen Tudor, had secretly married the widow of King Henry V, became a more vital factor in the stakes for royal power.

He had been taken into custody as a child after a rebellion of his uncle, Jasper Tudor, and apart from the brief six-months' restoration of Henry VI, when Edward IV temporarily lost his throne and went into exile, and Henry Tudor returned to Eton, he had remained in exile in Brittany virtually all his life. His danger as a Lancastrian candidate for the throne had long been recognised, and in 1475 Robert Stillington (that same Bishop of Bath and Wells concerned in the revelations of King Edward IV's pre-contract) had been sent to the Duke of Brittany in a vain attempt to obtain from him the surrender of young Henry Tudor, who had been granted an uneasy asylum in his territory.[14] It was not the only attempt of Edward IV to lay his hands on a potentially dangerous rival, not likely to be scrupulous about asserting his claim should Henry VI and his sole son (whose legitimacy was itself disputed) not survive.

Margaret Beaufort had hardly seen her son since infancy; but she was a highly ambitious woman, intensely conscious of her descent and the regal power which might one day be open to her only son. How far she carried her husband, Lord Stanley, with her is doubtful at this time; Richard, as we have seen, tended to trust him and very soon released him after Hastings' death. But Margaret was not content to carry the new Queen's train at the Coronation, and she seems already to have been scheming, with a Welsh physician named Lewis as go-between, with the ex-Queen, Elizabeth Woodville, in sanctuary.[15] It is possible that Dr Lewis went there first ostensibly to tend the younger prince, whom Elizabeth, according to More, claimed to have been ill. (The chronology is too undefined for one to assume that at the first visit Richard, Duke of York, had already left sanctuary.) At any rate, from subsequent history which confirms the accounts, it seems plain that Elizabeth was involved in a new idea, meant to recompense her for the elimination of her son, Edward V, from the throne. It was doubtless Margaret who thought of the plan to strengthen her son's dubious claim to the throne, and get him

Woodville, and possibly some dissident Yorkist, support. It was no less than his agreed marriage to the ex-Queen's eldest daughter, Elizabeth of York, now seventeen years old: thus the Yorkist claim would be united to the Lancastrian, and both Elizabeth Woodville and Margaret Beaufort become mothers-behind-the-throne, as it were.

Now if there is one thing apparent in Elizabeth Woodville's known character, it is that she was a realist, adept from long practice in the aggrandisement of her family. Given Richard's custody of the two boys (or even one of them), and his Council-supported position as Protector and later King, it must already have been obvious to her that the Woodvilles had lost the battle to control the government and throne. Her sons were out of her hands and unlikely to be restored to the succession. Her only hope lay in the armed support now being offered to her. And it was conditional on Henry Tudor, certainly not one of her sons, becoming King of England. A daughter as Queen of England was her only possible hope for a return to power; and in the circumstances it is not surprising that she seized on the idea.

There is no need to assume that she took for granted her sons were dead, or indeed in immediate danger. Had she looked ahead and at the matter more closely, she might have realised that in fact they were themselves a greater danger to Henry Tudor than to Richard (assuming she knew of Stillington's report); for if Elizabeth of York were accepted as legitimate, capable of representing the Yorkist claim on the throne, the two young boys, who under English hereditary rights took precedence to any sister as heir, must be legitimate also. Did a flicker of doubt on this count cross Elizabeth's mind? Literally, she was helping to place on the throne of England a man whose most dangerous rivals were, in fact, her own young sons. As early as these secret negotiations took place, there was no suggestion as yet that the princes were dead, whatever suspicions of Richard's intentions the Tudor plotters may have tried to plant in her mind. It is worth remembering that Elizabeth Woodville well knew Richard's loyalty and devotion to his brother, her husband, and his treatment of members of her own family, not related to him, would not necessarily extend to direct physical harm to his brother's own sons, his nephews, and the grandsons of his mother and of his father, Richard, Duke of York, to whose memory he had also shown consistent honour and affection.

Elizabeth of York

(Where, in fact, did the formidable Cecily, Duchess of York, his mother, stand in any supposed murder of her grandsons?)

In any case, and contrary to the impression conveyed by many writers on this subject (and, of course, the Lancastrian-inspired chronicles), Henry Tudor's bid for the throne of England was totally extraneous to, and indeed pre-dated, any question of Richard III's supposed tyranny and the murder of the Princes in the Tower. The claim was a longstanding Lancastrian claim, with Lancastrian support, and the debarring of the princes from the succession was no factor in the proposed invasion. It was merely an open gap through which Henry and his supporters could pass. If a rumour were put out that the princes had disappeared from view, and their uncle intended to murder them, or had already done so, so much the better for Henry's fortunes.

It is usually overlooked, though it may have considerable significance in connection with the disappearance of the princes, that Richard himself, who was no fool, and his advisers, were probably well aware of the danger to his nephews *from Henry*. His own claim to the throne had been legalised; Henry Tudor's most emphatically had not. Whatever Henry might do, although he might (and in fact did) get ratification of his kingship from Parliament in the unalterable event of his victory, his right to the throne would be "by right of conquest" only. He could strengthen it by marrying Edward IV's daughter, but hardly his sons. What would he have done had the boys remained alive? If there is a sinister implication here, it arises legitimately from the situation.

In fact, the first "rumour" of the murder of the princes, if one excepts Mancini's inexplicit identification of tearful men who suspected it *might* happen before his return to France early in July, seems to have appeared, most usefully for Henry Tudor and the Duke of Buckingham, at the climax of preparations for Henry's invasion and the outbreak of Buckingham's rebellion. This was at earliest late September and at latest mid-October, when Henry sailed. And on 24 September a letter written by the Duke of Buckingham to Henry Tudor on the proposed invasion, which being mentioned later in Parliament obviously got into the hands of Richard's agents, gave the "liberation" of the princes, not their murder, as one aim, although the Duke must have been fully aware that Henry had no intention of restoring them, only of taking the throne himself. John Morton, Bishop of Ely, had already fled *via*

Ely to Flanders, apparently deserting Buckingham at the height of his preparations. Why?

Chronicles and lives of Morton (a private MS of 1610 on Morton does not even mention Buckingham) say he "escaped" from Brecknock to the Isle of Ely, which suggests that in spite of the elaborate narratives of More and others in which he is depicted as persuading Buckingham to desert Richard and support Henry, the two men proved at variance in their objective. As Margaret Beaufort remained (probably deliberately, in view of her contacts with Elizabeth Woodville) in London, we can dismiss as the usual muddling of material the story that the Duke of Buckingham, aiming for the throne himself, was diverted by meeting near Brecknock Margaret's agent, Reginald Bray, and even Margaret herself, and thus being persuaded that Henry Tudor's was the better chance. It has not been overlooked by many historians that Buckingham himself had a minor claim to the throne, also by descent from the prolific Edward III, which as it did not include doubts about legitimacy could be ranked as superior to Henry's.

Why, in any case, did he fall out with Richard, and where was Richard in the meantime?

Within three weeks after the Coronation, possibly well aware as to how little he was personally known in the south and midlands, and how small was likely to be the understanding of people outside London of the circumstances of his accession, Richard set out on a royal progress, mainly to the midlands. He had already assembled the judges and enjoined on them the necessity for impartial administration of justice, sitting in the Court as Edward IV had done early in his reign: yet another indication of Richard's intention to get the governance of England back to the best and most moderate form for which his brother's reign had been notable before the slackness of his later years. On 18 July he issued a royal signet "for the payment of 52£ and 20d., resting due to divers persons for their services done his dearest brother the late king, and to Edward bastard, late called Edward V", the wording of which hardly suggests a man about to murder the sons of his "dearest brother". [16] He created Buckingham Constable of England for life, and confirmed his appointments as chief justice and chamberlain of the North and South Wales,[17] among other grants. John Howard, Duke of Norfolk, was made admiral of England, Ireland and Aquitaine for life, and relatives and followers of Richard such as the Earls of Surrey and Lincoln, Stillington, Sir James Tyrell, Robert Brackenbury and William Catesby were also suitably rewarded.[18]

Only one, the Duke of Buckingham, who received most, was to prove traitorous to Richard. Lincoln, eldest son of the Duke of Suffolk who had married one of Richard's sisters, was always particularly close and loyal to Richard, his uncle, and was made Governor of the king's household and demesnes in the North Later, Richard was said to have named him as his heir. Killed himself at the Battle of Stoke on rebellion against Henry VII, Lincoln's claim devolved on his younger brother, the Duke of Suffolk, who was to be one of the last of the many Yorkist "heirs" executed by Henry VII or his son and successor, Henry VIII.

On 23 July Richard left Windsor for Reading, where he granted to Katherine, Lady Hastings, his full pardon for the treason of her husband and lifted the attainder on her title and estates, promising "to protect and defend the widow and to suffer none to do her wrong."[19] At Oxford he was received at Magdalen College by the founder, Bishop Waynflete, and lodged there overnight. The next day, "at the command and desire of the king", two disputations were heard by him: in Moral Philosophy by Thomas Kerver, and in Divinity by John Taylor and William Grocyn (a friend and patron of Erasmus). He suitably rewarded the disputants, and thoughtfully paid the President and scholars "two bucks and five marks for wine". The next day he visited other parts of the University and heard further disputations, proceeding then to Woodstock.[20]

He was accompanied by the Bishops of Durham, Worcester, St. Asaph and St. David's, as well as Lincoln, Surrey, Lord Stanley (aware or not aware of his wife's treasonable activities in London?) and others. It is to the Bishop of St. David's that we owe an indication of the warm regard and optimism for the future with which the new king was received. In a letter to the Prior of Christ Church, Canterbury, dated sometime in August, he wrote: "He contents the people wher he goys best that ever did prince; for many a poor man that hath suffred wrong many days have be relevyd and helpyd by hym and his commands in his progresse. And in many grete citeis and townis were grete summis of money gif hym which he hath refusyd. On my trouth I lykyd never the condicions of ony prince so wel as his; God hathe sent hym to us for the wele of us al."[21]

Thomas Langton, Bishop of St. David's, was to remain faithful to this estimate of Richard III's character, and was later sent by the King to Rome, to join Dr John Sherwood, the Bishop-elect of Durham, in representing England at the Vatican.[22] Langton, like Russell, was a prelate-administrator of capability and the duplicity attributed to Russell, on the assumption that he wrote the entire Third Continuation of the Croyland Chronicle, is as without firm basis as any like distortion of Langton's loyalty to Richard would be. Alison Hanham's attempt to modify even Langton's obviously sincere panegyric of Richard, by what she admits to be a questionable reading of an almost illegible later passage in his original letter — criticising, according to her reading, the "sensual" nature of Richard's Court — has no basis as *fact,* although characteristically it has become "fact" in a later article by her.[23] Not only could Richard's influence on the Court hardly have been established by July 1483, when he left London on progress, but his letters and acts of government make quite clear the rather puritanical nature of his outlook and disapproval of his brother mainly in this respect. He had two avowed illegitimate children (hardly an excessive indication of adultery in a nobleman of that time, and often attributed in fact to before his marriage); but there are many indications in contemporary accounts, and even in antagonistic sources later, of the success of Richard's marriage and the blamelessness of his private life. Alison Hanham's contention that this private reputation of Richard can be ascribed only to the influence of Richard's 1955 biographer, Paul Murray Kendall, is totally untrue on historical and contemporary evidence, as many of us who were studying the subject before Kendall can attest.

The fact is indisputable that Richard won golden opinions on his progress both by his acts of beneficence and careful righting of wrongs, both personal and civic, where they were brought to his attention.* What is disputable is just what happened when Buckingham last visited him at Gloucester. That Richard at this stage still believed in Buckingham's loyalty seems indicated by the fact that it was only when he reached Leicester, where on 17 August he issued a mandate commanding "2000 Welsh bills or glaives" to

* One of the most interesting and helpful of his acts for the universities was to enable strangers to bring printed books into England and sell them by retail.

be made in haste, and commanding the impressment also of smiths, that he showed any signs of political unease.[24] He also sent for seventy knights and esquires of Yorkshire, to join him at Pontefract. Yet his alarm was still not great, for he proceeded to York with his wife Anne (who had joined him) and there held what was long described as "a second coronation", and which was in any case an elaborate ceremonial in the Cathedral. For this his young son Edward made the journey from his father's castle of Middleham, where he still lived and was under tuition. He was by now officially designated Prince of Wales. The lingering pageantry at York, which included dinners and plays, went on until the middle of September: dangerously late for the quelling of the Buckingham rebellion which was now well beyond planning stage. Richard had incontestable news of it only when he reached Lincoln, at the beginning of October.

In drama, it has become associated with the presumed fact of Richard's ordering of the murder of the princes while on progress, and his failure to recompense Buckingham for his services. The main More/Shakespeare story ascribes the murders not to Buckingham (said to be revolted by them) but to a bedraggled hanger-on named Tyrell, to whose lack of fortune and of scruples the King's attention was drawn by a page, and who was afterwards knighted for carrying out the murder. There is hardly need at this date to repeat at length this fantastic rigmarole. It has long been known that James Tyrell in fact was knighted after the Battle of Tewkesbury, by King Edward IV, on 4 May 1471, and was made a Knight Banneret by Richard as early as 24 July 1482, during the war with Scotland.[25] He had been created Master of the Horse in succession to his brother Thomas immediately after Richard's coronation (this was a post of the utmost importance: Queen Elizabeth's devoted Robert Dudley, Earl of Leicester, held it hardly a century later throughout his life). He had done notable service to Edward IV as well as Richard, and had been made Sheriff of Glamorgan some time before October 1477, with control of much other property in Wales. "The revenues he was drawing", writes T.B. Pugh, "gave him an income which put him among the richer members of the English gentry ... Tyrell's wealth shows what a great office of profit the sheriffdom of Glamorgan could be in the later Middle Ages."[26]

It was in this connection that he probably first became attached to Richard, who was "Lord of Glamorgan" as well as Governor of the North. But his rise to wealth and high office seems to have taken place after 1475, when prior to accompanying Edward IV's army on the French expedition which ended at Pecquiny, he made a Will in favour of his recent bride, Anne (there was as yet no child of the marriage). This Will shows some concern about his unpaid "dettes", incurred partly, he claims, through his sister's marriage (for which he had presumably had to pay both the expenses and dowry).* His association with the two Yorkist kings and his offices make it obvious he was in later years a long-trusted official and make nonsense of the Thomas More story.

This circumstantial account of the princes' murder by smothering (in which Tyrell was helped by named murderers, John Dighton and Miles Forrest), although it has been repeated *as fact* by certain historians down to our own day, is, however, supplemented even in More's work by the remarkable statement that "the lamentable murder of his innocent nephews ... hath nevertheless so far comen in question that some remain yet in doubt whether they were in his days destroyed or no."[27] The suggestion that Sir Robert Brackenbury, the Tower's Governor, was first approached through Richard's agent John Green to do the deed, but refused, and then yielded up the keys of the Tower meekly to Tyrell on command, is even more obvious fantasy. Not only would the Governor of the Tower not yield his office to anyone unless he were himself officially and finally displaced: "gentle" Brackenbury remained Governor of the Tower and loyal to Richard throughout his reign. He died with him at Bosworth Field.

In fact the rumours of the methods used to murder the two princes are so various and so conflicting that the tales positively emphasise the only certainty: that no one knew or knows how they died, or even if and when they did. The rumour that one survived (if only briefly, in one account, by hiding under the bed) was also persistent, and was noted long into Henry VII's reign. As Morton's biographer, Woodhouse, states categorically: "on proofs, which even stagger inquirers in our times, a belief had become very prevalent among the people that the Duke of York, younger son Edward IV, still survived".[28] It is typical of the kind of

* This Will, of which I appear to be the first to have obtained a copy, is among other neglected Tyrell family papers in the Suffolk County Record Office at Ipswich.

embroideries that circulated abroad that the French historian Molinet gives the following tale, quite different from but as affecting as More's:

"The eldest was simple and very melancholy, aware of the wickedness of his uncle, but the youngest was joyous and witty, nimble, and ever ready for dances and games; and he said to his brother, who wore the order of the garter, "My brother, learn to dance'; and his brother answered, 'It would be better for us to learn to die, for I think we shall not long remain in the world.' They were prisoners for about five weeks; and Duke Richard had them secretly slain by the captain of the Tower. And when the executioners came, the eldest was asleep, but the youngest was awake, and he perceived their intention, and began to say, 'Ha! my brother, awake, for they have come to kill you.' Then he said to the executioners, 'Why do you kill my brother? kill me, and let him live.' But they were both killed; and their bodies cast into a secret place.''[29]

Another foreign account claims they were killed falling off a bridge (i.e. trying to escape?).

More's story of their interment ("at the stair foot, meetly deep in the ground, under a great heap of stones''[30]) is itself incredible, if the burial were meant to be unheard and unnoticed by the Tower community of over 600 people. If the murders and burial occurred as tradition suggests, it is more than curious that none of these questioned the sudden disappearance of the boys from their midst or even, safely, in Henry VII's reign, came forward with a tale of noisy nocturnal operations. At least some of the Tower inhabitants must have looked after them, washed their linen and provided them with food. According to Sir George Buck, in fact diligent search was made for their bodies in the Tower after Henry's accession, and nothing found. Certainly More's suggestion that Richard, in an unlikely burst of religious scruple, arranged for an unknown priest to remove the bodies later to an unnamed but more hallowed spot, more suitable for a king's sons, seems made expressly to meet the discrepancy of this failure of Henry VII to discover the bodies, in spite of the detailed story of their murder and burial.

It must be added that More himself, though inclining to this version of the events which took place when he was a tiny child, is entirely honest that he heard totally different tales from others about Richard's "lamentable murder of his innocent nephews, the young king and his tender brother, whose death and final infortune hath nevertheless so far comen in question that some remain yet in doubt whether they were in his days destroyed or no".[31] According to Buck, whose scholarship is now acknowledged by good historians, the boys were "living freely and securely (and without question) long after this murder was said to be done."[32] Walpole repeats the story of a heavy chest containing the bodies in a "shyppe goynge to Flaunders". Concealment of the live princes on a journey to Flanders (where one of them at least was later claimed to be) is a story repeated in various forms, one of them suggesting they were, dead or alive, concealed in a chest thrown overboard, into the Thames or at sea. Muddled and overlapping versions of the "murder" abound.

It might be here worth noting that More, trying to be honest according to his lights, is not totally blind also to his one-time patron Morton's ambition: "lacking no wise ways to win favour".[33] Morton's character, in fact, particularly as a statesman later, has revolted even his biographers at times. He certainly cannot be taken as an unprejudiced witness in anything, and perhaps More began to realise this.

More, even so, was not the only Tudor-based writer to hear conflicting stories on the fate of the princes. Even Polydore Vergil, who arrived in England in 1502 and later came under the direct patronage, as an historian, of Henry VIII, admitted that it was generally reported and believed *"that the sons of Edward IV were still alive, having been conveyed secretly away, and obscurely concealed in some distant region".*[34]

The one thing that seems incontestable is that the boys were seen less frequently at the windows or playing in the Tower gardens after Richard's coronation, but even here dates become confused.

The Great Chronicle of London (written some time before 1496), for instance, states: "But afftyr Estyrn much whyspering was among the people yt the King hadd putt the childyr of King Edward to deth".[35] Yet "after Easter" in 1483 King Edward was only just dead, and the reference can only be to 1484. The date of 1484 might well be interesting, because the Act of Parliament which confirmed Richard's title and the illegitimacy of the princes, Titulus Regius, was passed in January 1484, and it writes of the princes in the present tense, as if they were still alive. It was in March, 1484, near Easter, that Elizabeth Woodville was to make her peace with

Richard and leave sanctuary. I shall return to this later.

Another passage in the Great Chronicle claims that during the mayoralty of Sir Edmund Shaa (October 1482 - October 1483) "the children of King Edward were seen shotying and playng in the garden of the Towyr by (*sic*) sundry tymes".[36] But the year indicated again seems 1484, when the Mayor was Sir Robert Billesdon. This kind of inaccuracy litters the evidence, and adds to the ambivalence which is so notable a feature of this whole mystery.

NOTES AND REFERENCES

IV — *Rumours of Murder and Invasion*

1 Fabyan, p.514.

2 Kendall, *Richard III,* p. 222.

3 *Chronicles of London* (ed. Kingsford), p.191.

4 *Excerpta Historica,* p.384. Halsted, ii.522.

5 Complete Works, Vol. 5, pp.233-8.

6 *Historia de Regibus Anglie,* B.M. MS. Cotton Vesp. A.XII. Hanham, p.118.

7 More, p.78.

8 Ibid, pp.16-7.

9 Edmondson's *Constables of England,* p.30. Halsted, ii.245n.

10 MacGibbon; *Elizabeth Woodville,* p.224.

11 Mancini, p.75.

12 *Excerpta Hist.,* p. 153. Halsted, i.32n, ii.242n.

13 For genealogical table, see Halsted, i.34, etc.

14 *Robert Stillington* by A.J. Mowat. *Ricardian,* Vol. IV, No. 53, June 1976. p.24.

15 MacGibbon: *Elizabeth Woodville,* p.174. Hall, *Historical Mag.* III, 53, 1791.

16 Harl. MSS. 433 fol. 104. Halsted, ii.142.

17 Rymers Add. MSS, 4616, art. 23. Halsted, ii.143.

18 Harl. MSS. 433. Halsted, ii.144.

19 Reading, 23 July; Harl. MSS. 433, p.108. Halsted, ii.147.

20 Gutch's *History of Oxford,* Edit. 1792, p.638. Halsted, ii.525-7.

21 *England Under the Yorkists,* pp.121-2.

22 Kendall, p.290.

23 Hanham: *Richard III and his early historians,* p.50. *Ricardian,* Vol. IV, No. 60, March 1978. p.24.

24 Harl. MSS. 433. fol. 110.

25 Dictionary of National Biography (W.A.J. Archbold). W.H. Sewell: *Memoirs of Sir James Tyrell* (Suffolk Inst. of Archaeology, Vol. V, p.128). Harl. MSS. 293. fo. 208.

26 *The Marcher Lords of Glamorgan and Morgannwg,* 1317-1485 (Glam. County History, Vol. III, 1971) p.201.

27 More, p.84.

28 Woodhouse: *Life of John Morton,* p.83.

29 Molinet, ii.402. Commines, ii. 63n. (Footnote by Editor, Andrew R. Scoble, 1856).

30 More, p.88.

31 Ibid, p.84.

32 Buck, p.84.

33 More, p.92.

34 Gt. Chronicle, fol. 209 vo. MacGibbon: *Elizabeth Woodville,* p.170.

35 Gt. Chronicle, p.234. Armstrong, p.127, Note 88.

V
The Buckingham Rebellion

What seems irrefutable, in the mystery surrounding the princes, is that the rumours of the boys' death coincided with the Buckingham rebellion and Henry Tudor's planned invasion. The two events are clearly linked in the narrative of the Third Continuator of the Croyland Chronicler, who had earlier commented only that "the two sons of king Edward before-named remained in the Tower of London, in the custody of certain persons appointed for that purpose. In order to deliver them from this captivity, the people of the southern and western parts of the kingdom began to murmur greatly, and to form meetings and confederacies".

"The people" were mainly, in these parts, under Lancastrian-orientated knights and squires and these were, in fact, the spearhead of the Tudor sympathisers. That their support among the inhabitants was limited seems indicated by the fate of the rebellion. Communications where the generality of people were concerned did not exist, except through spokesmen in some authority: a fact which is too little borne in mind when the word "people" is used of medieval times. But let Croyland continue: "At last, it was determined by the people in the vicinity of the city of London, throughout the counties of Kent, Essex, Sussex, Hampshire, Dorsetshire, Devonshire, Somersetshire, Wiltshire and Berkshire, as well as some others of the southern counties of the kingdom, to avenge their grievances before stated; upon which, public proclamation was made, that Henry, duke of Buckingham, who at this time was living at Brecknock in Wales, had repented of his former conduct, and would be the chief mover in this attempt, *while a rumour was spread that the sons of King Edward before-named had died a violent death, but it was uncertain how.*"[1]   [Italics mine).

It seems to me quite clear from this that the rumour was "spread" directly to help the insurrection, and was not the cause that originally gave rise to it. Any other interpretation is wishful thinking to support the opinion that *only* because of the murder of the princes did this rebellion arise. In fact, nothing could have been produced more aptly than this rumour for Henry Tudor's purpose, the seizure of the throne of England; and Buckingham, too, had certain purposes of his own. It would be easy enough for the rumour to be accepted as fact, among a general populace without newspapers or any reliable form of communication, to whom the displacement of the princes and Richard's succession were still unexplained. The widespread ignorance of the reasons for these was to make Henry Tudor's task easier, after he took the throne, in suppressing Titulus Regius, the Act of Richard's later Parliament, and obliterating it from men's minds. How much the public, largely illiterate, relied on mere rumour was to be crystallised by Shakespeare in his "rumour" Prologue to *King Henry IV*, Part II.

When, according to Rous,[2] Buckingham requested the custody of Morton, Bishop of Ely, was it because he already had some complicity, not realised at the time, in the Hastings/Morton plot? His Woodville wife may have advised him more than we know of what was actually going on, and Woodville support has often been suggested as a motive for this conspiracy. There is really no solid evidence that Buckingham was involved in the Tower Council meeting on Richard's side, and duplicity soon at any rate was to prove a factor in his makeup. It is surely worth noting that the letter written by the interestingly informative Stallworth to Stonor on 21 June, after the death of Hastings, ends: "All the lord chamberlain's men are switching allegiance to the Duke of Buckingham."[3] Why? Could it be because they *knew* Buckingham was involved in the same cause? No one seems to have noticed that not only was Buckingham's wife a Woodville, sister to the ex-Queen, but Hastings' wife Katherine was a cousin of Reginald Bray, the notorious Lancastrian go-between used by Margaret Beaufort and a steward of her household. He was later a prominent minister of Henry VII, alongside Morton. A letter exists written from Katherine, Hastings' widow, to Bray, thanking him for kindness to her children, but stressing her comparative poverty in Henry VII's reign, in spite of the generosity with which Richard III had treated her.[4] The connecting links in both conspiracies may well have been on the distaff side. Men are often influenced by their wives and it can certainly never be ruled out, even in politics.

What did Buckingham say or suggest to Richard when he visited him at Gloucester? Anything published on this is pure conjecture, including More's assumption that they "departed, as it seemed, very great friends at Gloucester", so that "a man would marvel whereof the change grew".[5] The next we know is that Buckingham, obviously disaffected, is with his "prisoner" Morton at Brecknock, and the nature of their discussion was presumably given out by Morton himself (as Buckingham did not survive) to have been of the kind later so often repeated. In More, Morton is made to play cunningly on Buckingham's pride and stirring jealousy of Richard, and the account (and indeed the whole work attributed to More) ends with a most significant remark to Buckingham: on the "excellent virtues meet for the rule of a realm, as our Lord hath planted in the person of your grace".[6]

The abrupt breaking off of the narrative at this point may have been due, not only to More's fears that what he had been finding out in Richard's favour was leading him on to dangerous ground, but also that a gulf was opening beneath his feet in the matter of Henry, Duke of Buckingham. It has been summarized by A.F. Pollard: "Incitement to treason was no safer in 1514 than in 1483; there was a third Duke of Buckingham in the field ... just as ready to be incited and with the same claims to the throne." In August, 1509, when Henry VIII had ascended the throne as a minor, Lord Darcy was reporting to Richard Fox, the lord privy seal, a plot in the north to make Buckingham Protector; and on 20 February 1514 Buckingham is said to have remarked to his future son-in-law, Ralph earl Westmoreland: "there be two new dukes created in England, but that if anything but good should happen to the king, he, the duke of Buckingham, was next in succession to the crown of England".[7]

It was this succession to the crown of England that seems quite widely to have been believed to figure in the schemes of the earlier Duke of Buckingham. "And surely the occasion of their variance is of divers men diversely reported", wrote More of Buckingham's break with Richard III, adding: "Very truth it is, the duke was a high-minded man and evil could bear the glory of another, so that I have heard of some that said they saw it that the duke, at such time as the crown was first set upon the protector's head, his eye could not abide the sight thereof ...." Sir George Buck too mentions his "Ambition and aime to be Soveraigne". [8]

If Morton did escape from Brecknock, it may well have been that he found his plan for the accession of Henry Tudor *not* congenial to Buckingham, who had plans for the crown himself. And if true it puts a new light on what might have happened to the princes. Buckingham was Constable of England with access to the Tower: was it he who murdered the children (if they were murdered), not on Richard's behalf, *but his own*? His possible implication in their supposed murder has certainly been widely reported: even Commines states it was Buckingham "who had put the two children to death, for Richard himself a few days afterwards ordered his execution". [9] This juxtaposition of the murder of the princes with Buckingham's execution after the October, 1483, rebellion is interesting: Commines' remark almost reads as if Richard executed Buckingham *because* he found he had killed the children, although it oddly contradicts statements by Commines elsewhere, painting the by then accepted picture of Richard and his crimes, which he would have learned from the followers of Henry Tudor, whom he himself admits to have known and conversed with.

Whether Buckingham did it for his own sake (as Kendall among biographers of Richard III has suggested as a possibility) or with the connivance of Morton on behalf of Henry Tudor, is also a viable question. Alternatively, it is worth noting that Morton fled to Flanders, where the princes, or one of them, were so often rumoured to have been taken. Possibilities abound; but the mystery remains.

It is only just to add that if we must consider Buckingham's wife, Catherine Woodville, as a possible factor (the human factor so many, in writing on history, overlook) in swaying him towards Woodville schemes, we must also remember that the princes were her nephews, no less than they were Richard's, and closer to the Woodville side of the family in their upbringing. There are plenty of examples in life of hatred within families, especially where inheritance is involved, but it rarely applies to children, and human nature does not change in this or its essential basics. We must bear this in mind both in the case of Richard and of Catherine Woodville. If Buckingham had any hand in murdering the princes, it certainly would not have been with his wife's knowledge.

It is not impossible that, if Buckingham did murder them, Richard discovered it, even if he did not order the murder himself, as is so often assumed. His fury against Buckingham in a postscript to a letter he wrote the Chancellor, John Russell, following the rebellion, has more than Richard's usual anger at disloyalty; lambasting "the malice of him that had best cause to be true, the Duke of Buckingham — the most untrue creature living".[10] It is a ringing cry at betrayal which might well have been something deeper and more agonising. For Richard, if he had discovered the death of the princes, and its cause, would have been far too intelligent not to know that if he publicized these deaths few would believe, in the circumstances, that he himself was not implicated. It is, in fact, the best argument for his innocence that he never proclaimed their deaths, and therefore he knew the deaths were useless to him. If faced with a *fait accompli*, his situation was a cruel one, and his rage understandable on his own account, as well as that of his brother's innocent sons. It is inconceivable that if he had really murdered the princes, and knew Buckingham knew it and was deserting him for this reason, he could have experienced such rage and apparent *surprise,* unless both were feigned. This is not the impression one gets at all from his handwritten postscript to the letter to Russell: it reads as a genuine outburst.

The King was not the only person to describe Buckingham's betrayal as malicious. Edward Plumpton, in the north, wrote to Sir Robert Plumpton: "The Duke of Buckingham has so mony men, as yt is sayd here, that he is able to goe where he wyll; but I trust he shalbe right withstanded and all his mallice: and els were great pytty."[11]

Buckingham indeed, whatever his motivations, was "withstanded". Richard may have been slow to perceive he was being betrayed (there seems to have been a curious streak of naivety in his political makeup), but once he recognised the certainty he was, as always, swift in action to meet the crisis. He wrote at once to York demanding aid, and that they should send troops to meet him at Leicester. (The ill-equipped troops from York brought by Northumberland to London had early been sent back, and on complaints of the local people of their marauding and pillaging on the journey Richard had quickly marched north and hanged a few, convicted of these offences, as examples and to stop the practice. He shared, as the laws and actions of his brief reign show, his brother's concern that the common people should not suffer from the ravages of the armies on either side.)

Whatever was the truth behind the Buckingham rebellion, it is clear that in the event, although it linked up with the mainly Woodville-Lancastrian insurrection in the south, probably already set in motion by Morton, it did not gain the support he had anticipated. It was, in fact, a partisan revolt not generally supported, in spite of attempts to spread the rumour of Richard's murder of the princes. The Chronicles of London are a vivid indication of the contradictions within this ambiguous situation. After claiming (under the year of Sir Robert Billesdon's mayoralty, which in October 1483 had only just begun) that "many knyghtes and gentilmen of Kent and other places" gathered together to join the Duke of Buckingham, "for anoon as the said kyng Richard had put to deth the Lord Chamberleyn and other Gentilmen, as before is said, he also put to deth the ij childer of kyng Edward, for whiche cause he lost the hertes of the people". But it seems the hearts of the "people" were not lost at all; for within the next few lines it appears that "whan the kyng knewe of the Dukes entent, anoon he went Westward; and there raysed his people, whereof the Duke ferid and fled, *because at that tyme his people were not come to hym*" (italics mine). Moreover, "when the Duke tooke contrary part aayn kyng Richard, the more party of the Gentilmen of England were so dismayed that they knewe nat which party to take but at all aventure".[12]

So much for the people's (or even the gentry's) awareness of Richard's wicked murder of two children, or belief in the rumour apparently fed to them.

Buckingham, it is true, was also betrayed by the English weather, which rose to thwart the occasion, as it so often does, with flood and storm. He was, moreover, betrayed by a former servant named Banaster, with whom he sought asylum, and who probably took advantage of Richard's prompt proclamation of an award of £1,000 for his capture. The marches of Wales, where Tudor's adherents might be expected to foregather, were heavily guarded, and Buckingham was quickly executed at Salisbury, after urging in vain that he might speak with the King. It was afterwards alleged, including by the third Duke of Buckingham (who suffered a similar fate under Henry VIII), that he had concealed a dagger about his person with which he intended to assassinate Richard. It might have been a last resource if the King failed to respond to the famous, if haughty, Buckingham charm, or to listen to whatever tale Buckingham may have had to tell about (perhaps?) the princes. We have no means of knowing.

The "Sir James Tyler" mentioned as delivering him into Richard's hands[13] was almost certainly a misspelling of Sir James Tyrell, to whom, in October, 1483 (before Buckingham's capture) was given the official commission to enter the castles of the Duke of Buckingham and seize his lands. On 12 October Richard's letter to John Russell, his Chancellor, had been principally written to ask him to bring or send the Great Seal, which had to be affixed to the warrant to apprehend Buckingham. It appears Richard was anxious that all legal formalities should be observed. In December, Tyrell was made Steward of the Duchy of Cornwall, and on 6 March following warrants were sent from London to reimburse him for money he had spent in the king's service, including the payment of his soldiers.[14] It is worth noting that not all monies lavished by a king on his followers were rewards: the followers themselves had to be prepared to pay out a good deal in the course of their service, bureaucracy then as now not always being quick off the mark in the matter of soldiers' pay and other financial recompense.

The names of those, like Buckingham, eventually executed or attainted for their part in this treason make interesting reading, for all were knights or squires definitely with Woodville or Lancastrian associations. The Croyland Chronicler makes clear his own political party when he laments in particular the execution of the dissident Sir Thomas St. Leger, whose history with regard to the outlawed Henry Holland, Duke of Exeter, had been by no means uplifting, including as it did the acquisition of Exeter's wife, already his mistress, after she obtained a divorce. The wife was one of Richard's sisters, which suggests nepotism was not to be a principle in his reign.[15] The suggestion that Richard's Chancellor, John Russell, Bishop of Lincoln, the receiver of the King's recent feeling letter on Buckingham's disloyalty, could have written this panegyric of treasonable Lancastrians seems, once again, highly questionable. At any rate, the City of Exeter received Richard with warmth and an oration of congratulation, as well as a purse containing 200 gold nobles and much costly entertainment. [16] When he returned in triumph to London he was also given a rousing welcome by both mayor and citizens, whose moral standards would seem to be peculiarly blunted if they really believed that he had very recently murdered his nephews.

Comparatively few were executed (about one dozen are recorded over the whole southern counties, from Kent to Cornwall), perhaps mainly because obviously few ringleaders were involved (Henry VII, later, with Morton pushing his sometimes reluctant elbow, executed rebels after revolts far more lavishly). Among those who escaped to Brittany were the ex-Queen's eldest son, the Marquess of Dorset, who had left sanctuary to join other Woodvilles in the rebellion and was reputed to have attempted to foster a rising in Yorkshire, Richard's most loyal territory.

On 19 December, Richard once again demonstrated his inexorable villainy by awarding Buckingham's widow (the sister of both Elizabeth Woodville and Lionel, Bishop of Salisbury, who had joined the rebellion and fled) an annuity of 200 marks, and granting her and her children and servants leave to join her sister, the ex-Queen, in sanctuary in London. The fact that she apparently asked this favour certainly shows she was still close to her sister. Richard also paid Buckingham's debts, so that she was not saddled with them. To widows of other rebels, such as Florence, wife of Alexander Cheyney, he was equally generous. Lord Stanley, apparently believed by Richard not to have helped the revolt in any way, was made Constable of England for life. [17] Other followers were rewarded, and Richard's secretary John Kendal was made "keeper of the princes' wardrobe within the city of London", an appointment which gives one food for thought: for Richard's own son, the new Prince of Wales, still lived in the north, and what other "princes" were there? [18]

What of Henry Tudor, the intended main benefactor of the rebellion? He had duly sailed, in spite of the storms, with fifteen ships and 5,000 men provided by the Duke of Brittany, but appearing off the Dorset coast near Poole, with only two ships (the others had been scattered by the storm), he had sensed there was no support there and sailed westward to Plymouth. Here he was met with the news of the failure of the rebellion and the escape of

Dorset and other chief supporters to Brittany. He had no option but to give up the attempt and set sail again for renewed exile. [19]

It was not his year; but he was to live to plot another day. His mother, so ready to let loose civil war and much bloodshed on the English people, was once again attainted but left in the charge of her supposedly loyal husband, Lord Stanley. One of her go-betweens at least was captured and imprisoned in the Tower for his part in the plot of autumn, 1483. It was Dr. Lewis of Caerleon, Monmouthshire.[20]

The baronage with one exception, Richard Beauchamp, Lord Seintmount, had remained faithful to Richard, and not a single town of consequence had been won to Henry's cause.

It was Lord Stanley, now, who had direct access to the Tower as Constable. No one ever seems to have noted the possibilities of this, if the princes were still alive there. Yet he was Henry Tudor's stepfather, and certainly switched allegiance at Bosworth. If others are suspected because of holding this office of Constable, surely Stanley, too, should not have been so conspicuously overlooked?

1 Croyland Third Continuator, pp.490, 491.

2 *Historia de Regibus Anglie,* Ed. Hearne, p.216.

3 PRO, SC1 46/207 (Ed. Kingsford, *Stonor Letters,* No. 331). Hanham: *Richard III and his early historians,* p.42.

4 Richard III Exhibition Catalogue, p.35.

5 More, p.91.

6 Ibid, p.96.

7 A.F. Pollard: *The Making of Sir Thomas More's Richard III,* pp. 237-8: quoting *Letters of Richard Fox,* P.S. Allen (1927) pp. 43-4; *Letters and Papers of Henry VIII* (1920), iii, p. 491.

8 More, pp.91 and 92. Buck, p.35.

9 Commines: *Memoirs,* ii.64.

10 Halsted, ii.261.

11 Plumpton Correspondence, pp.44-5. *England Under the Yorkists,* p.130.

12 *Chronicles of London* (ed. Kingsford), pp.191-2.

13 Stafford MSS (in Blakeway), p.241. Halsted, ii.271.

14 Sewell: *Memoirs of Sir James Tyrell* (Suffolk Inst. of Archaeology, Vol. V), p.135.

15 Halsted, ii. 277.

16 Ibid, ii.278. Jenkins, *History of Exeter,* p.88.

17 Ibid, ii.284. *Foedera,* xii, p.209.

18 Ibid, ii.285. Harl. MSS. 433, fol.133.

19 Kendall: *Richard III,* p.274.

20 Article in *Isis* 43 (1952) pp.100-8, by Pearl Kibre, quoted *Ricardian,* No. 50, Sept. 1975, p.29.

VI
Laws, Reconciliations and Foreign Observers

For the time being, at least, Richard seemed lulled into a sense of security. According to Croyland, he "gradually lessened his army", having "triumphed over his enemies without fighting a battle". [1] But the rebels who had fled needed to be dealt with in the usual way in cases of treason, and it may be that now there was not only time, but the obvious necessity, to call a Parliament and ratify Richard's assumption of the throne.

Richard returned to London before December, and the first and only one of his reign met in January 1484. Its principal Act passed was that of Titulus Regius, setting out in detail the reasons for the bastardizing of King Edward's children and the circumstances under which Richard had been offered, and accepted, the throne. [2] In addition, the Earl of Richmond, the Earl of Pembroke, the Duke of Buckingham, the queen's son, the Marquess of Dorset, and her brothers, Sir Richard Woodville and Lionel, Bishop of Salisbury, with Morton, Bishop of Ely, and the Bishop of Exeter, were attainted of high treason. [3] The comparatively few knights named included Stallworth's correspondent, Sir William Stonor, and John Cheyney, a notorious giant in physique whom Richard was to unseat from his horse (with his "wither'd arm"?) at Bosworth Field. The Woodville element, strongly represented alongside Buckingham and Morton, had mainly escaped. Margaret Beaufort was, in the circumstances, lightly treated, and Richard's trust of her husband unimpaired.

Parliament now proceeded to issue a number of acts, both civil and intended to promote foreign trade, which combined were to make this reign one of the most liberal and beneficial to the people: anything but the "tyranny", in fact, that later chroniclers and historians ascribe to it. "Free was he called of dispense, and somewhat above his powers liberal", as More wrote of Richard.[4] Richard III's reputation for good laws was to ring bells in many men's minds well over one hundred years, notwithstanding the gradual acceptance of the princes' murder story so assiduously fostered by those who overthrew him. Lord Bacon, writing in early Stuart times, has already been quoted; but whatever they secretly thought about the murder, even Tudor citizens of London held fast to their knowledge of Richard as a lawgiver.

"In 1525 Cardinal Wolsey was pressing the mayor and aldermen of London for a benevolence. To their objection that this demand was contrary to a statute of Richard III the cardinal retorted: 'I marvell that you speak of Richard the third, which was a usurper and a murtherer of his owne nephewes.' The reply to this is noteworthy, and one sentence in it might serve as a partial epitaph on Richard III: 'although he did evil, yet in his tyme wer many good actes made'."[5]

As early as 26 June 1483, according even to More (and corroborated in city records), "the protector, with a great train, went to Westminster Hall and there, when he had placed himself in the Court of the King's Bench, declared to the audience that he would take upon him the crown in that place there, where the King himself sitteth and ministreth the law, because he considered that it was the chiefest duty of a king to minister the laws". He set out to win nobles, merchants, artificers, "and, in conclusion, all kind of men, but specially the lawyers of this realm".[6] (More was himself a lawyer.).

It is possible More already knew the London Chronicle written up, some years before, under the title of the mayoralty of Edmond Shaa:

"And vpon thursday aftir, the said Duke of Glowcetir wt a greate company of lordes and Gentilmen, wt also the Mayr and the Craftes, went vnto Westmynster, and there toke possession of the Regalite sittyng in Westmynster halle; wher vpon his right hand satte the Duke of Northfolk, and vpon that other hand the Duke of Suffolk.

"And he, there so sittyng, called byfore hym alle the Juges of the Temporall lawe, gyuyng theym straitely in Commaundement to execute his lawes Justly and indifferently to euerych persone aswell to powre as Riche.''[7]

There seems much indication, as I have said, that Richard consciously modelled himself on his brother's actions early in his reign: for Edward, too, in 1462, had ''sate in the King's bench three daies together, in open Court, to understand how his lawes were executed''.[8] (Edward also, like Richard, had travelled through his ''realm with his justices, sparing none even of his own household, but rather that they should be hanged, if they were caught in theft or murder''[9]:as Richard had done when hearing complaints against the soldiers returning to the north.) Now the Parliament of 1484 began to set in motion a general scheme of justice and reform anticipated already by Richard in his acts for the ''common weal'', including the encouragement of his subjects' personal appeal to him, as on his progress a few months before. There was an Act against benevolences, raised by a more grasping Edward IV in his extravagant later years:

''The king remembryng howe the Commens of this his roialme by new and unlawful invencions and inordinate covetise, ageynst the law of this roialme, have be put to gret thraldome and importable charges and exactions, and in especiall by a newe imposicion named a benevolence, whereby dyverse yeres the subgettes and comens of this lande agaynst their willes and fredome have paid greate sommes of money to their almost utter destruction; ... Therefore the King woll it to be ordeigned ... that his subgiettes and the comynalte of this his roialme from hensfurth in nowise be charged by none suche charge exaction or imposicion called benevolence, nor by suche lyke charge ... but it be dampned and anulled for ever.''[10]

In and out of Parliament, the reforms continued. Part of the fee-farm of Winchester was remitted, because of the town's decayed and impoverished condition, and similar towns had similar assistance.[11] Trade with Iceland (already of great importance to the fishing industry) was fostered by licences, and by the appointment of a ''fishing admiral'', ''William Combreshall, captain of our ship named the Elizabeth''.[12] Italian merchants were rapped over the knuckles for storing up goods in their warehouses ''unto the tyme the prices thereof been greatly enhaunced for their most lucre'', and moreover for employing only their own countrymen when selling in our English markets, and then departing "out of this said roialme" and spending "the same goodes often tymes among the King's adversaries".[13] A land law was introduced (anticipating a reform ascribed to Henry VIII); the King repeated Edward IV's efforts to establish law and order; and it was made easier for the poorer people to present petitions directly to him, when unable to cope with the cost or prevarications of justice.

He also introduced a law preventing the seizure of a person's goods while he was in prison, before the trial and verdict; thus deliberately harking back to a notorious abuse by the powerful Woodvilles, led by Anthony, Lord Rivers, whose servants in 1467 had ransacked the house and possessions of Sir Thomas Cook, an Alderman and one-time Mayor of the City, when he was impeached for supposedly lending money to Queen Margaret. Cook was found not guilty of treason and fined on the lesser charge of "misprision of treason", but although he managed to get some damages for the loss of his goods, jewels and plate, Elizabeth Woodville, the Queen, claimed an ancient right of "queen's gold" and other gifts which Cook was more or less forced to pay. The judge who ruled in his favour, Sir John Markham, was dismissed from office at the suit of Rivers and his wife.

This case rankled still in City memories and records. "Who is of you either so negligent that he knoweth not, or so forgetful that he rembereth not, or so hardhearted that he pitieth not that worshipful man's loss", cries More nearly fifty years later, in fine rhythmical lament. It is only one of the indications as to why the authorities were so ready to support anyone, such as Richard, against the Woodville influence. Richard certainly knew of the Cook case and framed his law accordingly.[14] His laws also conferred power on magistrates to accept bail, and aimed to protect juries against intimidation. Their intention in many cases was the checking of corruption.

Perhaps it was with this in mind that the statutes of Richard III's Parliament were the first to be published in English. The literate public at large could read them, and know their rights. It was, perhaps, a gesture towards the trend of the coming Reformation; the Bible too — "Wyclif's Bible" — had recently at last been translated into English; and a New Testament in English was among Richard's own possessions.[15] Soon the power of both Church and State, so long locked together to exclude the general people, would begin to be challenged, as what was really said in the New Testament, and in the laws of state, began to be understood by others than ecclesiastics, statesmen, and the wealthier Latin-educated aristocracy and merchants. Bernard Shaw's Saint Joan, ahead of her time, and dying only half a century before Richard, represents what one of her judges recognises as the new flood of "protestantism", the beginnings of a new trend in which the individual at last is beginning to interpret religion and politics for himself. That was not the name yet given to the movement; but although he would certainly not have recognised it, Richard's reign already was touched by the new age, the age that left the middle ages behind and swept in the Renaissance. Henry VII, establishing of necessity a harsh new dynasty on uncertain foundations, was to attempt to stem the tide; but his son, for quite different reasons and while still clinging to the swaying rock of tyranny, was to let in the first floodwaters, rather less graciously than Richard.

In any case, the markedly untyrannical nature of Richard's Parliament has always been acknowledged by those who studied it dispassionately. As Lord Campbell wrote: "We have no difficulty in pronouncing Richard's parliament the most meritorious national assembly for protecting the liberty of the subject, and putting down abuses in the administration of justice that had sat in England since the reign of Henry III."[16] It is not in the partisan gossip of chroniclers, but in the written laws, acts of parliament, the whole recorded governance of a reign, that we read incontrovertible truth.

Even the ecclesiastics praised Richard. A convocation of clergy addressed to him, shortly after the Parliament, a petition setting forth certain of their grievances, among them the suggestion that there should be far greater attention to religious offices in the ecclesiastic community, too long tending to be absorbed in more ambitious secular affairs. As Caroline Halsted writes: "it is scarcely credible ... that the whole body of English clergy, embracing so many individuals of piety, learning, and independence, could have so far departed from their sacred profession, as to address, in the following language, a monarch whom they considered to be a usurper, and looked upon as the murderer of two innocent children, his unoffending orphan nephews, the only sons of his deceased brother!"

The preroration contained the following:

"SEEING YOUR MOST NOBLE AND BLESSED DIS-

POSITION IN ALL OTHER THINGS, we beseech you to take tender respect and consideration unto the premises; and of yourself, as a most Catholic prince, to see such remedies, that under your most gracious letters patent the liberties of the church may be confirmed and sufficiently authorised by your high court of parliament, — rather enlarged than diminished." [17]

It was signed among others by John Russell, Bishop of Lincoln and Lord Chancellor, "a wise man and a good" (the phrase is More's); Waynfleet, Bishop of Winchester, admired by the saintly Henry VI and known for "piety, learning, and prudence"; [18] and John Fisher, friend of Erasmus, later Bishop of Rochester, and eventually executed by Henry VIII. The complete ecclesiastical list of signatories also included Thomas Bourchier, Archbishop of Canterbury, (reputed the previous year to have pledged his life and honour to Elizabeth Woodville for the safety of the young prince she yielded to him), and Rotherham, Archbishop of York, a known Woodville adherent who had been pardoned by Richard after brief arrest at the time of the Hastings affair. That some of these princes of the church might be time-servers one can well believe; but that *all* would unhesitatingly add their names to such an appeal, addressing a man "of most noble and blessed disposition" who they believed to be the murderer of his child nephews, is surely incredible. Not only do I believe many clergymen and believers of our own time (or any time) would reject this; as an atheist, but with considerable respect for some ecclesiastics, I reject it totally myself.

A still more startling psychological phenomenon was soon to take place. For in March, 1484, Elizabeth Woodville allowed herself at last to be persuaded to leave sanctuary. She did so, it is true, on the assurances of the Lord Mayor and Aldermen that if she allowed her daughters to come out of sanctuary with her, Richard would guarantee their safety, and that the King would provide good marriages for them, not below their dignity as a king's daughters. The offer was as follows:

"I, Richard, by the grace of God, &C., in presence of you, my lords spiritual and temporal, and you, my lord mayor and aldermen of London, promise and swear, *verbo regio,* that if the daughters of Elizabeth Grey, late calling herself Queen of England, that is to wit, Elizabeth, Cecily, Anne, Catherine and Bridget, will come to me out of the Sanctuary of Westminster, and be guided, ruled and demeaned after me, then I shall see that they shall be in surety of their lives, and also not suffer any manner hurt by any manner person or persons to them or any of them in their bodies and persons to be done, by way of ravishing or defiling contrary to their wills, nor them nor any of them imprison in the Tower of London or other prison; but I shall put them into honest places of good name and fame, and them honestly and courteously shall see to be founden and entreated, and to have all things requisite and necessary for their exhibitions and findings as my kinswomen; and that I shall do marry (cause to be married) such of them as be marrieageable to gentlemen born, and every of them give in marriage lands and tenements to the yearly value of 200 marks for term of their lives, and in like wise to the other daughters when they shall come to lawful age of marriage, if they live. And such gentlemen as shall hap to marry with them I shall straitly charge lovingly to love and entreat them, as wives and my kinswomen, as they will avoid and eschew my displeasure.

"And over this, that I shall yearly content and pay, or cause to be contented and paid, for the exhibition and finding of the said Dame Elizabeth Grey, during her natural life, at four terms of the year, that is to wit, at Pasche (Easter), Midsummer, Michaelmas, and Christmas, to John Nesfeld, one of the esquires of my body, for his finding to attend upon her, the sum of 700 marks of lawful money of England, by even portions; and moreover I promise to them that if any surmise or evil report be made to me of them by any person or persons, that then I shall not give thereunto faith nor credence, nor therefor put them to any manner punishment, before that they or any of them so accused may be at their lawful defence and answer. In witness whereof to this writing of my oath and promise aforesaid in your said presence made, I have set my sign manual, the first day of March, in the first year of my reign." [19]

It may be noticed that nothing whatever is said about the girls' brothers, although the reference to not imprisoning them in the Tower of London may slantingly indicate the princes. Interpretations of this quite naturally will rest with the reader. It is also fair to note that no woman, and Elizabeth Woodville in particular, could be expected to contemplate for ever being in sanctuary, however many of her goods and chattels she may have contrived to be around her. Elizabeth was used to Court life and she loved power. One must not under-estimate these things, nor her possible concern for the future of her daughters. Nevertheless, it was still a remarkable concession to Richard if she truly believed him to have murdered her small sons; for if so her daughters too were vulnerable as heirs. Her son by a first marriage, and her brother, had already incontestably been executed.

What makes her capitulation the more questionable, however, is that there seems a general acceptance that she made her peace with Richard in every way. Even her biographer, who accepts Richard's guilt and the whole traditional story without question, uses the words "almost inconceivable". There are, however, certain questions about this whole business which never seem to be asked. It is said the daughters went to Richard's Court, but in fact only two of them (Elizabeth, b.1466, and Cecily, b.1469) were in March 1484 fifteen years of age or over. Anne, Catherine and Bridget were eight, five and three years of age respectively. Obviously they must have stayed with their mother.

So where did Elizabeth Woodville live? Only one historian/ biographer seems to have thought this might be worth considering: Paul Murray Kendall. And he suggests "it seems reasonably probable that she had secretly agreed to retire to a country house, under the nominal wardship of Nesfield".[20] I shall return to this shortly.

To Nesfield, certainly, was committed her by no means ungenerous pension of 700 marks. She was no longer even Queen-Dowager: she was "Dame Elizabeth Grey", and ex-Queen-Dowager. There was no special place for her at Court, and there is no evidence, until the following Christmas, even that her elder daughters went there, and lived at Westminster in a royal palace or in the Tower apartments. Did Richard really trust her? And what did she think of him? Quite irrespective of the fate of the princes, he had, after all, executed her brother and son. It is quite possible a realistic woman in politics at that time would accept this, whatever her personal feelings: the Woodvilles had played hazard for control of a throne, and the laws against treason were quite explicit. Did she secretly even blame herself a little, knowing the ambitions her own position had given rise to had led them, inexorably, to their deaths? It is not beyond the bounds of probability.

Young children, incapable of plotting, are a different proposition. Had her own boys really disappeared, that she seems in the end to have trusted Richard so much? For that she *did* trust him now, and not only with the girls (his record of kindness and generosity to his foes' womenfolk cannot be gainsaid), is shown by the letter Vergil claims she wrote, probably the next year, to her son Dorset, urging him to abandon the party of the Earl of Richmond and return to England.[21] Although Vergil's story has been questioned, it seems substantiated by the fact that Dorset, before Henry's final invasion, does seem to have made a bid to flee from Paris, and was overtaken at Compiègne. Henry prudently did not include him in his army when he sailed: nor did the Marquess return to England until some months after Henry took the throne. His ambiguous position seems stressed by Richard's own proclamations: one of 7 December 1484, against Richmond, was reissued on 23 June 1485, but with Dorset no longer mentioned.[22]

So were his small half-brothers still alive, that Elizabeth was prepared to take risks with her one remaining son? Apart from the rumours already described, what are the other possibilities?

It is claimed by Mancini that a physician, Dr. Argentine, "the last of his attendants whose services the king [Edward V] enjoyed, reported that the young king, like a victim prepared for sacrifice, sought remission of his sins by daily confession and penance, because he believed that death was facing him".

This doctor, in Armstrong's 1936 edition of Mancini, was described, owing to a faulty reading of the MS, as "a Strasbourg doctor", but Armstrong on good evidence has identified him as John Argentine in his 1969 edition. Argentine certainly existed. S.T. Bindoff, Professor of Queen Mary College, University of London, has supported his identification as a doctor to Edward V from a MS in King's College.[23] He moved in what might be called Mancinian circles, meeting Mancini later in France and in fact returning to England when Henry Tudor took the throne, to become doctor to Henry's heir, Prince Arthur. Whether he knew Mancini when he was in England, and told the Tower story to him then, we do not know. It could have been a "wise after the event" comment; it could have been dramatised by either the doctor or Mancini from what was, in fact, the case of an ailing child preparing for death from natural causes. More, as many have commented, repeats that the boy king lost heart and "pined" in the Tower.

There remains the curious and indubitable fact that no subsequent "pretender", in Henry VII's reign (and there were at least three), claimed to be the presumptive king, Edward V. Lambert Simnel seems to have been hailed briefly as Richard, Duke of York, before settling into the rôle of Edward, Earl of Warwick, Clarence's son, in whose name, as Edward VI, he was crowned in Ireland. The most serious "pretender" of all, Perkin Warbeck, also claimed to be Richard, the second son of Edward IV, and his supposed aunt, Margaret of Burgundy, supported him in this. The inference seems inescapable that it was *known* the elder boy was dead. In this case the Dr. Argentine story would link up with natural death, unless one boy were murdered and the other escaped. The first hyothesis seems rather more likely, although Warbeck's "official" confession, which so suspiciously suited Henry VII's book that torture has been assumed by historians as far apart in outlook as Buck and Hume, gave this story of one murder, and one escape, remarkably vague in its details.

Dr. Argentine was not the only foreigner in London who had connections with Mancini. "Pietro Carmeliano", suggests Armstrong, "could have introduced Mancini to the court";[24] and Carmeliano, like so many in this story, had a foot in both English camps, according to the political winds of change. A humanist and Latin poet eager for patronage, he had come to England in 1470 and on 7 April 1482, apparently while working at the Rolls House, he dedicated a Latin poem to Edward, Prince of Wales (later Edward V). He was befriended by Richard's friend, Sir Robert Brackenbury, described as "gentle" in the Chronicle of Calais,*[25] and in a Preface to a poem on St. Catherine dedicated to him Carmeliano praised Richard III as a model king. But Brackenbury, as we know, died with Richard at Bosworth Field and Carmeliano, once more without a patron and indefatigably anxious to please, in 1486 celebrated the birth of Henry VII's heir, Prince Arthur, with yet another poem, in which he obligingly states what Henry wanted to hear, that Richard, ex-model king, "destroyed both his nephews" (*geminosque nepotes sustulit*). The grateful new father rewarded him by making him his Chaplain and Latin secretary, and

* Was this known character a reason why, in the legendary tale of the murder of the princes, Brackenbury's responsibility as Governor of the Tower had to be explained away by the story of his refusal to commit the murder, and his handing over of the keys to Tyrell?

also Archdeacon of Gloucester.[26]

"An undated edition of the *De quatuor Virtutibus* (B.M., 8406, d.19: Bodleian, Arch Ae 99)", writes Armstrong, "contains on the title-page a few lines of Latin verse by Carmeliano in praise of Mancini and his work as though to suggest that the two men were known to each other."[27]

In July 1483, when Mancini appears to have left London to write his report, Carmeliano would still have been, at least ostensibly, attached to the Brackenbury-Richard III party; but by the time of Argentine's association with Henry Tudor he, too, was equally involved in anti-Richard propaganda. Once again, therefore, we have a rumour spread through French/Lancastrian associations.

Can it be irrelevant that Angelo Cato, who sent Mancini to England, was, according to Armstrong who studied the papers in his possession, "something of a specialist on Breton affairs among the Councillors of the French king"?[28] The Brittany-Henry Tudor link once again obtrudes.

NOTES AND REFERENCES
VI — *Laws, Reconciliations and Foreign Observers*

1 Croyland Third Continuator, p.495.

2. Rot. Parl. vol. vi, p.240. Halsted, ii.540-46.

3 Rot. Parl vol. vi. p.244 et seq. Halsted, ii.546. Woodhouse, *Life of John Morton,* p.71.

4 More, p.9.

5 A.R. Myers: *The Character of Richard III. History Today,* vol. 4, No. 8, August 1954.

6 More, p.83.

7 *Chronicles of London* (ed. Kingsford), p.191.

8 Stow's *Annals,* p.416b. *England Under the Yorkists,* p.168.

9 *England Under the Yorkists,* pp.168-9.

10 Ibid, p.157. Statute Rolls II, 478.

11 Ibid, pp.231-2. PR.1 Rich. III, pt.2, m.20.

12 Ibid, pp.213-4. *Letters of Richard III and Henry VII* (RS) II, 287, fr. Harl. MS. 433, f.159b.

13 Ibid, pp.216-8. S.R.II, 489-93.

14 Ross: *Edward IV* pp.99-101. Scofield: *Edward IV,* I.461. *Chronicles of London* (ed. Kingsford), p.179. Sylvester (ed. *More,* p.71n) identifies Markham and Cook but not the Woodville connection with the case.

15 Richard III Exhibition Catalogue, National Portrait Gallery, 1973. p.29.

16 *Lives of the Lord Chancellors,* i.407. Markham: *Richard III,* p.134.

17 Halsted, ii.295. *Wilk. Concil.,* vol.iii, p.614.

18 *Archaeologia,* vol. xxv, p.2.

19 Ellis' *Original Letters,* Second Series, I.149, from Harl. MS. 433. Gairdner, *Richard III,* pp.165-6. MacGibbon: *Elizabeth Woodville,* pp.178-9.

20 *Richard III,* p.287.

21 Vergil, p.210, 214.

22 Hanham: *Richard III and his early historians,* p.19.

120

23 Lecture at Nat. Portrait Gallery, 24 July 1973. Report fr. Folger Library, Vol. 10, No. 1, April 22, 1961.

24 Intro. *Mancini,* p.19.

25 Ed. J.G. Nicols, Camden Soc., 1846, p.1.

26 Poems: BL Royal MS 12A.xxix, Add., MS. 33736, Bodleian lib. MS Laud 501. See also: Armstrong, Intro. *Mancini,* p.19n. Peter Hammond, *Ricardian,* IV, 57, June 1977, p.23.

27 Intro. *Mancini,* p.19n.

28 Ibid, p.24n.

VII
A Tradition, Heirs and Journeys

There is ambivalence throughout this history in the case of children. One still unexplained item concerns the Tower Wardrobe Account, which in March, 1485, listed expensive clothes made for "My Lord Bastard", who appears by the measurements to have been a boy of approximately Edward's then age. No other aristocratic children are known to have been in the Tower at the time, and Edward IV's sons were officially designated "Bastard" in all documents. Edward remained a Lord, retaining the Earldoms of Pembroke and March conferred on him by his father. The reference could have been to Richard's own bastard son, John of Gloucester — who was not, however, a Lord. The entry, once again, could have been wrongly dated.

Mysterious children occur again in an Ordinance made by Richard III for the regulation of his household in the North. Richard's nephew, John, Earl of Lincoln, seems to have been both highly capable and attached to him. In 1484 Richard made him his successor and chief representative in the North, leader of the "King's Council" there as it now became known. [1] And on 24 July the King's Ordinance was issued and included the following items:

"Item, my Lord of Lincoln and my Lord Morley be at one breakfast; the children together at one breakfast; such as be present of the council at one breakfast ....

"Item, the costs of my Lord of Lincoln, when he rideth to seesions, or any meetings appointed by the council, the treasurer to pay for meat and drink ...

"Item, that no liveries of bread, wine, nor ale be had, but such as be measurable and convenient, and that no pot of livery exceed measure of a pottle, but only to my lord and the children ...."[2]

Who were "the children", so obviously near in status to my Lord of Lincoln? They could have included Edward, Prince of Wales, but he died before July 1484; although one or both of Richard's illegitimate children, the boy John or girl Katherine, could have been referred to. If so (and we know nothing of their respective mothers) they were certainly treated as of considerable importance. Or were the princes themselves sent for their protection to the North? One local rumour did maintain that Edward V died at Middleham, but it almost certainly derived from a confusion with Richard's own son Edward, who died there. The Council centre, in any case, was at Richard's other castle, Sheriff Hutton.

At this stage, it seems more likely, assuming they were still alive, that the princes lived with Elizabeth their mother when she came out of sanctuary. So where *did* she live? I come here to the longstanding and specifically-worded tradition in the Tyrell family, going back well before the eighteenth century, and handed down from generation to generation. This was (and I quote Kathleen Margaret Drewe) "that the princes and their mother Elizabeth Woodville lived in the hall by permission of the uncle". The reference is to Gipping Hall, near Stowmarket, Suffolk, which Sir James Tyrell rebuilt in 1474 as a gift, it would seem, to his bride, and which remained the home of the Tyrells until it was finally pulled down early this century.

One reason this story was never produced outside the family, at least to anyone interested in publishing it, was that the Tyrells themselves, understandably in view of Shakespeare and the English history books, had long accepted the established legend that James Tyrell had murdered the princes in the Tower; they had therefore assumed the Queen and princes had lived there before this. But this could only have been in Edward IV's reign, and not only was Sir James still fairly penurious (as his Will of 1475 shows) and in debt, probably partly from his building transactions, until about 1477, but the elder prince was as early as 1473 taken to Ludlow to live under the tutelage of his uncle, Lord Rivers, and others. There is no record of Elizabeth, although she sometimes visited other towns, being in this area while Queen, after the birth of her sons, nor would one expect her to *live* anywhere but at Westminster, in the palace or Tower apartments.

A Tudor agent, Bernard de Vignolles, wrote in 1496 that Thomas Tyrell, whose house was frequented by the Perkin Warbeck conspirators (*"conjurés"*), liked to recall that King Edward *"avoit fait aultrefoiz bonne cherre chez lui"*. It is not clear if Gipping Hall is referred to. [3] J.A. Speares has deduced an early official connection between the families of William Tyrell, Sheriff of Norfolk and Suffolk, and of Richard, Duke of York, at Fotheringhay. If so, James Tyrell could have known Edward and Richard from childhood, and Vignolles' reference could be to visits of Edward during the time of Tyrell's father. There is no record of Edward IV visiting there later when King, and it does not square with the specific tradition of his Queen *living* there with his sons "by permission of the *uncle*", which could only mean Richard III.

The assumption must be, I think, that the Tyrell tradition, if true, applies to some time *after* Elizabeth Woodville left sanctuary, and Kendall's conjecture that she may have lived in "a country house" was more important than he realised. The story may certainly link up with Tyrell's own recorded mysterious mission for Richard in 1484.

This mission is recorded in a warrant sent to the collectors of customs at the port of Sandwich, in connection with payment to the Cinque Ports in respect of shipping. It is as follows:

"Warrant to the Privy Seal in order towards the repaying the Mayor, &c, of Dover four marks, by them advanced for defraying the passage, &c, of Sir James Tyrell, the king's councillor, and knight of his body, who was of late sent over the sea, into the parties of Flanders, for divers matters concerning greatly the king's weal." [4]

What did so "greatly concern" the king's weal in the Flanders connection? Caroline Halsted conjectures that it might have been an attempt by Richard to discover the whereabouts of the princes, possibly smuggled abroad by the Queen's adherents. But Halsted did not know of the Tyrell family rumour, which if true might well suggest this was a journey of another nature, by Tyrell to Margaret of Burgundy to prepare the way for, or actually take, one or both princes out of the kingdom — with the knowledge of their mother who was living with them, in the meantime, at his house.

There might, of course, be other reasons for the journey, including Morton's sojourn in Flanders, and Tyrell may well have acted as one of Richard's spies on the Earl of Richmond's activities. Both the year and the name Tyrell are in any case suggestive. What is clear is that Tyrell was a confidential agent of Richard's of considerable importance and trust.

It must be noted that Gipping Hall is not that far from the coast and Ipswich; a useful spot if it became necessary to get the princes (or one surviving one) away should the danger from Henry Tudor loom again. Tyrell was just the man for such a purpose.

Is there anything at all in the records to suggest that Elizabeth could have been induced to leave sanctuary on the promise that she could then have her sons to live with her? When we re-examine More in the light of this story, we do in fact find that indeed *this was suggested* on the *first* occasion she was pleaded with, and induced to part with the Duke of York. Let us re-read More:—

"And we all, I think, content that both be with her, if she come thence and bide in such a place where they may with their honor be." [5]

Was this proposition repeated to Elizabeth in March 1484, and did she this time accept it? It would explain her own attitude to Richard, and at least be psychologically more understandable than her making her peace with the boys' murderer.

There is not only Elizabeth Woodville to be considered in this. What of Richard's own mother, the once-lovely Cecily Neville, "the Rose of Raby", with whom he had been living in 1483 and whose minstrels (and therefore quite possibly she herself) were with him on progress in 1485, suggesting a continued intimacy between mother and son? [6]

What of Elizabeth of York and her sisters, said to have danced at Christmas 1484 at Richard's Court? Mother, grandmother, sister of the boys — could *all* have shown such ruthless expediency in propitiating, and accepting favours from, the boys' murderer? They must either have known Richard's innocence, or believed the boys were still alive. No other human explanation seems possible.

The living of Elizabeth for a time with the boys (and possibly of course also the girls) at Gipping would be in character too with another earlier story, that it was feared "that some of the king's daughters should leave Westminster, and go in disguise to the parts beyond sea"; [7] and a similar suspicion is expressed by Buckingham in More relative to the younger boy, Richard himself, "that she shall send him somewhere out of the realm". [8] In other words, the fate of King Edward IV's children is inextricably, and confusingly, mixed with the idea of escape abroad. Could it in the end be the *timing* that was confused in the chronicles, as provably so much else of their dating? It would not be unknown in the creation of a legend. In this case, Tyrell's own place in the story may show a distorted link with the truth.

Before we leave the matter of the supposed murder before Elizabeth left sanctuary, it is not only Richard, Tyrell and Buckingham who have had their supporters as principal murderer or agent. Although to my mind the case is tenuous and highly improbable, John Howard, later Duke of Norfolk, has been put forward by S.T. Bindoff as a serious candidate.[9] This rests on the somewhat disputable ground that Howard was Constable of the Tower early in 1483, and needed the death of Richard, Duke of York (who was also Duke of Norfolk) in order to inherit the title, from which he had been displaced as co-heir through the child Richard's marriage to the heiress Anne Mowbray. The fact that Howard's Household Books (ed. by J.Payne Collier, London, 1844) contain an entry of payment for the making of three beds, and two sacks of lime, as Tower expenses, has been taken to suggest a sinister purpose of murdering the princes in the beds and disposing of the bodies by means of the lime. As P.W. Hammond has pointed out,[10] these could be quite innocent acquisitions and Howard's position as Constable was granted in 1479, to take effect only until the death of the present holders, Lords Dudley and Dacre. James Ramsay states Dudley appeared still to be holding the post at the death of Edward IV. Sir Robert Brackenbury was appointed Constable in July 1483, except for a short period when the Marquess of Dorset held the post as deputy.

At the best, it seems very unlikely that someone already so close to Richard would murder a child for a title which the King would almost certainly allow him, as his right, after the bastardizing of Richard, Duke of York, who held the Norfolk title only through marriage to another dead child. In fact, Howard was made Duke of Norfolk, which carried with it the honour of Earl Marshal, so that he was able to carry out this function traditionally attached to the King's coronation, which took place on 6 July. He was a tough customer in war at sea but also a generous lord of his estates, not only supporting those in need but providing education at Cambridge for those "promising youngsters around the countryside'' whose talents and impecuniosity attracted his attention. Like the much younger Richard III, also, he was a lover and patron of music. [11]

If the Tyrells came to accept a story about their ancestor as a murderer, given as irrefutable historical truth in many history books, the same of course applies to the family of Howard in respect of Richard III. Lord Henry Howard, in the year 1583, one hundred years later, wrote ''A defensative against Poison of Supposed Prophecies'', in which he refers to King Richard's ''heinous fault''. In view of Richard's connection with the earlier Howard, A.L. Rowse characteristically seized on this as ''*corroboration* of Richard III's guilt'' (italics mine). [12] If this private family tradition (as Rowse calls it) is acceptable, obviously the Tyrell family tradition about the princes living at their home with their mother, ''by permission of the uncle'', must be equally so: more especially as at least the last few generations of the family living at Gipping Hall had failed to realise its significance in possibly clearing their ancestor of the crime of murder.

Neither story, in fact provides proof; but the Tyrell one seems to me by far the more important, in that it is explicit, and throws a possible wholly new light on a mysterious affair. It is also a reasonable proposition, viewed alongside other evidence. Of nothing put forward on the fate of the princes can more be claimed in honesty.

Could it be significant, in connection with Elizabeth's leaving sanctuary, that John Foster, Hastings' adherent and later, in Henry VII's reign, associated with Morton and Bray, was released from the Tower on 10 March 1484? [13] Was Richard's and the City's persuasion of Elizabeth Woodville this same month part of a general scheme of amnesty for those concerned in the Hastings conspiracy? An Easter amnesty rather seems indicated in the circumstances. According to the Great Chronicle people began whispering about the disappearance of the princes after Easter, and they were no longer seen in the Tower. This would be quite natural if their mother now took them away to live with her.

The Buckingham insurrection had been suppressed five months before, and although in December Henry Tudor, for the first time openly, had solemnly, in front of the Woodville exiles, committed himself in Rennes Cathedral to marry the Princess Elizabeth after obtaining the crown, [14] Richard had reduced his army and felt himself at least for the time being secure. It is often overlooked that after Elizabeth's release there was a lapse of nine months before her daughters were reported at Richard's Court. In fact, Richard and his Court went north, and stayed there so many months that there were murmurings in the south and definite fears that the King, whose attachment to Yorkshire and his homes there was well-known, intended to shift his capital from London to York.

If, indeed, he had had any hand in murdering his nephews, Nemesis soon followed; for shortly after he arrived in Nottingham on 20 March, news reached him and his wife of the sudden death of his ten-year-old son, Edward, Prince of Wales. The suddenness and severity of the blow can be guessed from the fact that only in February, during the lifetime of his Parliament, Richard had brought together "shortly after mid-day, nearly all the Lords of the realm, both spiritual and temporal, together with the higher knights and esquires of the King's household". These dignitaries, who met "in a certain lower room, near the passage which leads to the Queens apartments" were required to subscribe to an oath "of adherence to Edward, the King's only son, as their supreme Lord, in case anything should happen to his father". [15]

All Richard's care to ensure the succession of the crown to his only legitimate son crashed with this death, and with it the hopes of the Yorkists for an undisputed direct heir. "Then", wrote the Croyland Chronicler and this time we can perhaps believe him, "you might have seen his father and mother in a state almost bordering on madness by reason of their sudden grief." [16] It is said that thereafter Richard referred to Nottingham as his "Castle of Care". One need hardly add that the Third Croyland Continuator vindictively seized on the "Nemesis" aspect, its not being a part of the morality of such theologians to comment on the fact that the God they worshipped, and whose actions they so approved, had incidentally visited the supposed sin of the father on the entirely innocent child.

It was perhaps because of the prince's delicacy that he so rarely travelled or saw his parents, although the separation of children from their families at a very early age was a regular practice of the times, as has been seen in the case of Edward IV's own heir, of Richard himself when young, and many others. It is actually pointed out to Elizabeth Woodville, in More's dialogue, that she had apparently not minded parting with and seeing little of her elder son, so why should she object to giving up Richard, Duke of York? In any case, the fragility of Richard III's son may have been hereditary; his mother was to die within a year, at thirty years old (it is strange that the stalwart Warwick the Kingmaker should have left only delicate daughters).

Was it because of Anne Neville's health that she and Richard, in over ten years of marriage and in days when contraception was unknown, should have had, as far as we know, only this one child? Anne travelled with and to the King constantly; far more, as has been pointed out by Caroline Halsted, than was often the case with Queens. There is, of course, one other possibility: that Richard's reaction from his brother's lasciviousness, which seems to have bred in him (as is shown in some of his letters and statutes) a streak of puritanism and open repudiation of "vice", caused in him a certain impotence, or unwillingness, in actual sex relations. In modern psychological knowledge, this would certainly be possible. He made no bones about acknowledging two bastards, but there is strange lack of evidence about their mother or mothers, and it is viable, I think, that they were born in his early life, while still under the influence of, and perhaps (as young hero-worshippers do) trying to emulate, his magnificent elder brother. He seems totally to have taken charge of them, even the girl. But why only one legitimate child? Did Anne, on her part, become barren or unwilling? If so, any evidence of Richard's finding satisfaction elsewhere is markedly lacking. A question mark hangs over his personal character, in this as so much else in the enigma of his reign.

Certainly Richard gave no indication, after his only son's death, of expecting he himself might father another heir; although the story soon to be narrated may have carried the implication that he desperately needed one. In the meantime he is reputed (there seems no confirmation in government papers, perhaps because there was no other Parliament in his short reign) to have made Clarence's young son, Edward, Earl of Warwick, briefly his heir, and later displaced him by nominating the adult and faithful son of his sister, John, Earl of Lincoln, heir to the Duke of Suffolk and virtually now governor of the North. There seems to be a general historical assumption that Clarence's son was slightly feeble-minded; although accounts are quite untrue that, as Mancini writes, Richard kept him "in confinement, for he feared that if the entire progeny of King Edward became extinct, yet this child, who was also of royal blood, would still embarrass him". [17]

In fact, as Rous (who was present) makes clear, young Warwick was with his uncle in 1483 when the royal progress reached Warwick: an act of special kindness, perhaps, owing to his title, of which the attainder on his father had not robbed the child. It was Dorset, and later Henry VII (who ultimately executed him at the age of twenty-four), who kept the ill-starred Warwick immured in the Tower. Even Mancini concedes he was confined "in the household of his [Richard's] wife, the child's maternal aunt". He was, of course, very closely related to both the new King and Queen (he was their brother's and sister's child respectively); but it may also have been because of the attainder on Clarence that Richard had second thoughts about making one so young his heir. If he lifted the attainder on his brother's children, the disinheritance of Edward IV's two sons too might come in question again. Indeed, J.A. Speares has speculated that it is not beyond the bounds of possibility that, after the death of his own son, Richard did actually contemplate reversing the disinheritance of Edward's sons too, in order to make the ex-King Edward V, when fully grown, his heir. The illegitimacy could have been reversed, on papal authority, for this purpose as is made clear in Mary O'Regan's revealing article, discussed earlier in this book.

It has been noted that Langton, Bishop of St. David's, later (in 1484) was sent by Richard to Rome. J.A. Speares points out that in December of that year Sir John Kendall, Grand Prior of St. John, was also sent to Rome. Kendall was subsequently involved with Thomas Langton in supporting Perkin Warbeck. [18] It is a beguiling theory, because it fits in with Tyrell's immense position of trust at this time, his appointment to the post at Guisnes (a key continental entry-point for Yorkist heirs travelling to Flanders, as will subsequently appear) in January 1485, and the approximate dates of the death of Richard's son and Elizabeth Woodville's decision to leave sanctuary, and possibly accept Tyrell's hospitality at Gipping Hall. I suggest myself that there would probably be no question, during Edward V's minority, of actually reinstating him as heir; but the Rome visits may have included discussion with the papal authorities about the possibilities.

In the meantime, the able and trustworthy Earl of Lincoln was obviously a better answer if the kingdom were not to be plagued with the rule of a minor again. Could he have been looked on, in the case of Richard's early death, as a future *Protector,* rather than direct heir? And did Elizabeth Woodville know of this? We do not know the exact date of her leaving sanctuary in March, but by the 20th of that month or very soon after Richard's son was dead. Some of this might explain her attitude in Henry VII's reign, to be discussed later, as also that of Lincoln in supporting a pretender to the throne, without ever attempting to assert his own possible rights as Richard's heir.

Nothing, in March 1484, after the death of Richard's son, would be as indisputable in men's minds as a direct heir, or one through the male line. Had Edward, Prince of Wales, lived long enough, Henry Tudor might have had a rougher passage to the throne. In the meantime, it is perhaps worth noting that Warwick may have been one of the unnamed "children" with Lincoln at Sheriff Hutton in July 1484 (he was certainly there when Henry Tudor won the Battle of Bosworth) and his sister Margaret, later that Countess of Salisbury executed in her old age by Henry VIII, another. It has been suggested that although Richard's son Edward died at Middleham, he may have been buried at this other favourite castle of Richard's, at Sheriff Hutton, which is less of a backwater than Middleham, and ten miles north-east of York.[19] It was, as we have seen, the headquarters of the Council of the North.

There is no record of the prince's funeral, but by 1 May Richard and Anne were at York, and later in the month they visited Middleham (for the last time), Durham and Scarborough before returning to York. The King spent the whole summer travelling between York, Pontefract and Scarborough, returning to Nottingham at intervals.[20] It has been conjectured Nottingham was chosen because it was near the centre of England, a place from which the King could take an army reasonably quickly to any point of the coast at which Henry might land. The east coast, too, had been suggested as a possible landing-place, hence the visits to Scarborough. But Henry in 1484 did not come (he was still having difficulties getting the French support he now desperately needed, possibly because the French agents in England had not been able to report a strong enough movement against Richard, in spite of Lancastrian efforts to convince Mancini's successors). Nevertheless, Richard's long stay in the north may have been a miscalculation which weakened his potential support in the south. It was here he needed to be to become more widely and intimately known, and win hearts to his cause.

At Pontefract a foreign visitor, one of the few to write a later travel diary (written between 1490 and 1494) not angled to Tudor susceptibilities, met Richard, and was impressed. Nicolas Von Poppelau was of a noble Silesian family, and according to Armstrong "one of the first modern diplomats".[21] He arrived at Pontefract on 1 May 1484, and presented to the King letters of introduction from the Emperor, Frederick III. After his delivery of a Latin oration, which was greatly admired, King Richard took him graciously by the hand and ordered a chamberlain to conduct him to his lodgings. The next day Von Poppelau attended a mass at which the King was present, and which included music of high standard (Richard was particularly fond of music and an order of his exists for the acquisition of men and boys with good voices to be trained for the royal choirs). After dinner he spoke alone with the King, who made interested enquiries about the Emperor and European princes and when told of the recent victory of the King of Hungary over the Turks exclaimed, according to Von Poppelau: "I wish that my kingdom lay upon the confines of Turkey; with my own people alone and without the help of other princes I should like to drive away not only the Turks, but all my foes."

Doubtless he was thinking of Henry Tudor: it is the cry of a man harassed by the thought of that threatening invasion. Von Poppelau gives no hint of any deformity in Richard, but claims he was three fingers taller than himself, but thinner, "with delicate arms and legs also a great heart". Von Poppelau was less impressed by the English than by their King: they had wealth and were hospitable, but also ostentatious and natural pilferers, while their women were impudent (English women in medieval times had far more freedom, and sometimes control of their own or their husbands' estates, than in most periods later). His wail about the standards of English cooking was to be echoed by European visitors down the centuries. Nevertheless, he received from the King of this country of deplorable *cuisine* a golden necklace, taken by his own hands "from the neck of a certain lord". Whether Richard repaid the deprived lord is not recorded: almost certainly, being "somewhat above his power liberal", he did so.

A Privy Councillor of Scotland, acting as Secretary to the

Ambassador from Scotland at this time, was also warm in praise of the King, even allowing for the flatteries of a diplomatic oration. In Richard, he stated, "all the excellent qualities of a good king and great commander are happily united ... You show yourself gentle to all, and affable even to the meanest of your people". He also comments on Richard's stature: "Nature never united to a small frame a greater soul, or a more powerful mind". He describes his face as having "a princely majesty and authority royal".[22]

It is worth noting that Von Poppelau, unlike the French commentators after Richard's death, gives no hint of having heard that this King is supposed to have murdered his nephews, although the Dutch Chronicle of Holland, Zeeland and Friesland (known as the Divisie Chronicle) certainly does so. Its version is that the Duke of Gloucester "their foresaid uncle made them starve to become king himself". It adds, however, (once again), the interesting alternative that "Some others will say that the Duke of Buckingham killed these children hoping to become king himself". According to Huizinga, the Dutch historian, the Divisie Chronicle was written about 1500, that is within fifteen years of Richard's death. It was first published in 1517. [23]

A good deal of building, for which he has often been praised, was set in motion by Richard at Nottingham Castle, at Pontefract, and at the royal palace of York (possibly it was the last that gave rise to southern anxiety that Richard was to make York his permanent capital). Less noticed, is the fact that he also gave the order for a good deal of rebuilding and repairs of "some part of the Tower of London towards the Thames: in memory whereof, there be yet his arms impaled with those of the Queen his wife, standing upon the Arch adjoyning to the sluice-gate". [24]

No one seems to have commented that to set building craftsmen and labourers to work within the Tower was surely a rash action by a monarch confidently stated to have murdered his nephews and had them buried in some unspecified spot there, "under a great heap of stones". Suppose the workmen in their rebuilding activities had discovered these?

Richard did not return to London until 9 November, when "the Mayr, and his brethren thaldermen, wt the citezeins in violet clothyng, fet in kyng Richard, metyng wt hym beyond Kenyngton, and so brought hym to the Warderobe at the blak ffreris, where he was loged". [25]

Here he was at last to act as host to Elizabeth Woodville's daughters, including at least the eldest girl, Elizabeth of York, who had inherited the red-gold hair of the Plantagenets, which she was destined to pass on to her son, King Henry VIII, and her grand-daughter, Queen Elizabeth I. But this genealogical strand was as yet only dreamt of by an ageing woman recently disgraced in England, and her exiled son across the Channel, plotting to make her dream a reality.

For Richard, his niece was to be the instrument of one more rumour, soon to explode in his face.

1 *Letters and Papers of Richard III and Henry VII* (RS), 1, 56-9, July 1484.
England Under the Yorkists, pp. 148-9.

2 Harl. MSS. No. 433, fol. 265. Halsted, ii. 524-5.

3 Jean-Didier Chastelain: *L'Imposture de Perkin Warbeck*, (Brussels, 1952), p.42.

4 Halsted, ii. 369.

5 More, p.29.

6 *Annals of Cambridge*, Cooper. This reference to the "Lady of York" in the
Cambridge treasurers' accounts, misread by Cooper as "Duke of York" and
excitingly drawn attention to by V.B. Lamb in a letter to the *Sunday Times*
about 20 years ago, was corrected by A.R. Myers, who investigated the original
MS translated by Cooper and found "domine" (presumably Cecily, Duchess of
York), not "ducis" was meant by the abbreviation.
It is only one example of the false trails which turn up in the forests of this
complex mystery.

7 Croyland Third Continuator, p.491.

8 More, p.30.

9 National Portrait Gallery lecture, 24 July 1973. Also "Report from Folger
Library", Vol. 10, No. 1, 22 April 1961.

10 *Ricardian*, IV, No. 60, March 1978. pp.26-7.

11 Kendall: *Richard III*, pp. 194-5.

12 *Elizabethan Renaissance — The Life of Society*. Quoted in *Ricardian*, No. 39,
Dec. 1972, p.37.

13 Geoffrey Wheeler, *Ricardian*, No. 40, March 1973, p.18.

14 MacGibbon: *Elizabeth Woodville*, p.177.

15 Cal. Close Rolls, p.229. Rot. Parl. VI, p.234. Hammond: *Edward of
Middleham*, p.20 Croyland, p. 496.

16 Croyland Third Continuator, p.497.

17 Mancini, p.89.

18 Chastelain: *L'Imposture de Perkin Warbeck*, p.38.

19 Hammond: *Edward of Middleham*, pp.22-3.

20 Harl. MSS. 433, f. 172d et seq.

21 Appendix to Mancini Report, ed. Armstrong, pp.136-8.

22 Buck, pp. 39-40. Translation from Latin in Halsted, ii.358.

23 Divisie Chronicle (Die xxxi Divisie, folio cccxcii, kat. x, recto and verso). *Ricardian,* III, No. 46, Sept. 1974, pp.12-13, on information supplied by Miss Maaike Lulofs.

24 Buck, p.139.

25 *Chronicles of London* (ed. Kingsford), p.192.

VIII
Elizabeth of York

Perhaps aware of the feeling that he had deserted his capital city too long, Richard saw to it that the Christmas festivities were on a particularly lavish scale. It was a return to the famed magnificence of the Court of Edward IV, and whatever Richard's inner puritanical compulsion he had already shown, at the coronation and the subsequent ceremonies in York Cathedral, that he had an astute political grasp of the need for a king to dazzle by splendour (the English monarchy clings to this tradition in the ceremonies that attract the public and foreign tourists today). The glittering richness of even Richard's clothes pointed, less to the vanity of the man conscious of his own lack of height, than to his urgent realisation that he must be seen to be a king in all the power and glory suggested by regal trappings.

Was there, too, a lingering psychological uncertainty about the means by which he had acquired the throne, over the heads of, even if not by the deaths of, his brother's sons? Was he trying to convince himself of his impregnable position, when he and his Queen wore their crowns so conspicuously on Epiphany, at a court revel? Were they both trying, too, to drown in opulence and gaiety the memory of their dead son?

There was perhaps a desperation behind this magnificence, during which indeed Richard learned "from his spies beyond sea, that, notwithstanding the potency and splendour of his royal state, his adversaries would, without question, invade the kingdom during the following summer, or make an attempt to invade it. Than this, there was nothing that could befall him more desirable, inasmuch as he imagined that it would put an end to all his doubts and troubles."[1]

But Richard had anticipated this, with proclamations against Tudor and the summary execution, after trial, of William Collingbourne, who had been in proved treasonable communication with Henry regarding his projected invasion. The crown did not always sit easily on his head; but at this Christmas-time it was firmly worn, and shiningly in view. It was symbol of his supreme authority, and he must have known it.

The Woodville girls, or those of them old enough to attend, seem to have been taken into the Queen's special care. According to Croyland, in sour disapproval, "far too much attention was given to dancing and gaiety, and vain changes of apparel presented to queen Anne and the lady Elizabeth, the eldest daughter of the late king, being of similar colour and shape; a thing that caused the people to murmur and the nobles and prelates to wonder at". It seems an innocuous enough thing to wonder at, and "the people" (once again) can safely be left out of it, as no ordinary citizens would have attended such a Court function. Croyland, throwing up his hands in puritanical horror (the humanist method of history dramatised to point a moral is here very marked) has more important fish to fry: with this sprat he proposes to catch a mackerel. " .... it was said by many that the king was bent, either on the anticipated death of the queen taking place, or else, by means of a divorce, for which he supposed he had quite sufficient grounds, on contracting a marriage with the said Elizabeth. For it appeared that in no other way could his kingly power be established, or the hopes of his rival be put an end to."

Now "the anticipated death of the queen" (in spite of her sprightly revels and changes of apparel only a few lines before) is "anticipated" by the Croyland Chronicler (wise after the event) but not, surely, at this moment by Richard; and Croyland indeed has to cover his statement by a falsification in the opening to his next paragraph: "In the course of a few days after this, the queen fell extremely sick, and her illness was supposed to have increased still more and more, because the king entirely shunned her bed, declaring that it was by the advice of his physicians that he did so. Why enlarge? About the middle of the following month, upon the day of the great eclipse of the sun, which then took place, queen Anne, before-named, departed this life, and was buried at Westminster, with no less honours than befitted the interment of a queen".[2]

In fact, Anne died in the middle of March 1485, after an illness which, like that of her sister, Clarence's wife Isabel, seems to have had many attributes of tuberculosis, and probably began in an obviously dangerous form many more than "a few days" after Christmas. If late medieval medical knowledge matched that of today, Richard's and the Queen's doctors may well have warned him of the dangers of contagion, as well as the further weakening of the Queen by a sexual relationship. We can perhaps assume her decline was accentuated by grieving over the death of her son, not by any neglect of Richard's, for they seem to have been conspicuous for being frequently in each other's company, whatever his cares of state. How much was she his *confidante* and comforter? Possibly, a good deal. Sir Frances Lovel, his closest friend since his youthful days in the Earl of Warwick's household, cannot have been so constantly at his side; and both Richard and Anne would have retained childhood memories, and surely been bound by some of the similar vicissitudes they had experienced, as playthings in the power game. Richard's grief at her death is recorded, even if it did not take the extravagant emotional form of that of his royal namesake, King Richard II, at the funeral of another beloved Queen Anne, a century before. No hints of poisoning her — even in the poisonous Croyland Third Continuator — appear until the later Tudor chronicles, used with such propaganda force by the unsuspecting humanitarian Shakespeare.

Nevertheless, that the rumour that Richard intended to marry his niece, Elizabeth of York, existed, and he was aware of it, we know from his later (and remarkably prompt) official denial. (Why did he not similarly deny the rumour that he had murdered the princes? Was it because in fact this was never recorded, and much more whispered and less prevalent than his enemies later proclaimed? Neither Buckingham's rebellion nor Henry's invasion had openly been based on it: it was long known that Henry claimed the crown for himself from his Lancastrian descent and through his mother's machinations. Only through reading of the chronicles, written later, do we know of it ourselves; and Richard's spies in France were at times curiously inefficient — for instance in judging Henry's proposed landing plans — and the speech of Guillaume de Rochefort in the French Parliament may not necessarily have reached Richard's ears. If it did it might not have registered with him except as an enemy country's inevitable propaganda — which from the nature of the speech it obviously was. There was no form of journalism to repeat and record the speech in England. The citizens of London, Exeter, and the many other towns which welcomed him can have given no hint to him of these rumours. To some extent, in all this, we make assumptions on hindsight.)

What of Elizabeth? She was a girl of eighteen in the first flush of young womanhood, and it is possible she had inherited some of the charm and sexuality of both her parents. Richard could have been attracted to her, and no king in his not unprecarious position, knowing of the Queen's decline in health or approaching death, could ignore the necessity of remarriage and a possible heir. Moreover, at least by now Richard must have known about Henry Tudor's use of her to help consolidate his claim. Whatever the secrecy of Margaret Beaufort's original proposals to Elizabeth Woodville in sanctuary, Henry at Rennes had openly declared his intentions.

Had the girl been consulted, and what did she think of this proposed alliance, for reasons of state, to an unknown young Welshman? No one knows. But Elizabeth was the daughter of Edward IV, and there is often a close bond between a womanising father and his daughters. There is nothing necessarily perverted in this; the man of this type is attracted by women as a sex. He tends to be closer to a daughter than to a son. There is certainly evidence that Elizabeth as a child was introduced into Court life and its attractions by her father. In September, 1472, when she was six and a half years old (by no means an unobservant age in a girl), Edward IV staged a great entertainment at Windsor for the Lord of Gruthuyse, the Duke of Burgundy's ambassador. Two chambers "richeley hanged with clothes of Arras, and beddes of astate", were prepared; and when the ambassador had supped in his chamber, "my lord Chamberleyn had hym againe to the Kinges chamber, and incontinent the Kinge had hym to the quenes chamber, wher she sat plainge with her ladyes at the morteaulx* .... and dauncing .... Also the Kinge daunsed with my lady Elizabethe, his eldest daughter ...."

The next day, after hunting, the "quene did order a grete banket in her owne chambre .... And when they had sopt, my lady

* A game resembling bowls.

Elizabeth, the Kynge's eldest doughter, daunsed with the Duke of Bokingham ..."[3] Given the bond between the King and his dazzled young daughter, she must have known, especially as she grew older, his affection for and appreciation of his loyal brother Richard; and at an impressionable age this could have ended in her sharing her father's devotion. Richard was only thirteen years her senior; still a young man in 1484, and according to the Countess of Desmond, who claimed at an immense age to have danced when a girl at Edward's Court, Richard was "the handsomest man in the room except his brother Edward, and was very well made".[4] The old Countess may not have been quite the advanced centenarian that this suggests: the story could have come to her from a predecessor, and she could have made herself the important heroine of it, as old ladies sometimes do in telling tales of the remote past. But Horace Walpole in the eighteenth century heard corroboration: "With regard to the person of Richard, the earl of Shaftsbury was so good as to inform me, that his ancestor the lady Ashley, who lived to a great age, had conversed with lady Desmond, and gave from her the same account that I have given, with this strong addition, that Perkin Warbeck was remarkably like Edward the fourth".[5]

It is certainly true that Richard, from his portrait, the earliest of which was probably based on a contemporary original, has good features, and that curious air of slightly careworn sadness that often attracts romantic young girls.

If Elizabeth grew up impressed by her loved father's devotion to her young uncle, how, in fact, did she react to her mother's fear of Richard in sanctuary, and the attempted power bid of her maternal uncle, Rivers, and her half-brother, Richard Grey? She probably had not seen a great deal more of them than she had of Richard, if they were so often in Ludlow with her brother the Prince of Wales, whom she also could not have known well. Is it possible she clung to her memories of her father's faith, and Richard's devotion to him, and resented betrothal to the unknown young Welshman who intended to take the throne from the Yorkists? (Her mother was in slightly different case. Her family, and her first husband, had been Lancastrian, and she may, self-interest apart, for this reason have been more amenable to Margaret Beaufort's suggestions than other Yorkists. Her Woodville relations, certainly, had no difficulty in switching allegiance to Henry Tudor when it suited them.)

What did she think (if at first she knew) of the bastardizing? She was surely old enough in Court ways, and aware enough of Edward's openly-flaunted mistresses, to realise there might be truth behind it. Girls of this age do not always follow their mother: frequently they rebel against them. Was it Elizabeth, in the end, who helped to persuade the ex-Queen to leave sanctuary and let her go to Richard's Court? Sanctuary must have been irritatingly confining to an adolescent girl of any spirit, and her nearest sister may have backed her in this.

If so, one thing seems clear, and indeed arises from her obviously equable appearance dancing at the Court nine months later; *she could not have believed Richard had murdered her young brothers.* We are dealing with human beings, not with history book ciphers; and Richard of York, at least, she had known well all his life.

There is, of course, a reason for this scrutiny of her character and the suggestion of her marriage to Richard. It was not necessarily against the law, and papal dispensations for the marriage of uncle to niece were certainly not unknown. As she eventually married the triumphant Henry VII, Tudor chroniclers naturally stress her repugnance to a suggestion which they maintain came from her uncle; and it was not until Sir George Buck wrote his *History of the Life and Reigne of Richard III* in the early seventeenth century, after the end of the Tudor dynasty, that it was claimed that she herself had taken a leading part in this proposed match. Buck stated categorically than when the Queen failed to die in February as her physicians had expected, Elizabeth wrote a letter to the Duke of Norfolk, "intimating first, that he was the man in whom she most affied, in respect of that love her Father had ever bore him, &c. Then she congratulates his many courtesies, in continuance of which, she desires him to be a mediator for her to the King, in behalf of the Marriage propounded between them, who, as she wrote, was her onely joy and maker in this world, and that she was his in heart and thought: withall insinuating that the better part of February was past, and that she feared the Queen would never die."

"All these be her own words, written with her own hand; and this is the sum of her letter, which remains in the Autograph or Original Draft, under her own hand, in the magnificent Cabinet of Thomas Earl of Arundel and Surrey ....."[6]

Was the letter, of which Buck gives only this summary, genuine?

Naturally, it has been furiously denied by both pro- and anti-Ricardians, the first assuming it reflects on his own character and wishes, and the second wishing to believe that although Richard was capable of any wickedness (and to the morality of Victorian historians this marriage of course was beyond the pale), the angelic wife of the hardly less angelic Henry VII (*vide* Croyland and Vergil) could not possibly have had any hand in it.

Setting aside such partialities, however, the marriage was not beyond the pale among royalty or the aristocracy according to Vatican rulings of the period; it merely had to have papal approval like many other less close ties of consanguinity (Richard's marriage to Anne Neville should have had this dispensation). It was, however, a nearer relationship than many people, in England especially, even at that time might be prepared to accept. Nor would it have been greatly approved of by the readers of Buck's own period. We therefore come to the interesting question (which no one ever seems to ask) as to why he should *make up* such a letter, which many (in spite of his claim that Richard himself "had no real intent to make her his wife") would take to reflect on Richard adversely? For Buck's book was definitely intended as a *vindication* of Richard III.

There are other reasons for accepting its authenticity. It is true that John Howard, the first Duke of Norfolk, to whom it was addressed, was known to have influence with Richard; and the home of a descendant, the Earl of Arundel and Surrey, was certainly the most likely place for it to be preserved, for on 4 February 1495 Elizabeth's younger sister Anne was married to Thomas Howard, the Earl of Surrey and later third duke of Norfolk (the Duke to whom the letter was addressed had been killed with Richard at Bosworth Field). Elizabeth herself, as Queen to Henry VII, died eight years after this, and her sister, eleven years her junior, may well have been instrumental in preserving her letter in the Norfolk family archives.

As only a summary is given, and prolonged search never produced the original, it has, of course, been suggested that Buck's memory of the contents was faulty and even that it could have concerned the delayed marriage of Elizabeth later to Henry VII. As it stands it certainly could not fit this theory, and the remarks on the Queen's death do not themselves throw an especially amiable light on Elizabeth in the matter. We must, in this, nevertheless allow for her age and the fact that the Queen's death was assumed to be certain in any case. It seems to me questionable, in Buck's wording, if the preliminary " he" before "the man", "in respect of that love her father had ever bore him", applies to Norfolk or to Richard himself. I have already suggested King Edward's affection for and trust of Richard may have impressed his daughter, and this could just possibly be verification.

Why did she feel she needed a mediator with Richard? It is a letter showing both ardour and impatience, stamping her as her father's daughter in matters of the heart. The assumption would seem to be that Richard was not as responsive as she would wish, though this could have been his genuine anxiety and grief over the Queen. It seems to me unlikely that he had not at least contemplated the possibility of such a marriage, if only to frustrate Henry's attempt to bolster his dubious claim. He was not a demonstrative man in his affections, and certainly lacked his brother's sexual passions. Did the girl's too-obvious infatuation begin to irk him? It may not have been only to keep her at a distance from Henry, whose invasion was now known to be imminent, that he sent her to Sheriff Hutton to join the other Yorkist, Edward, Earl of Warwick.

At any rate, as early as March ("a little before Easter") in the great hall of the Hospital of Saint John in Clerkenwell, the King "in the presence of the mayor and citizens of London", denied the rumour "in a loud and distinct voice".[7] It was the same month that Anne, his Queen, had died.

Croyland's animosity, of course, must still make the whole affair seem derogatory to Richard: he claims that the King only yielded to the persuasions of twelve Doctors of Divinity, "who asserted that the pope could grant no dispensation in the case of such a degree of consanguinity". If they did so, they were wrong, as an ecclesiastic minister as experienced as John Russell, Bishop of Lincoln, would have known. He also maintains that "Sir Richard Ratclyff and William Catesby, Esquire of his body" (Richard's Chancellor should also have known Catesby was Speaker in his Parliament and Treasurer of the realm) urged against the plan, for fear that when Elizabeth became Queen "it might at some time be in her power to avenge upon them the death of her uncle, earl Antony, and her brother Richard, they having been the king's special advisors in these matters."

As Croyland is considered sacrosanct, no one has remarked on the extraordinary nature of this claim. Nothing whatever is said about the murder of her small brothers, the princes, by Richard, the man she was to marry: her objection might only be, not to becoming the murderer's Queen, but to the continued influence of those alleged to have urged the execution of her uncle and half-brother for treason.[8] Is it possible that the Third Continuator, after all, did not really believe the rumour which he claimed had been "spread", at the time of the Buckingham rebellion, that the princes had met a "violent" death, presumably at Richard's hands?

There is, of course, more possibility in Croyland's other statement that Catesby and Ratcliffe advised Richard that he might lose some support in the North, on whose loyalty he had always been able to count, if he proceeded with this match. But Croyland's partisanship of Henry Tudor makes him too unreliable a source for the story of Richard's own original intentions to be accepted without reservations. He seems, on his prompt denial, almost immediately after the Queen's death, to have rejected the idea even politically. He had, after all, through his Council and Parliament been instrumental in the bastardizing of Edward IV's children, and such a match, for him though not for Henry (who intended to repeal the Act and indeed suppress all future knowledge of it), would have been tantamount to admitting Elizabeth still had a Yorkist claim.

It may have been to his advantage to allow the rumour to proliferate for a short time, in order to circumvent Henry: which indeed it did, for it was at this time that Henry appears to have abandoned the idea of marrying Elizabeth and started seeking the hand of the sister of Sir Walter Herbert, whose influence and lands on the borders of Wales were considerable. Sir Walter, however, failed to respond and remained true to Richard: in fact the messengers Henry dispatched to him feared to venture into the limits of his territory. [9] Lord Bacon's claim that Henry VII was a "cold" husband, and the evidence of his two-year delay in allowing Elizabeth of York to be actually crowned (there was some open protest at this), may have some basis in his suspicions of her interest in the proposed marriage to Richard.

It is true this repulsion would have been greater if he genuinely believed Richard murdered his wife's brothers, and she was willing to overlook it; but there is considerable indication that in fact Henry did not really know what had happened to them, and this lack of exact knowledge bedevilled his own reign.

At the best, Elizabeth of York was a pawn in the power game, and in the making and unmaking of kings. If as a spirited young girl, and her father's daughter, she once tried to play a card of her own in the game, it is not necessarily unbelievable or even out of Neville or Woodville character. Warwick the Kingmaker, Richard Neville, was her grandmother's nephew, and the ambition of the Woodvilles was a byword in society of the time. If she inherited a little of her father's romantic susceptibility, that too would be in keeping. For had not Edward risked his throne, and lost his strongest ally, when he married in secret the gilt-haired widow of a Lancastrian knight?

The history of Henry's subsequent relationship with his wife's mother, Elizabeth Woodville, belongs to another chapter, but again it provokes speculation and suggests inner tensions which have never been adequately explained.

NOTES AND REFERENCES

VIII — *Elizabeth of York*

1 Croyland Third Continuator, p.498.

2 Ibid, p.498-9.

3 Record of Bluemantle Pursuivant: Kingsford, *English Historical Literature,* pp.386-8. *England Under the Yorkists,* pp.241-2.

4 John Harvey: *The Plantagenets,* pp.137-8.

5 *Supplement to the Historic Doubts.* Complete Works, p.216.

6 Buck, p.128.

7 Croyland, p.500.

8. Ibid, pp.449-500.

9 Leland's Itinerary, vi.p.30. Halsted, ii. pp.426 and 438.

IX
Bosworth and the Tudor Dynasty

Richard was now alone: within a year he had lost both heir and wife, and the enemy was thundering on his shores. Henry had at last won generous French aid, and he was to sail with the full support of the nation which had for centuries been Britain's principal target for invasion. Richard had his hands too full with Lancastrian rebellion or threats of rebellion to pursue the old Plantagenet claim to the French throne; but he had been brought up a warrior.and had already proved himself, at Pecquiny, antagonistic to the idea of peace with France for the sake of an annual pension, and although he had since signed peace treaties with Scotland, France and other countries, the French were perhaps understandably suspicious. Their agent had presented them with a useful rumour of the new English king's intention to murder child rivals, and they had already promptly seized on it and presented it as fact, *via* their Chancellor. To have another king on the English throne, dependent on *them* now for aid and grateful in future negotiations, was a chance not to be missed. When Henry sailed it was with French money and an army of three thousand Normans, "the loosest and most profligate persons in all that country", commented Commines.[1] The commander of the French troops was Philibert de Shaundé.[2]

Richard's spies had informed him of the coming event, but the secret of the place of Henry's proposed landing was well–kept: even when it occurred Richard found his agents had bungled. He had issued yet more proclamations against Henry Tudor as a "bastard" line whose armies and treatment of the English could be expected to be atrocious; and he certainly had some support in the nature of Henry's army. It was a band of official French troops with an acknowledged element of unruly mercenaries: in other words a foreign invasion, aimed to put what the French government may well have hoped to be their English puppet on the throne. To give Henry his due, he had no intention of becoming anyone's puppet, French or otherwise: he was to rule England with a rod of iron, through his main instrument Morton, and under constant rebellion and protest; but as an English king, though with a diplomatic gesture towards his Welsh blood which he well knew had brought him his support in the west.

Nevertheless, his support, as well as the later supposed peace and stability of his reign, have reached purely mythical proportions in many accounts, simply because of the equal myth of Richard's tyranny. Henry Tudor's triumph at Bosworth was an accident of history, owing nothing to the size of his army and support but a great deal, in the end, to the last-minute decision of his relatives – by-marriage, Lord and Sir William Stanley, to throw in their lot on his side. It owed even more to Richard's impetuosity and courage, and also to his lack of luck (it was said that Napoleon always asked those he intended to make his generals, "Are you lucky?") But that the main body of peers supported Henry is based on pure propaganda. At least twenty of the thirty-four peers supported Richard, and even Croyland contradicts the estimates of Henry's support, stating of Richard's forces: "it became necessary to move the army, though its numbers were not yet fully made up, from Nottingham, to come to Leicester. Here was found a number of warriors ready to fight on the king's side, *greater than had ever been seen before in England collected together on behalf of one person* (italics mine)[3].

Every evidence supports this. In fact when the parties on either side came to be named, Henry's once again were mainly the same Lancastrian knights and squires who had long supported him in exile: including the Earl of Oxford, "who had beene partly prepar'd by Dr Morton"[4], and whose wife had been most generously treated by Richard while he was in exile, in spite of his treasonable support of Henry Tudor.

In the south, it is possible Richard lost support both by his concentration on and love of the north; and although accounts of his northern followers being given almost total control of the lands of the south is exaggerated (a surprising number of historians, including Kendall, have assumed Tyrell was a northerner and not realised his family had been based for centuries in East Anglia), there is no doubt this did occur, partly through the loss of Lancastrian and Woodville rebels' lands by attainder, and partly owing to Richard's noted generosity to his friends and followers.[5] In addition, some of the feudal aristocracy may have been alienated by the very moderation and legal reform which characterised his reign. There is nothing new in this; history, and especially English history, is peppered with the still-hot ashes of argument and confrontation, in a land where every boy and every girl that's born into the world alive is, as W.S. Gilbert noticed, "either a little Liberal or else a little Conservative". That Richard's efforts were deliberately aimed to level unjust distinctions in the law is incontrovertible, for the evidence is in the law books and other records.

In December 1484, Richard had issued a Proclamation "for the love that he hath for the ministracion and execusion of Justice for the common welthe of this Royme", that if any should find himself wronged by any officer or other person then he shall show it to the King and "according to Justice and his lawes they shal have Remedy". In the second year of his reign he had called "all the justices before him in the inner Star Chamber and asked of them 3 questions .... The first question the King put to them was: 'If anyone brought a false writ and action against some man by which he was taken and imprisoned and kept in prison, shall there be any remedy in that case for the party or for the King, etc. The King then specified a case where a Thomas Staunton had had a judgement in chancery against a Thomas Gate and had had execution but Thomas Gate had ignored the judgement against him and had re-entered the disputed lands and had imprisoned Staunton by a false action. The justices found that the false action could not be known as such until it was tried and only then did the king have his fine. For the contempt of the judgment by Gate the Chancellor might imprison him. The second question was also no doubt, says Miss Hemmant, about a specific case but no names have survived. It ran: 'If some justice of the Peace had taken a bill of indictment which had not been found by the Jury and enrolled it among other indictments "well and truly" found etc., shall there be any punishment thereupon for such justice so doing?' To discuss this the justices withdrew apart from the council and then returned to say that in such a case an inquiry should be made by a commission and if the justice of the peace were convicted he should lose his office and pay a fine to the king according to the degree of his misprision. The third question concerned the erasure of a court record when a plaintiff, discovering that he had had writs made out in the wrong name of John Barret, had the correct name of William Barret inserted. There followed a very lengthy and complicated discussion of this case, for the offence appeared to be a felony against the statute 8 Henry VI cap. 12, but the statute had made no provision for such an offence. The case involved the plaintiff and his attorney, the keeper of the writs, J. Mundus, who had erased the original writ, and a clerk of one of the compters of London. There were so many ensuing complications that King Richard was 'perturbed' that these offenders should escape unpunished. Four of them were finally indicted for misprision concerning the erasure and in the King's Bench, Westminster, they were found guilty and fined, the King himself being present."[6]

That the King should be so interested in legal points and the administration of justice that he personally involved himself in getting legal opinion on difficult cases is evidence of a genuine concern for what he called "the common weal"; and even Lingard, one of the historians most totally committed to the black legend of Richard's own crimes and general infamy, refers to "his extraordinary zeal" for the "suppression of crime".[7] His interest in preventing a repetition of the Thomas Cook case has already been noted, and Anne Sutton, who quotes the above account of Richard's participation and "three questions", gives further details.[8] This is not the record of a criminal tyrant but of a particularly enlightened monarch concerned for the welfare of all his people, not only the feudal aristocracy, and in fact looking beyond the feudal age well into the future. Corruption in particular he aims to check, spreading justice to all classes. Anyone who has attempted this in history has always met entrenched opposition from some of the privileged, and Richard is not likely to have been an exception.

Charles Ross has also commented on Richard's "conspicuous loyalty to, and generous treatment of, the men who had been in his service as Duke of Gloucester. This continued patronage extended even to people of humble or comparatively obscure origin".[9] Undoubtedly this sometimes aroused jealousy, as we can detect in some of the expressed resentment (in Croyland and elsewhere) of William Catesby, who was Speaker in Richard's Parliament and controller of the Treasury. His knowledge as an able lawyer probably cemented Richard's interest in him.

Nevertheless, with his glittering army which took hours to wind out of Leicester that sunny August morning in 1485, his record for justice, his faithful personal retinue and his own long experience as a military tactician, Richard should have won the Battle of Bosworth. Why didn't he? There were no significant desertions until the last-minute defection of the Stanleys, and if it is true that Richard kept Lord Stanley's son, Lord Strange, as hostage, it is also true that the young man survived the battle and in fact never was executed, as Richard's enemies claimed he threatened. Henry Tudor was no fighter and kept out of the action, well behind his standard bearer.

What went wrong? The one thing that emerges clearly is Richard's own sudden impetuous attempt to end the threat to his throne by this Welsh-Lancastrian upstart here and now. One senses a crisis of temperament, the rage of a man who had shown rage before, in cases of disloyalty, and now felt in his bones the climax of his year of sorrows, waiting on tenterhooks for an invasion and now faced with an army of foreign mercenaries and French troops, masquerading as supporters of a Lancastrian claimant to the English throne. Was it for this that his dead father, that often admired Richard, Duke of York, had laboured so long, and his dazzling, handsome, flawed brother Edward had faced exile and triumph? Perhaps the whole Yorkist genealogy boiled in Richard's veins at that moment. He had everything to gain, and everything to lose. Norfolk, the steadfast old seadog and adherent of York, had just been killed before his eyes. Was this the final spur that sent him rushing headlong down the hill at Bosworth, his close personal followers and many knights behind him, the hooves of his favourite horse, White Surrey, pounding on the turf towards the Red Dragon of the Cadwalladers, Henry's standard? Was it something more — a Schopenhauer Death Wish before his time, an expiation? We still do not know: perhaps we shall never know. He fought like one possessed right through almost to Henry himself, unseating the giant Sir John Cheyney and killing Henry's standard-bearer, Sir William Brandon. It was as they thundered down the hill that Sir William Stanley made the final decision that was to be Richard's death warrant, and moved his forces forward to intercept. Almost within reach of his enemy, Richard was felled to the ground, and died fighting, overwhelmed by numbers.

Partisan hatreds had not finished with him, even now. The Great Chronicle of London paints us the picture.

"Rychard late kyng as gloriously as he by the mornyng departid ffrom that Toon, soo as Inreverently was he that afftyr noone browgth Into that toon, ffor hys body Dyspoylid to the skyn, and nowgth beyng lefft abouth hym soo much as wold covyr his pryvy membr he was trussyd behynd a pursevant callid Norrey as an hogg or an othyr vyle beest, And soo all to besprung wyth myyr and ffylth was browgth to a church In leycetyr ffor all men to wondyr uppon. And there lastly Inreferently buried. And thus endid this man with dys honour as he that sowgth It, ffor hadd he contynnyd styll protectour and have suffyrd the childyr to have prosperid accordyng to his Alegeance and ffydelyte, he shuld have been honourably laudyd ovyr all, where as now his ffame is dyrkid and dyshonourid as fferre as he was knowyn, but God that ys all mercyffull fforgyve hym hys mysdedys." [10]

This was, of course, written in Tudor times. And overlooks the fact that, princes or no princes, Henry Tudor would have invaded England, given the foreign support he needed, in any case. Even the Croyland Third Continuator, grudgingly, remarks that Richard's treatment after death was "not exactly in accordance with the laws of humanity". [11] It did not affect his adulation of the "glorious conqueror".

Ten years later, Henry belatedly erected a tomb over the spot where Richard's body lay in Greyfriars, at Leicester. The cost of it was the meagre sum of £10.1s. [12] Both tomb and body were despoiled and destroyed at the dissolution of the monasteries.

The President of the Immortals had finished his sport with Richard. But there is one odd postscript to the Bosworth story.

On 1 September 1733 Thomas Brett, LL.D., wrote to William Warren, LL.D., President of Trinity Hall, an account he had heard from Lord Heneage, the Earl of Winchelsea, at Eastwell House, of a bricklayer named Richard Plantagenet, who according to the Eastwell church register was buried on 22 December 1550. According to this account, which Lord Heneage was studying from papers concerning the house, when Sir Thomas Moyle built Eastwell

Place, as it was then known, "he observed his chief bricklayer, whenever he left off work, retired with a book". After a time, he was even more startled to find that the unexpectedly literate bricklayer was actually reading Latin. When he enquired how he came by this learning the man told him, as he had been a good master to him, he would trust him with a secret he had never before revealed to anyone. It was as follows (and I quote Thomas Brett, who in his turn is of course paraphrasing Lord Heneage):

"That he was boarded with a Latin schoolmaster, without knowing who his parents were, 'till he was fifteen or sixteen years old; only a gentleman (who took occasion to acquaint him he was no relation to him) came once a quarter, & paid for his board, and took care to see that he wanted nothing. And one day, this gentleman took him & carried him to a fine, great house, where he passed through several stately rooms, in one of which he left him, bidding him stay there.

"Then a man finely drest, with a star and garter, came to him; asked him some questions; talked kindly to him; & gave him some money. Then the 'forementioned gentleman returned, and conducted him back to his school.

"Some time after the same gentleman came to him again, with a horse & proper accountrements, & told him, he must take a journey with him into the country. They went into Leicestershire, & came to Bosworth Field; & he was carried to K. Richard III. tent. The King embraced him, & told him he was his son. But, child, says he, to-morrow I must fight for my crown. And, assure your self, if I lose that, I will lose my life too: but I hope to preserve both. Do you stand in such a place (directing him to a particular place) where you may see the battle, out of danger. And, when I have gained the victory, come to me; I will then own you to be mine, & take care of you. But, if I should be so unfortunate as to lose the battel, then shift as well as you can, & take care let no body know that I am your father; for no mercy will be shewed to any one so related to me. Then the king gave him a purse of gold, & dismissed him.

"He followed the king's directions. And, when he saw the battel was lost & the king killed, he hasted to London; sold his horse, & fine cloaths; &, the better to conceal himself from all suspition of being son to a king, & that he might have means to live by his honest labour, he put himself apprentice to a bricklayer. But, having a competent skill in the Latin tongue, was unwilling to lose it; and having an inclination also to reading, & no delight in the conversation of those he was obliged to work with, he generally spent all the time he had to spare in reading by himself.

"Sir Thomas said, you are now old, and almost past your labour; I will give you the running of my kitchen as long as you live. He answered, Sir, you have a numerous family; I have been used to live retired; give me leave to build a house of one room for myself in such a field, & there, with your good leave, I will live & die: and, if you have any work that I can do for you, I shall be ready to serve you. Sir Thomas granted his request, he built his house, and there continued to his death." [13]

The Parish Register at St. Mary's Church, Eastwell, in Kent, certainly records the death of this Richard Plantagenet under the heading "Ano Domine 1550", and it has even been suggested his story of being Richard's son might have been a cover for a more interesting truth, that he was in fact one of the princes in the Tower, who after Bosworth understandably decided concealment was the better part of valour. Brett computed that his age in 1550 would have been "about 81", which would have made him fifteen to sixteen years of age in August 1485: near enough to the age of Edward V had he lived, but certainly older than Richard, Duke of York. His year of birth must have been 1469 or 1470, and as Edward V was not born until November, 1470, he is more likely perhaps genuinely to have been the son of Richard III, as he claimed. In this case he would have been born before Richard's marriage, and when his father was seventeen or eighteen years old. This would fit in well with my own surmise that Richard in his early life could have been trying to imitate his admired elder brother in many ways, including sexual prowess. Could Edward considerately have provided the lady, for his hardly more than sixteen-year-old brother's initiation? It would appear Richard Plantagenet was a "solitary" who never married. Might not this too be a hereditary factor if, as I have suggested, Richard III himself was later rather a-sexual in nature?

The boy Plantagenet, whoever fathered him, was wise to submerge his identity in a country backwater, and a humble trade. Few Yorkists heirs, under the Tudors, came to so peaceful an end.

At Bosworth, Northumberland, not showing his hand like the Stanleys, had sat on the fence, metaphorically driving the last nail into Richard's coffin. He was to serve Henry from now on, and try unsuccessfully to subdue the undefeated, rebellious, followers of Richard in the north, who eventually murdered him. Already the Town Recorder was making his historic entry in the York City records: "King Richard, late mercifully reigning upon us ... with many other lords and nobility of these north parts, was piteously slain and murdered, to the great heaviness of this city". The date was 22 August 1485. Less than two months later, in October, the York clerk, John Harrington, was to refer to a grant to the city made by "the most famous prince of blessed memory, King Richard, late deceased."[14]

And was the realm, as so often stated, now at peace? "Through this battle peace was obtained for the whole kingdom",wrote the Croyland Third Continuator, still glowing from his panegyrics of the new king's angelic nature, showing "clemency to all". This idealised picture of the first of the Tudors has reverberated through the centuries in writings on Richard. The truth is rather different.

Those of Richard's followers who had not died with him, like Norfolk and Brackenbury, were quickly and summarily executed, Catesby among them. Stillington was immediately and urgently sought, by an edict issued the day after Bosworth, and imprisoned (he escaped, or was let go free, and supported the later Simnel rebellion at the Battle of Stoke. He was then recaptured and seems to have spent the rest of his days in a Windsor dungeon). At the November Parliament Richard was attainted of high treason, and with him the clement conqueror attempted to condemn for treason all who had supported him. This vindictive and unheard-of convolution of historic practice, making men who supported a reigning king guilty of treason to his eventual conqueror, so upset the Commons, and caused such murmuring, that Morton, some years later in the Parliament of 1497, was forced to quell the fears expressed by the nobility about following the king in the Warbeck and other rebellions, by introducing a "statute protecting from the pains of treason all who act under a *de facto* king".[15] In other words Henry eventually found himself hoist with his own petard.

Richard's Act of bastardising the princes, of course, was at once carefully suppressed. "Justices advised against its recital in repeal, in order to avoid the perpetuation of its terms. But they considered the record could not be deleted without authority of parliament. Every person having a copy of Richard III's act was ordered to hand it into the Chancellor before Easter, on pain of imprisonment".[16] But although Henry produced his own Titulus Regius, "it passes rapidly over Richard's acts of tyranny", admits Alison Hanham with a certain wonder. There is, perhaps, no reason to show surprise. Could it be that the "acts of tyranny" — especially compared with those of Morton and Henry about to be enacted — were too well known by Parliament and the City hardly to exist? The only reference to the princes, if so it can be called, is the obscure "shedding of infants' blood", making quite clear nothing specific was known or it certainly would have been published. Because they were so much more dangerous to Henry's right of succession (on the repeal of Richard's Act of Titulus Regius), it has often been conjectured that they were still in the Tower and murdered by agents of Henry. There are flaws in this theory, discussed elsewhere, but on evidence it cannot be totally dismissed.

As for peace, Henry had not ended the Wars of the Roses, he had revived them. "The ghosts of York could not be laid by Act of Parliament", writes S.B. Chrimes: ".... many guilty and innocent heads were to roll so that the Tudors might sleep more easily in their beds. Throughout the history of that dynasty, indeed, the problem of the succession was never to be very far from the thoughts of any member of it." [17]

Morton's speech as Henry's Chancellor on 3 November 1488 — three years after Bosworth — is revealing of the unsettled state of the country, and a contradiction of the story that Richard's reign was so tyrannous, and he so hated as a widely-known murderer, that Henry's accession was hailed as a deliverance. "He next comes to the government at home", writes Morton's biographer R.I. Woodhouse, "and states that no king ever had greater cause for the two contrary passions of joy and sorrow ... joy, in respect of the rare and visible favour of Almighty God in girding the imperial sword upon his side; sorrow for that it hath not pleased God to suffer him to sheath it as he greatly desired, otherwise than for the administration of justice, *but that he had been forced to draw it so oft to cut off traitors and disloyal subjects..* (italics mine). [18]

The north simmered with revolt and occasionally burst into flames, and so it seems did the midlands. In November 1485, Robert Throckmorton, appointed in September, was replaced as Sheriff of Warwickshire and Leicestershire and petitioned for a pardon of fines and arrears connected with his office, ... "in which time of occupation was within this your realm such rebellioun and trouble, and your lawes not stabysshed'', that he could not execute his office. [19] On 17 October Henry VII had written to Henry Vernon of Haddon of his ''knowledge that certeyne our rebelles and traitours being of litell honour or substance ... made insurreccion and assemblies in the north portions of our realm, taking Robin of Riddisdale, Jack St. Thomalyn at Lath, and Maister Mendall for their capteyns ...'' [20]

A fierce rebellion of Cornishmen later in the reign was one of several to be sparked off by virulent and it seems justifiable hatred of Morton, Henry's Chancellor, and ministers such as Margaret Beaufort's one-time go-between, Reginald Bray. They were ''threatened and rayled upon, as the suckers and caterpillars of the commonwealth, rather then wise councellors and faithfull officers ... they raged against them as parricides and uultures praying upon the poore and oppressed ...'' This was in an account of Morton written in a 1610 MS by John Budden to Sir George Morton, the great-grandson of one of Morton's two heirs, his nephew John Morton. [21] He was by the time of ''the miserable slaughter of these Cornishmen'' both Cardinal and Archbishop of Canterbury: which did not prevent the Pope in Rome receiving letters, in 1489, complaining of his ''molestations'' against other Bishops. [22] He aroused, according to the Chronicle of London,''greate haterede of the commons of this lande'', and even his 1610 biographer, writing to one of the Morton family, echoed this: ''He much stomached the com'on people, excommunicating them, I know not upon what contumacy, and rebellious occasions .... but it is now convenient to pass over, then com'emorate these things ...'' [23] Morton had, he admitted before so conveniently passing over things better not remembered, ''a kinde of artificiall cunning to insinuate with the favour of greatt men''.

The ''haterede of the comons'' was so intense in the north that a demand for the surrender of the Archbishop of Canterbury, Chancellor Bray, and a few others made by ''some 20,000 men''. [24] Under Morton and Henry, according to Morton's biographer Woodhouse, the Star Chamber's powers of arbitrary government were greatly extended, giving rise to a ''growing love of freedom''; despotism intensified; and the exactions of benevolences were made the principal instrument of policy known as ''Morton's Fork''. Richard had made these illegal, and although reluctantly forced to revive them in 1485 to pay for the resistance to Henry's invasion, he had treated them as loans, giving "good and sufficient pledges as surety for repayment".[25]

That Henry's assumption of the throne was challenged, and dissidents ruthlessly dealt with, we can gather from the riot in his presence in the Parliament Chamber on 15 December 1485. "There were eighty persons concerned in it, all charged with a design to destroy some of the king's great officers and Privy Council; and six of the ringleaders being seized, were immediately by the Parliament declared felons, convicted, their goods and chattels forfeited, as if attainted, according to the course of the common law, and, *without being admitted to the benefit of the clergy, ordered to be executed as felons without delay, or other process to be made on their behalf*"[26] (italics mine). Yet certain historians and chroniclers write of Richard's summary execution of Hastings as an example of supreme tyranny and hail Henry VII's reign as ending a "reign of terror"! Richard pardoned more than he executed: in fact it was the magnamity he showed to so many of his enemies that helped to precipitate his own downfall. The Tudors, at least until the reign of Queen Elizabeth (who had many Plantagenet characteristics), did not fall into that error. This is what I meant by double standards in the writing of history, and genuflection to the winning side.

But Henry's problem was not just one of social unrest and revolt; it was one of challenge to his succession, and the very survival of his dynasty. The Yorkist ghosts indeed would not be laid, nor would those of the princes. Their fate was to remain a recurring question mark in Henry's reign, no less than it had in Richard's.

1 Commines: *Memoirs,* ii.64. Lingard, *History of England,* IV, p.125.

2 Vergil, p.559: Gairdner: *Richard III,* p.213.

3 Croyland Third Continuator, p.502.

4 Buck, p.58.

5 A.J. Pollard: *The Tyranny of Richard III.* Pollard thinks Tyrell was a "midlander", but although his article reasserts a traditionalist view of Richard's "tyranny", his evidence of the grants of lands and offices to the king's followers in the south is valuable and interesting.

6 Anne Sutton: *The Administration of Justice Whereunto We Be Professed. Ricardian,* IV, 53, June 1976, pp.6-7. Harl. MSS.433, fol. 273.

7 Lingard, IV, p.117.

8 *Ricardian,* IV, 53, June 1976, pp.7-8. See also: H.C. Hanbury: *The Legislation of Richard III.* American Journal of Legal History, Vol. 6, 1962. "A very favourable assessment", writes Anne Sutton.

9 *Some 'Servants and Lovers' of Richard in his Youth: Ricardian,* IV, 55, December 1976, pp.2-4.

10 fol. 214. *England Under the Yorkists,* pp.134-5.

11 Croyland, p.504.

12 *Excerpta Historica,* p.105. Lingard, IV, p.127.

13 *Desiderata Curiosa,* pp.249-51.

14 York City Town Books, 2-4 f.169b. Hanham : *Richard III and his early historians,* p.60.

15 Woodhouse: *Life of John Morton,* p.83.

16 Chrimes: *Henry VII,* p.66.

17 Ibid, p.158.

18 *Life of John Morton,* pp.80-1.

19 W.E. Hampton: *Ricardian,* IV, 55, December 1976, p.27.

20 Henry Kirke: *Sir Henry Vernon of Haddon.* Derbyshire Archaeol. and Nat. Hist. Soc., Vol. 41, 1919, pp.11-12. *Ricardian,* IV, 55, December 1976, p.27.

21 Budden, p.67.

22 Woodhouse, p.155.

23 Budden, p.67.

24 Woodhouse, p.149.

25 Fabyan, p.518. Halsted, ii,372.

26 Woodhouse, p.100.

X
Warbeck: King or Pretender?

The Yorkist menace became dangerously apparent in 1486, with the rebellion ostensibly putting forward Lambert Simnel, who claimed, with the support of more genuine Yorkist heirs, to be Edward, Earl of Warwick. This almost coincided with the birth of Henry's heir, diplomatically named Arthur as a reminder of Henry's totally unwarranted claim of descent from the most famous of British kings. If it helped to draw Henry and Elizabeth of York together, it must be noted that on his progress north he had left her at Winchester, under what looks suspiciously like the spying eye of his mother, Margaret Beaufort. (She was later placed under Margaret's wing at Kenilworth.) Her own mother, Elizabeth Woodville, seems conspicuously to have been precluded from this tight family circle. Winchester was, of course, chosen as the ancient seat of English kings: yet another indication of Henry's nervous hold on the throne.

It has been suggested by John Lingard that it was because of this birth of a Tudor heir that the Yorkists made their first move to put forward a counter-candidate. It may be true, because it was far too early for Richard, Duke of York (if, as later claimed, he had survived) to make a personal bid, and endanger his future success as an adult; and Edward, Earl of Warwick, had already been displaced by Richard's other nephew, John, Earl of Lincoln, as his official successor. Yet this John, Earl of Lincoln, so devoted and loyal to his uncle, now became leader of this rebellion to place Simnel, as Edward Earl of Warwick, on the throne!

Simnel was the handsome young son of an Oxford joiner, put forward by one Richard Simons, a priest of that town, who can only, in the circumstances, have been acting as a cover for more important Yorkists. In Ireland, where the magnanimous rule of Richard, Duke of York (Edward IV's and Richard III's father) had never been forgotton, and made for strong Yorkist allegiance among the Irish leaders, Simnel was acclaimed and crowned as Edward VI, as we have seen. (Thus early it can surely be assumed that it was believed Edward V was dead.) The amazing instigator and supporter of this crowning was Richard's heir-apparent, Lincoln, who had landed in Dublin with 2,000 veteran soldiers provided by his aunt, Margaret, Duchess of Burgundy, whom he had recently visited. As Lingard comments, "At every step of this affair we meet with new mysteries". As he points out, "Lincoln himself had a better claim than the prince in whose right he pretended to draw the sword".[1] Well might Henry VII anxiously remark, after Lincoln's death at the Battle of Stoke, that he wished the Earl had lived, that he might learn from him "the bottom of his danger".

Was Lincoln, in fact, coming from Burgundy (on which rumours of the escape of the princes to their aunt already concentrated), attempting to establish one of the princes, if not himself, on the throne? One object of the rebellion may have been to force Henry to produce the living Earl of Warwick, who had been brought south from Sheriff Hutton after Bosworth and who was, with one brief episode about to take place, to remain imprisoned in the Tower for the rest of his life. But given the oft-repeated rumour of his slightly retarded mentality, the attainder still not lifted from his father, and Lincoln's own prior claim, the assumption that the rebellion was to make Warwick King of England seems untenable. Its real objective was something much more dangerous, as Henry seems to have realised.

It forced him, before its end, into at least some gestures of conciliation. The "pardon" officially given those of Richard's adherents not executed or killed at Bosworth had been "clogged with restrictions", and as Lingard admits, "frequently violated". "He now published a pardon which was full, without exceptions, and extended to every species of treason".[2] He also conducted the real Earl of Warwick openly from the Tower to St. Paul's, and then for a short period to the palace of Sheen. The matter was finally settled at the Battle of Stoke, where Lincoln's estimated 8,000 men met a royalist army under the Earl of Oxford, and being ill-armed were decisively defeated by Oxford's heavy cavalry.

Lincoln perished, and with him his secret. The young Simnel Henry found it politic to treat with contempt, emphasising his low birth by making him an assistant in his kitchen. He later rose to the position of falconer.

One immediate result of the rebellion was the long-delayed coronation of Elizabeth of York, who had now been married to Henry approaching two years, and borne him an heir, without any form of recognition of her Yorkist royal blood. Even the House of Commons had begun to murmur. She was therefore at last released from obscurity and brought to the Tower to be crowned at Westminster, dressed in white cloth of gold of damask, with a mantle of the same furred with ermine. "Her faire yellow hair hung downe pleyne byhynd her bak, with a calle of pipes over it." On her head was a circle of gold ornamented with precious stones. In this dress she was borne though the City reclining in a litter, with a canopy of gold carried over her by four knights of the body. The king was conspicuous by his absence, viewing "both the coronation and the dinner from behind a lattice".[3]

What were her thoughts, this lovely, helpless pawn in the game of kings, a forced sleeping partner to the man who had taken her family's throne "by right of conquest", little more than a breeder of his heirs until she died, still young, in that breeding process fifteen years later? Her king and master so resented her own claim that he could not even bring himself to take part in the ceremony that crowned her. Did she ever think of the dead king she may have thought, for a tragically brief moment of time, she loved, and who might have made her his queen? Why did Henry so humiliate and distrust her, that he could not even bring himself to be present at her coronation? She moves like a lonely wraith through a short period of our history, founding a dynastic line of two generations and then vanishing for ever.

Her mother's rôle is even more enigmatic, and possibly significant. For in spite of efforts to evade or gloss over the fact, there is evidence even many Tudor-partial historians have been forced to admit that Elizabeth Woodville suffered some disgrace at this time, which can only have been in connection with her support, or suspected support, of the Simnel rebellion. Her allowance was reduced; her lands transferred to her daughter (which means, virtually, to Henry as her husband); and she was committed to the custody of the monks of Bermondsey, being seen thereafter at

Court only rarely, and apparently so that she could be noted by visiting ambassadors. Henry's reported reason for this treatment of her is even more remarkable: it was that after promising her daughter to Henry in marriage she had left sanctuary and allowed her to attend Richard's Court: a fact he had known at the time he took the throne.

The question therefore arises: why should Elizabeth Woodville, having a daughter married to a king (although not yet crowned), prefer that a son of the Duke of Clarence, reputedly executed owing to the enmity of the Woodvilles, should be on the throne, or even the son of her late husband's sister, the Earl of Lincoln? It has sometimes been conjectured that the Simnel affair was a kind of "try-out" of public opinion and support, with the intention of producing one of the princes — still too young to be personally risked and his whereabouts made known — if the rebellion succeeded. It is in many ways a more reasonable hypothesis for Lincoln's involvement, especially as he had recently been to see his aunt in Burgundy. If Richard, as suggested, had before his death made a tentative movement to reinstate Edward V or the other surviving son of Edward IV as his heir, with Lincoln as Protector during a minority, something of Lincoln's attitude might be explained. Descent through a male line would always be preferable (and more easily established) than to a female. Margaret indeed might have insisted on her preference for her brother Edward IV's own children, and given her armed support only on this condition. The bastardizing had been recently revoked in Parliament, the only way in which Henry had been able to strengthen his claim by his marriage.

If the Queen-Dowager was not suspected, it is still notable that her retirement from Court and her financial losses occurred at this time, and it is certain that her pension from Henry Tudor was considerably less than the 700 marks she received from Richard. There exists in the Public Record Office a receipt signed by Elizabeth Woodville for the sum of thirty pounds, the arrears of her annuity of £400, payable half-yearly, which had been granted in February 1490. She describes herself as "Quene Elyzabethe lete wyffe to the excelent prynce King Edward the iiijth", and the date is 21 May 1491. On 14 December 1490 she also received a small grant of fifty marks, made "vnto oure right dere and right welbeloued quene Elizabeth moder vnto oure most dere wif the quene ... aynest the fest of Cristemas next commung".4 It was a small enough gesture, although by then, after the birth of several children, including another son, Henry understandably seems to have been feeling more gracious towards his Queen and her mother, at least as regards outward forms. Elizabeth Woodville's Will, neverthless, plaintively indicates her poverty: "Item where I have no worldly goods to do the Queen's Grace, my dearest daughter, a pleasure with, neither to reward any of my children, according to my heart and mind ..." She gives "all the aforesaid my children" her blessing, but there is no indication of the princes. The year was 1492.5 By the time the Perkin Warbeck affair grew serious, Elizabeth Woodville was dead.

Not so Margaret of Burgundy, who strongly supported this new Yorkist claimant as her nephew, Richard, Duke of York — who would now have been the right approximate age. According to most historians he suddenly appeared in Cork harbour, on a merchant ship from Lisbon, and on stepping ashore was soon hailed as Richard, Duke of York, in view of his striking likeness. This idea never having occurred to him before, he was so much struck by it that he went along with it, and thus began, by pure chance, his long and serious commitment to asserting his claim.

Now this is pure poppycock and should long ago have been recognised as such. For Warbeck's involvement with Yorkist exiles began well before stepping on to Ireland's shores, which was doubtless carefully planned. Gairdner, author of the only English academic short biography of Warbeck (printed, in its final form, as supplement to the third edition of his biography of Richard III in 1898) is far from disinterested in his study of Richard as a murderer and tyrant, and his account of Warbeck is based on highly questionable material, much of it taken from Warbeck's alleged "confession" before execution. And one thing Gairdner certainly missed was the true nature of Perkin's early Yorkist connections; he merely repeated from the claimed "confession" the fact that after studying with a merchant in Middelburg he "afterwards went into Portugal with the wife of Sir Edward Brampton, an adherent of the House of York". Here the alleged confession conveniently drops all mention of the Bramptons, and we get the story that he reached Ireland in the service of a Breton merchant named Pregent Meno, where the Cork citizens, "seeing him dressed in the silk clothes of his master (probably the goods in which his master traded), insisted on doing him honour as a member of the Royal House of York."[6] It must be added that this "confession" was only published by Bernard André, Henry's own official historian, in his *Memorials of Henry VII*, devoted to panegyrise the Tudor who employed him.

The story that Warbeck went into Portugal only with *Lady* Brampton has often been repeated; but Gairdner was partly wrong and this could have been ascertained long ago by studying the work of an expert researcher into the life of Sir Edward Brampton, Cecil Roth, who after two articles on this most interesting character of the reigns of Edward IV and Richard III, the first published in 1922 and the final summing-up in 1956[7], made clear not only Brampton's close association with the Yorkist cause but that it was with *Sir Edward himself,* as well as his wife, that Warbeck went to Portugal.

Some of Sir Edward's career is given in Kendall's biography of Richard III, but it does not mention this or Brampton's subsequent history, after Bosworth. He was a Jew from Portugal, originally named Duarte Brandão, who, having an adventurous bent, turned up in England in 1468 at the *Domus Conversom* (a Home for Converted Jews) in Chancery Lane. "Those who were baptised under its auspices generally had the king as their godfather and adopted his name", writes Roth, and the future Governor of Guernsey, Edward Brampton, was in fact described later in official documents as godson ('filiolus') of King Edward IV. He was at first known as Edward Brandon, but after giving "good service to the King in many battles", as official documents state, and lying low/ during the brief restoration of Henry VI, he reappears as "Edward Brampton", appointed with others to the command of an armed force "which the King is sending to sea to resist his enemies and rebels". The following year he was granted estates in the City of London without fee; now "a naval commander, a property owner and an English subject, with easy access to Court because of his special relationship with the sovereign".

Kendall does record some of his later career, both under King Edward and King Richard[8]; and it was Richard who knighted him (the first converted Jew in England to receive this honour). He had conspicuously fought the Woodville faction at sea and in the first month of Richard's reign received a grant of £350 secured on the custom-dues of London, Sandwich and Southampton. He also seems to have helped to quell the Buckingham rebellion. It is not quite certain when he was made Governor of Guernsey, which appears to have been in those days a nominal post with no necessity to step on shore there, although its strategic position in any naval clashes with the French is obvious. He gave up this position in March 1484, but continued to receive favours, including a £100 annuity in August 1484, and a rich Northamptonshire manor. There is no record of his fighting at Bosworth, but he certainly went into exile as a marked Yorkist adherent, and in Henry's Act of Resumption his estates — largely the confiscated property of Lancastrian supporters in exile — reverted to the original owners.

Roth, rather taking the traditionalist line on Richard, tends to label him an unscrupulous adventurer and *parvenu*, but there is really no evidence for this, or his leaving Portgual originally under some youthful cloud, as Roth admits. He fought well for two Yorkist kings and remained loyal to them, and was suitably rewarded. When he fled he settled in Bruges, in Flanders, the English inhabitants of which town had enthusiastically celebrated Richard's coronation on 7 July 1483 (a day late, it appears, because on 6 July "the child count of Flanders, Philip the Fair, paid a state visit to Bruges and the municipality monopolized all festivities on his behalf".9)

Obviously there was feeling for Richard among the inhabitants here, and once again we get the significant link with the rumour of the escape of the princes and Margaret of Burgundy's knowledge of at least one of them. It is worth noting that Brampton re-established himself as a merchant and Warbeck, in his supposed confession, claims to be the son of a Jean Werbecque (in England the name became anglicized to "Warbeck") or Osbeck, controller of the town of Tournay, who is elsehwere described as a "converted Jew" and merchant. His wife, Katherine de Faro, had a Portuguese name, as has often been pointed out, and hers may have been the Jewish blood. The possible link with Brampton in this case is obvious. There is no record that Werbecque had a son named Peter, or Perkin, living with him from babyhood, and Warbeck's "confession" rather remarkably, although he gives the Werbecque genealogy, makes no reference to himself until as a boy, of unspecified age, he was taken by his "mother" to Antwerp to learn Flemish, and returned to Tournay only in the year 1483 or 1484. "From this date he gives a minute account of his time for about three years".[10]

Gairdner of course makes no comment on this, but if one thing stands out it is that Warbeck turns up indubitably in Tournay, with the Werbecque family, in 1483 or 1484, as Henry's agents doubtless discovered, and can thereafter loquaciously trace his movements, including the passage to Portugal with "the wife of Sir Edward Brampton". (Obviously, he was shielding Sir Edward, and in fact he had refused to give the name of anyone who had helped his original escape from England, as the child Richard, Duke of York. Could Brampton as well as Tyrell have been concerned in this?) It is surely interesting that these two years, the very years in which the princes' murder or escape must have taken place, are specifically given as the starting point of his "minute account".

Gairdner's belief that he really could, at some eighteen years of age, have learned English properly for the first time in Ireland, when Warbeck's fluent English was one of the factors that convinced so many people of his identity, shows how little an historian wedded to a theory is inclined to "think through". Gairdner, however, is correct that one statement by Warbeck, that he was "under age" in 1495, suggests, if correctly reported, that he believed the prince was born in 1474. 17 August 1473 is assumed from the Shrewsbury town records. Lawrence E. Tanner further verified this by quoting a document in which the Chester Herald, Thomas Utine (Whiting), acknowledged a gift of money from the Duke of Burgundy on 3 September 1473, and included news of the birth of a second son to the King, Edward IV.[11] Four months is not, however, far out, and Warbeck may have been misreported.

The fact that Warbeck was taken up by Sir Edward Brampton, who as an exile of distinguished Yorkist service is bound to have been known to Margaret of Burgundy, is certainly significant. He could have given Warbeck many details of Edward IV's Court, but his service took him much to sea and some of the rest of his free time he certainly spent on his estates. There is an equal difficulty in ascribing the breadth and detail of Warbeck's knowledge, which convinced so many of his authenticity, in regard to Margaret of Burgundy. She had left England to be married on 23 June 1468, before either of the princes was born, and had returned only for a brief visit to see her brothers in 1480. Short of a voluminous correspondence with friends and relatives in England, which has never been discovered, it is hard to see how much detailed and meticulous account of the younger prince's history she could have given Warbeck.

"Lord Bacon", writes Gairdner, it is true not without that scepticism he normally deplores in history writing,[12] "assures us that she instructed him carefully in the family history of Edward IV, and *in everything that concerned the Duke of York*" (italics mine), as well as "the personages, lineaments, and features of the king and queen, his pretended parents; and of his brother and sisters, and divers others that were nearest to him in childhood, together with all passages, some secret, some common, that were fit for a child's memory, until the death of King Edward". She also "told him all about the death of his father Edward IV, his own imprisonment with his brother in the Tower, the murder of the latter, and his own escape". Truly a formidable lady, of pronounced psychic powers.

It is unclear exactly what story Warbeck told about this escape, and if he really did claim his elder brother was murdered by Richard or anyone else. Kendall quotes him as declaring in a proclamation that "though desire of rule did bind [King Richard], yet, in his other actions, he was noble, and loved the honour of the realm, and the contentment and comfort of his nobles and people".[13] It is a curious tribute, if true. Did Warbeck subtly try and convey that he did not believe Richard intended to murder his brother or himself? If smuggled secretly out of the country he would not necessarily have been told the full story, and if Morton, Buckingham or the Woodvilles alone were involved they would presumably have told the child that King Richard threatened his life.

There are, of course, other possibilities which might explain the Plantagenet resemblance. Warbeck could have been a bastard of Edward IV. Unfortunately, unless he were several years older than he claimed, the dates here do not quite fit, for Edward, who may well have left a Flemish lady or two in an interesting condition, was in exile in Flanders only six months, and left in 1471. If one account is true that Werbecque as a merchant visited England and met Edward on matters of commerce, this could of course be explained, if his wife travelled with him. It also came to light via Milan State papers some years ago that there was gossip about Margaret of Burgundy's own possible relationship with an ecclesiastic at roughly the right time — i.e. Warbeck's date of birth. It was made the basis of Christopher Hassall's play, *The Player King*. But it is the only reference and obviously pure guesswork that the association went that far and a child was secretly born. There would be nothing untoward in a boy of aristocratic family being placed in a respectable, well-to-do family such as the Werbecques.[14]

If Warbeck were a fraud, he was a remarkably able impersonator, impressing the King of Scotland enough to be given the hand of one of his kinswomen, Katherine Gordon, in marriage, and also gaining much support among European royalty, although expediency can, of course, never be ruled out in foreign diplomacy. Warbeck, to some of them, might be, as Henry Tudor had been, a useful pawn in later difficulties or negotiations. His likeness to Edward IV was widely attested and unquestionable (although of course Gairdner questioned it). The attributed Arras drawing of Warbeck, published here alongside a very typical painting of Edward IV, shows the same, slightly double, line of chin and faintly rétroussé nose (this nose of Edward's also figures clearly in a Flemish artist's illustration for a MS commissioned by Edward, in which the young king as Hadrian is depicted in profile, kneeling before Trajan, with his sister Margaret to his right).[15]

Gairdner produces a letter from Warbeck to his mother, telling her that certain Englishmen had made him claim he was the second son of King Edward of England, Richard, Duke of York, and asking for her help and *"un petit de argent pour moi aidier"*.[16] It was found in copy (not the original) in the Low countries, in the towns of Courtray and Tournay. Its authenticity seems highly doubtful (Warbeck with his powerful friends hardly needed "a little money") and even if authentic he would probably have used this phraseology about his assumption of the identity of Edward's son in case the letter got into the wrong hands, and his mother were questioned. If his story were true she would have known he was not her own son, and correctly read the device. It seems an unlikely letter for Warbeck to dare to write in the circumstances, and if a forgery only too convenient for Henry's agents. A forgery seems suggested by its long and totally (for his mother) unnecessary reminiscence of past and quite irrelevant events in her life and that of his brothers and sisters. This was surely material produced by Henry's agents themselves about the activities of the family, and its composition.

How alarmed Henry was by Warbeck's threat to his throne can be gauged by the fact that the Venetian Ambassador reported that he had put his queen and his eldest son in a very strong castle on the coast, with vessels to carry them away if necessary.[17] Was this the way he also evaded the possibility of Elizabeth seeing and recognising her brother?

The Warbeck affair was prolonged, in the end, eight years, and there is no need here to go into its details. Warbeck moved about Europe, as we have seen, and visited (or re-visited) his "aunt" of Burgundy. When he finally plunged into armed insurrection he failed, and was captured after leaving sanctuary on a promise of pardon. Henry kept the promise (perhaps keeping him alive in the hope of finding out more), until Warbeck escaped. Soon after his recapture he was encouraged (it is generally agreed, by Henry's agents) to consort with Edward, Earl of Warwick, in the Tower, and plan their joint escape. This was duly reported by the agents, and both young men, although conspiring to escape was hardly a treasonable matter, were tried and executed: the ill-starred Edward, who had known so little of life and freedom, in the way reserved for the higher classes, by beheading on Tower Green; Warbeck, to emphasise his "common" birth, by hanging, drawing and quartering at Tyburn. It was now November, 1499. Warbeck died, it was said, meekly, confessing his "crime". It was the memory of Warwick, the innocent and child-like, that was to haunt Henry VII on his death-bed.

Why was he not haunted by Warbeck? One answer might be that he *knew* he was a pretender, and knew it because he himself had been responsible, in 1485, for getting rid of the princes. Or that he knew that others, two years before, had contrived their deaths on his behalf. It may not be so simple. Both in his comment on Lincoln's death and his anxieties in the Warbeck affair, Henry showed signs of genuinely not *knowing* if the princes, his possible supplanters, were still alive, or what had really happened to them. Morton might know, and Morton's rise to power was spectacular. There is some indication Henry kept him in office in spite of himself, being of a less revengeful and sanguinary disposition than his ministers.

The executioner's axe fell constantly after every rebellion, and plenty of times before Warbeck himself was finally disposed of. Most surprisingly, in January 1495, it fell on Sir William Stanley,

Lord Stanley's brother, whose timely support at Bosworth had helped Henry to the throne. He was betrayed by Sir Robert Clifford, who seems to have either renegaded from the Yorkist cause himself, and named Stanley to save his own skin, or been one of Henry's secret agents from the beginning, mixing with the Yorkist exiles in Burgundy. At any rate, on Clifford's information (for which he received £500 from the privy purse) Stanley was executed for treasonable involvement in the Warbeck affair, and was reported to have declared that if Perkin were indeed the son of King Edward, he would never fight against him.[18] The remarkable thing about this statement is, of course, its implication that his action at Bosworth had nothing to do with Richard's supposedly having murdered the princes. It is an admission that Stanley *still did not know*. Stanley's great wealth, which now accrued to the king, was said also to be a factor in his execution.

In another little-known work of fiction, Mary Shelley's *The Fortunes of Perkin Warbeck* (1830), Robert Clifford is the villain of the piece, and Warbeck a son of Edward IV: showing that in the world of the Shelleys (and Shelley was no romantic in politics) the work of Horace Walpole still bred literary queries.

Did Morton use some undivulged knowledge, or pretended knowledge, of the fate, or whereabouts, of the princes as a lever over Henry in his rise to power? His Flanders connections cannot be ignored, nor his involvement with Buckingham. In some ways of looking at it, Henry VII seemed as mystified by the whole matter as anyone else.

Then history forced his hand.

1 Lingard, *History of England,* IV, p.137.

2 Ibid, p.136.

3 Ibid, p.139n. Leland Coll., iv, 216-233.

4 MacGibbon: *Elizabeth Woodville,* pp.220-1.

5 Coll. of Royal Wills, p.150. Kendall: *Richard III*, p.495.

6 Gairdner: *The Story of Perkin Warbeck,* p.267.

7 Report and Transactions for the Year 1956: La Société Guernesiaise, Vol. XVI, Part II, pp.160-170.

8 *Richard III*, pp.186-7.

9 Armstrong (Ed. Mancini). Note 112, p.134.

10 Gairdner, p.267.

11 *Recent Investigations regarding the Fate of the Princes in the Tower.* Society of Antiquaries, Oxford, 1935.

12 Gairdner, pp.269-70.

13 *Richard III*, p.319.

14 Fortescue; *Commendation of the Laws of England,* Chaps. 44 & 45. *England Under the Yorkists,* p.244.

15 See Charles Ross: *Edward IV*, opposite p.208.

16 Gairdner, pp.329-30.

17 Ven. Cal. vol.i,   No. 756.

18 W.A.J. Archbold: *Sir William Stanley and Perkin Warbeck,* Eng. Hist. Review, XIV (1899), pp.529-34. Kendall, p.383.

XI
Tyrell: Murderer or Victim?

Perhaps it was impossible for Henry to produce any specific story of the princes' murder until the death of the three women closest to them: their mother, Elizabeth Woodville, who died in 1492; their grandmother, Cecily, Duchess of York, who died in 1495; and their eldest sister, Elizabeth of York, already subdued by her position as Queen and by the summer of 1502 suffering from an illness at Woodstock, probably from the effects of the pregnancy from which she died in February, 1503. An apothecary had been paid to attend her on 9 April, suggesting that she was ailing for some time.[1]

Early in 1502 there occurred a bitter blow to both Henry and Elizabeth: their heir, Prince Arthur, recently married to the young Spanish princess, Katherine of Arragon, died. Another boy, Edmund, had already died as a child, leaving only the second son Henry as possible male heir. One boy's life now stood between Henry VII and the extinction of his brief dynasty. And Isabella and Ferdinand, the Spanish rulers, had already made clear some worry about letting their daughter marry an English prince, unless assured that the régime was stable, and the Yorkist threat no longer a danger. (Isabella of Castile, long ago, had conveyed certain warm suggestions for a diplomatic alliance to Richard III through a message conveyed by her orator, Geoffrey de Sasiola,[2] and it may be she still felt some lingering doubts and distrust about the rights of his supplanter.) Now English hopes were bent on affiancing the widowed princess to Henry, the new heir.

It was a diplomatic moment to assuage Spanish doubts, and certainly aggravated by the recent Warbeck affair, emphasising as

Entry on death of Richard Plantagenet, 1550 (Register of St. Mary's Church, Eastwell, Kent)

Ano Domini:1550:

Ano Domini:1551:

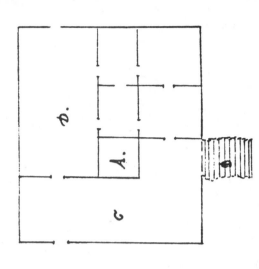

Plan of Tower where bones of princes said to be found in sealed room: from notes on book of 1647.

A. The "Little Roome".
B. The Stayres leading out of Cole Harbour to ye Kings Lodgings.
C. Passage to ye Kings Lodgings.
D. Ye Guard Chamber.

Opening lines of Will of Sir James Tyrell, 31 May, 1475.

End of Will of Sir James Tyrell, 31 May, 1475, with signature and seal.

Ruins of Middleham Castle

it did the need to prevent further pretenders or claimants. The action taken was both startling and unexpected. And it could be said to have killed several birds with one stone.

Morton had died in 1500, and Henry VII's more clement disposition may have been given freer rein. Early in 1501 the brother of the dead John, Earl of Lincoln — Edmond de la Pole, who had succeeded his father as Duke of Suffolk — had been arraigned for the killing of a vassal: whether accidentally is not known. He had fled to his aunt, Margaret of Burgundy (who else?), but was pardoned, and in September the same year he was present at the reception given to Katherine of Arragon. In November he attended the marriage of Katherine to Prince Arthur. Then suddenly the picture changed: Suffolk was, after all, Richard III's heir, by right of his mother, Richard's sister, and as presumed successor to his dead brother. Suffolk, perhaps on some warning of Henry's changed attitude, fled again, and with his younger brother Richard was given hospitality *en route* to Flanders by Sir James Tyrell at Guisnes.

Tyrell had been made commander of Guisnes, in Picardy — a key bastion, for Calais, against the French — by Richard III on 13 January 1485, in the absence of Lord Mountjoy. On 20 January, a week later, he received the strikingly huge sum of £3,000 (estimated by J.A. Speares to be almost the whole royal budget for twelve months) on behalf of the King. It was paid at Calais.[3] When Henry VII ascended the throne Tyrell lost some of the Welsh lands granted by Richard III and some held in association with his wife Anne, but he received compensation, and later was granted "for life" the office of Sheriff of the County of Glamorgan and others in the area, including the post of Chief Forester of all forests in the same county, and of Constable of Cardiff Castle. He received two General Pardons on 16 June and 16 July, 1486, a not exceptional occurrence into which it would be unjustifiable to read too much. (Some Ricardians have thought they were given for some great service, such as murdering the princes, for Henry. If Tyrell was a double agent without Richard's knowledge, this would of course be possible, but hardly otherwise.)

What is clear is that there was nothing particularly against him, and the new king, as most new kings do, decided to make use of an able and experienced official, not of powerful and noble enough family to be considered worth attainting for treason simply because he had served Richard III. On 25 November 1487 he was present at the coronation of Elizabeth of York, and on 13 June 1489 took part in the battle of Dixmunde in Flanders. He also played a prominent part in the ceremony attached to the Peace of Etaples in 1492.

In 1494, perhaps rather more interestingly, he was present when Prince Henry was created Duke of York. Did he therefore accept the fact that Richard, Duke of York, was dead, or did he simply keep his own council? Tyrell seems not the man to jeopardise his career unnecessarily. As early as December 1486 he was mentioned as again lieutenant of the Castle of Guisnes, in connection with the appointment of ambassadors to treat with those of the Emperor Maximilian, and thereafter he seems to have retained the Guisnes post which he had first received from Richard.[4]

The visit of Suffolk and his brother was to be his undoing; it once again labelled him as an unrepentant Yorkist, although he may well at the time have seen no reason why he should detain them. Obviously Suffolk knew he would be welcome: it is not possible to deduce more. But from Henry's point of view it was the second time Suffolk had used Guisnes as a temporary haven on the way to Burgundy, and this time he acted with a severity that seems strangely out of proportion to the offence. Tyrell was ordered to vacate Guisnes, and return to London on the ship sent by Henry. The Lord Privy Seal, Thomas Lovel, was on board and gave his surety for Tyrell's safety. As soon as Tyrell and his son Thomas, who had been with him at Guisnes, arrived on board, they were arrested: a trick that was to be remembered with bitterness and deplored by Lord Sandys in a letter to Thomas Cromwell as late as January 1537.[5] Edmond de la Pole also wrote confirming what had happened to Tyrell in a letter to Thomas Killingworth.

On Monday, 2 May 1502 Tyrell was tried at Guildhall with Sir John Wyndham, Wellesbourne (a "gentleman servant" to Tyrell) and a humble sailor, for "unspecified treason".[6] They were condemned to death the next day, and on the Friday, 6 May, Tyrell was beheaded with Wyndham on Tower Green, the more shameful death prescribed at the trial of hanging, drawing and quartering being commuted because of their rank. The unfortunate sailor, too humble in birth for such honour, suffered the more painful and degrading fate. On Saturday 7 May Sir John Wyndham's son and a James Holand, barber, of London, were tried at Guildhall and on Monday 9 May sentenced to be hanged, drawn and quartered. On the same two days, at Whitehall, Tyrell's son Thomas, with a Matthew Jonys and Pursevant Cursum, were tried, with Wellesbourne as witness (had he been spared to become King's Evidence?), Jonys and Cursum were sent back to Guisnes for execution. Thomas Tyrell and Wellesbourne were sentenced to remain in prison at the King's grace. Whether the Thomas Tyrell of Vignolles' 1496 report was Sir James's son or brother (both named Thomas), it would implicate the Tyrells in the Warbeck affair and explain Henry's anxiety to seize them.

It was in an Act of the Parliament of 1504 that James Tyrell was officially attainted: "of treason on account of his connection with 'Edmonde de la Pole, Earl of Suffolk' ''. His lands were declared forfeit to the King.[7] On 13 April 1504, Thomas Tyrell "of London, gentleman, received special pardon from the King".[8] Three years later, on appeal, he was restored to his estates at Gipping.[9] He did well under Henry VIII, by 1520 was Master of the Horse, and in 1550 and 1551 made Wills regarding his property. His son, John, on 12 July 1553 attended the Lady Mary (Tudor) at Kenninghall, Norfolk, and the day after her coronation was knighted as Sir John Tyrell.

It was 1534, in Vergil's account, before anything appeared in print connecting Tyrell with the murder of the princes, and Sir Thomas More's *History of King Richard III*, giving the detailed story of the murder with the aid of Forest and Dighton, did not appear in any version until 1543, in Grafton's edition of The Chronicle of John Harding. It is constantly stated and assumed that Henry VII or his agents "gave out" the story that before his execution Tyrell had confessed to the murder of the princes, but this could not have been until after 1504, when the Roll of Parliament still records his treason as "on account of his connection with Edmonde de la Pole, Earl (*sic*) of Suffolk." More, writing in 1514 or soon after, follows his elaborate and (where Tyrell is concerned) provably inaccurate account with the unhelpful remark: "Very truth is it and well known that at such time as Sir James Tyrell was in the Tower for treason committed against the most famous prince, King Henry the Seventh, both Dighton and he were examined and confessed the murder in manner above written, but whither the bodies were removed they could nothing tell."[10]

Was the confession ever made? As there is no proof even that Henry ever did give it out, and nothing in writing before More, it has to be dismissed, for the simple reason that had it been made, and especially in writing, it was obviously in Henry's interests to produce it and triumphantly prove not only that the princes were dead but that Richard III was definitely responsible for their murder. He would also surely have discovered, or tried ostentatiously to discover, the bodies. Any priest who heard such a confession verbally would have been bound by ecclesiastical practice to secrecy, as the Rev. Sewell has pointed out. Nothing whatever was ever produced, or has been found, in corroboration of any confession or of Tyrell's involvement in the murder. It can be believed only by those who press the saying that "there's no smoke without fire" to the uttermost it will go: which is not far.

It has been discovered that a John Dighton (in fact several John Dightons) existed at the period and one of them seems to have received rewards from Henry as well as Richard. There was no John Dighton in the Tower with Tyrell and his fellow conspirators: only the man Wellingbourne, one of Tyrell's servants, who escaped execution (but not, it seems, imprisonment) by acting as witness at the trial of the others. A Miles Forest was an attendant on Cecily, Duchess of York, and Richard helped his widow; but as Richard was always helping widows and this one was connected with his mother's household, it really proves nothing at all. At any rate, by the time of Tyrell's execution, he was already, and conveniently, long dead.

On hearing the tradition in the Tyrell family and that a picture of Gipping Hall could be obtained from the Suffolk Record Office at Ipswich, it occurred to me that there might be other papers there on so prominent a Suffolk family, including Tyrell Wills. Anthony Rivers and others made Wills, still extant in some cases, before execution, and it was customary in most cases, not only of course before execution, to add a rider on the hope of God's pardon. Could Tyrell have made such a Will and did he, if so, indicate a need for absolution on the specific case of the princes? A Will which did not include such a plea would rather suggest that no such confession had been made.

Perhaps this occurred to the State also, for no Will seems to exist made soon before death, either at Ipswich or in the Public Record Office. As pointed out to me by Miss M.M. Condon of the Public

Record Office Search Department, "as an attainted traitor, all James Tyrell's possessions, both realty and personalty, became the property of the crown. This meant that he could make bequests, even of his body, only at the king's pleasure". Probate, to judge by other cases, would be unlikely to be sought, and (confirms Miss Condon) "there is no probated will enrolled amongst the records of the Prerogative Court of Canterbury". His wife and family were, nevertheless, allowed to bury him in the church of Austin Friars, London.

The Will I obtained from the Suffolk Record Office, made in 1475 before Tyrell had a son and heir, can surely not be the last one he made, if only for the reason that he needed to amend it to include his heir or other children. His son, Thomas, made two Wills, in 1550 and 1551 as stated (it is the main evidence that he survived to those years: the Rev. Sewell thought the last reference to him was in 1520, when he was made Master of the Horse). There is no reference to Sir James in the last Will; the first Will, made a few years after the first printed publication of the story that his father murdered the princes, is incomplete, and it is the last page — the one that often contained some prayer for the souls of the writer and his family — that is missing, including the signature. This may or may not be significant, but it is certainly worth noting. John Tyrell, Thomas's son, also in 1548 (owing to sickness) and 1573, made wills, but again there is no reference to the soul of a murderous grandfather, perhaps in need of special prayers.

Both men, as I said, did well under the Tudors, and perhaps adjudged it better to let sleeping dogs lie. In 1483 Thomas would still be a child too young to know what his father was doing in another part of the country, and he may have accepted the later stories (it is difficult to imagine his being totally unaware of them). On the other hand he was obviously, as a young man in his twenties, in his father's confidence and company, and was involved with him in the supposed Yorkist "treason" at Guisnes. It would be interesting indeed to know what he really knew, or believed. Certainly it is clear that Tyrell, although he served Henry VII well, also kept his Yorkist loyalties. In the end, he died for one of its heirs. According to family tradition the ones he *is* supposed to have murdered lived, apparently in safety, with their mother at his house, with Richard's permission. It is interesting, if inconclusive, that Tyrell's connection with the princes, although in a different way, is suggested by this tradition, and also perhaps (we cannot of course be sure) by the record of his secret journey to Flanders on a matter of great concern to Richard in 1484. Was the immense sum he received at Calais on the King's behalf in January 1485 in connection with this mysterious errand of the previous year? Was he one of Richard's secret agents, and (assuming the worst) even a double one, acting both for Richard and Henry? If so, there might well be reasons why Henry felt it necessary to get rid of him, especially when his continued friendliness to a Yorkist heir became clear. J.A. Speares suggests the money would probably have been raised to meet Henry's threat of imminent invasion, which seems plausible.

In any case, Tyrell was a man very conspicuously in Richard's trust and an agent in matters of high policy, which could well have included the *protection* of the princes from Henry, the Lancastrian claimant.

It must be added that it is provably untrue that the Chapel rebuilt by Tyrell at Gipping was, as local tradition long maintained, erected in penance and expiation for the murders. Its dedication to St. Nicholas, patron saint of children, helped to encourage this idea. In fact, as Joyce M. Melhuish discovered and pointed out, the rebuilding took place in 1474, when a Will of Robert Cosyn, of Stowmarket, lists: *Item, lego capelle Sci Nichi de Gyppyng ad reficiendum et reparandum XXs.* [11] The intertwined J's and A's carved in lovers' knots well fit the date; like the rebuilt house it was probably meant as a gift for James' intended wife, Anne.

The inscription above the outside door reads: "Pray for Sir Jamys Tirell (tyrell knot) Dame Anne His Wyf". A later inscription inside the chapel reads (after translation):

"A.V.T.A. [Pray for the souls of (or, for the good estate of)] James Tyrell, Knight, Anne his wife, Thomas Tyrell, Esquire, son of the aforesaid James [and] Margaret [his wife] T.A.M."

These are, like Richard III's similar church inscriptions for the souls of himself, his wife Anne and his family, simply in the religious pattern of the time.

Roses en soleil (the Yorkist emblem) make clear Tyrell's allegiance, as Miss Melhuish remarks. It is worth adding, too, that the East window of the Tyrell Chapel at Gipping includes Sir James. This was installed almost certainly after his death and does not suggest his family considered him a murderer. The placing

Gipping Chapel, Suffolk

above the main altar of a church would be scandalous otherwise. Gipping discloses no other secrets. The mystery remains.

But the bones of the princes, it is claimed, were actually discovered two hundred years later, in roughly the place More specified. This matter, too, needs investigation.

NOTES AND REFERENCES

XI — *Tyrell: Murderer or Victim?*

1 Privy Purse Expenses, 8, 37. Dictionary of National Biography.

2 Harl. MSS. 433, fo. 235. Halsted, ii.527.

3 Harl. MSS. 433, fo. 202b. Sewell: *Memories of Sir James Tyrell* (Suffolk Inst. of Archaeology, Vol. V, 1886, pp.125-180).

4 W.A.J. Archbold: Dictionary of Nat. Biography. Sewell, see above.

5 *Letters and Papers of Henry VII* (Gairdner), xxii.i.151.

6 Vitell, A.xvi, 202 et seq.

7 Roll Parl. VI, 545.

8 Pat. 13 April, 19 Hen.VII, p.1, m.5.

9 Pat. 19 April, 22 Hen. VII, p.1, m.4 (or 27)

10 More, pp.88-9.

11 *Sir James Tyrell and his Chapel at Gipping. Ricardian,* Vol. III, No. 50, Sept. 1975. pp.10-14.

XII
The Bones in Westminster Abbey

This evidence did not come to light until 1933, when an urn in Westminster Abbey containing the presumed bones of the Princes was opened in the presence of representatives of the Society of Antiquaries and others.

These bones have a curious history, and indeed the urn when opened, in addition to very incomplete bones of two children, contained three rusty nails and a good deal of fine dust. In spite of legend, the fate and burial ground of the two boys had remained an entire mystery until July 1674, almost two hundred years after their alleged deaths, when workmen rebuilding the stairs to the royal chapel in the White Tower came across a wooden chest, containing bones to which they attached no importance, buried ten feet deep, so it is said, within or below the stairs. They threw the bones into the yard among other debris; but were soon made to recover them when their story and the possible nature of their discovery became known. Obviously some of the bones may have disappeared at this point, or even been disposed of as relics: certain finger bones were rumoured by Sandford to have reached the Ashmolean Museum in Oxford but Professor Wright, one of the examiners of the bones, found no trace of them could be found, or record of them confirmed, when he called at the Museum to check.

It is not true, as has sometimes been claimed by Richard's supporters, that they disappeared for four years, until the actual burial date (1678) in Christopher Wren's urn in Westminster Abbey. There are a number of dated accounts, given with references by John Morgan, an Australian Professor, in a very interesting and lengthy paper on this whole subject now in the possession of the Richard III Society. 1

The first written account was that of John Knight, Principal Surgeon to Charles II.

"A° 1674. In digging down a pair of stone staires leading from the Kings Lodgings to the chappel in the white tower ther were found bones of two striplings in (as it seemed) a wooden chest which upon the presumptions that they were the bones of this king and his brother Rich: D.of York, were by the command of K. Charles the 2nd put into a marble Vrn and deposited amongst the R; Family in H: 7th Chappel in Westminster at my importunity. Jo. Knight."

The second account, published in 1677, gives Knight as its authority but is a little fuller:

" .... in order to the rebuilding of the several Offices in the Tower, and to clear the White Tower from all contiguous buildings, digging down the stairs which led from the King's Lodgings, to the Chappel in the said Tower, about ten foot in the ground were found the Bones of two striplings in (as it seemed) a wooden Chest, which upon the survey were found proportionable to ages of those two Brothers viz. about thirteen and eleven years. The skul of the one being entire, the other broken, as were indeed many of the other Bones, also the Chest, by the violence of the labourers, who .... cast the rubbish and them away together, wherefore they were caused to sift the rubbish, and by that means preserved all the bones. The circumstances ... being ... often discoursed with ... Sir Thomas Chichley, Master of the Ordinance, by whose industry the new Buildings were then in carrying on, and by whom this matter was reported to the King".

A third anonymous account, "possibly also by Knight," adds: "there were pieces of rag and velvet about them ... Being fully recognised to be the bones of those two Princes, they were carefully put aside in a stone coffin or coffer".

The fourth account is by John Gibbon, Bluemantle Herald, dated 1674:

"July 17 Anno 1674 in diggin some foundacons in ye Tower, were discovered ye bodies of Edw 5 and his brother murdered 1483. I my selfe handled ye Bones Especially ye Kings Skull. Ye other wch was lesser was broken in ye digging. Johan Gybbon, Blewmantle."

The most interesting account to many, owing to the identity of the writer, is that of Christopher Wren, Surveyor General to Charles II, undated, which confirms that the bones were found "... about ten feet deep in the ground .... as the workmen were taking away the stairs, which led from the royal Lodgings into the Chapel of the White-tower". (It is quoted from Wren's Parentalia, p.333, and is also given by Tanner, p.8, note 4; but Morgan suggests Wren's account may have been second hand.)

The bones were put in the custody of Chichley for some months until removed to Westminster Abbey under a Warrant issued to Wren to design "a white Marble Coffin for the supposed bodyes of ye two Princes lately found in ye Tower of London and that you cause the same to be intered in Henry ye 7th Chappell in such convenient place as the Deane of Westminster shall appoynt." The Warrant is signed "Arlington", and dated 18 February 1675.

It would seem, therefore, that the bones were not lost and the delay occurred probably in Wren's designing and the manufacture of the marble urn ordered to contain them. Whether any (they were remarkably few) got sold in the meantime as relics, as suggested, and indeed if they ever were the full skeletons of the princes, is another matter.

Before passing on to the examination of the bones by medical experts, it is necessary to make some comment on the position in which they were supposed to have been found. It is certainly at first sight a striking and suggestive fact, not only that the skeletons of two children should be found in Tower of London territory, but that the place in which they were found should conform to a tradition mentioned by Sir Thomas More, that the bodies were hastily buried "at the stair foot, meetly deep in the ground". On the other hand, More states specifically that Richard later suffered rather belated pangs of conscience about this burial of royal children in unconsecrated ground, and had the bodies removed to another place, never revealed, by a priest of Sir Robert Brackenbury (that same "gentle" Brackenbury who had refused to murder them and remained faithful to Richard unto death). This very surprising addition to the narrative was necessary, as already suggested, owing to the obvious fact that, on learning from Dighton the place in which he buried the children, Henry VII must inevitably have ordered a search of the spot. An improbable tradition has also long been extant that the children were buried, not near the White Tower and royal apartments, but in the

"Bloody Tower", which was said to derive its name from this murderous deed. Unfortunately for this story, with which Tower attendants for many years regaled ghoulish-minded visitors, this Tower was in Richard's time, and for nearly a hundred years afterwards, known by the pleasant name of the "Garden Tower", because it was situated by the private gardens used by the Constable of the Tower. The name "Bloody Tower" derived from the fact that religious martyrs in the reigns of Mary and Elizabeth I were incarcerated there prior to execution. The Garden Tower in Richard III's reign was in fact a porter's lodge or gate, and the reference to the princes being seen shooting and playing in the garden of the Tower "sundry times" doubtless referred to this area. They would probably have been allowed to play and take exercise in the Constable's garden wherever they were lodged.

We are faced, then, by the curious fact that the bones were discovered in a similar place to that in which tradition originally buried them but from which it equally firmly removed them; and that Henry VII, after Dighton's and Tyrell's alleged 'confession', either for reasons of his own failed to institute a search, or the search when made failed to reveal what turned up accidentally one hundred and seventy years later. (Buck, as I have earlier noted, claimed the search was made, but unavailingly.)

The position in which the chest containing the bones is alleged to have been found in 1674 is in itself unaccountable; for it would have necessitated the removal of the steps, a long and inevitably noisy operation, and impossible in the course of the short time allowed by tradition to this hasty and supposedly secret dead-of-night burial. Rather desperately, it has been suggested that the bodies were found at the foot of the steps, not ten feet below them, but this is not the impression the contemporary accounts give.

By any standards of research the whole story is involved and strange, and Sir Philip Lindsay has indeed suggested that the bones may have been wall 'foundation sacrifices', which still occurred in civilized Italy for a century or more after the completion of the White Tower in 1078. This explanation — though it must be confessed rather a frantic clutching at a straw by a professed lover of Richard — is possible in date, since the examiner of the bones, Professor William Wright, appears to have admitted to Lindsay that, although he considered he could deduce the ages of the children (a fact which modern medical knowledge emphatically denies), he could not gauge within centuries the actual period in which they lived.

What of the medical deductions from the original examination of the bones themselves?[2] The examination by Professor Wright, who was Dean of London Hospital Medical College and President of the Anatomical Society of Great Britain and Ireland, established in his own mind conclusively that they belonged to children of roughly the ages of the two princes in 1483, and that by no stretch of possibility could the children have been the ages of the princes in August, 1485, when Henry VII came to the throne. This conclusion was arrived at through the ossification development, the condition of the vertebrae, and the odontoid process stage of the axis, which was not joined to the rest of the bone, or atlas — a process normally completed, he claimed, in a child's twelfth year. It was assumed the axis and atlas concerned both belonged to the elder child, mainly because of a continuous stain which discoloured them.

On the other hand, although Professor Wright was himself convinced by the bone condition that the skeletons were those of children who could not be as old as the princes were in August 1485, the heights he deduced from isolated bones were 4ft 9½'' and 4ft 6½'', which corresponded to the average of slightly older children when the last medical records on this were made (1913). It might, however, be taken into consideration that their father, Edward IV, was a conspicuously tall man: some 6ft 4'' tall appeared from his skeleton when his coffin was opened.

A further examination of the teeth was made by Dr. George Northcroft, late President of the Dental Association and British Society of Orthodentists; and dentition is still by far the most reliable of methods for age identification. In his opinion the dentition also supported Professor Wright's view, corresponding to the ages which the princes had reached in 1483. There was a disease of rarefying osteitis in the case of the elder, which could add to the age, but not in Dr. Northcroft's opinion as much as one year to one-and-a-half years. This condition could be consistent with death from natural causes. Septic conditions, such as those suggested in the teeth of both skulls, might themselves retard the ossification process, and I will return to this in connection with more recent analysis. Finally, it must be stated that the sex of even full skeletons could not then, and still cannot, be ascertained before children have reached the age of puberty, and it is therefore quite impossible to judge if these bones were even those of two boys.

The attribution of these bones to the two brothers, Edward V and Richard, Duke of York, could not therefore be certain on any count, even in 1933. The cause of death could not be deduced. It must be remembered that the examiners, although their integrity and specialised knowledge cannot be doubted, started on the exciting premise that these definitely *were* the bones of the two princes, and subconsciously this premise must have coloured their deductions. Both Lawrence Tanner and William Wright in their subsequent account refer to the bones specifically as those of the princes, and Tanner, accepting More's account in every particular as fact, makes assumptions which today must be realised are totally untenable.

We must now study the advances in forensic knowledge in this respect, since this analysis by Wright and Northcroft was produced. Paul Murray Kendall in his *Richard III* (1955) noted some observations by later experts which threw doubts on the 1933 findings, and included those of Dr. Richard Lyne-Pirkis, an anatomical expert of this country. Dr. Lyne-Pirkis subsequently greatly extended his medical investigations and in a talk to the Richard III Society in 1963 made valuable additions to our knowledge of bone analysis.[3] His talk was illustrated with photographs of the bones of the supposed princes which had been published by Tanner and Wright.

He reiterates the indication of osteomyelitis or chronic inflammation of the bone, in the jaw of the elder child: "It's a very slow, chronic disease; in those days there was no means of curing it so it just went on for years until either the body was able to defeat the infection and leave itself with a disorganized and rather odd-looking bone, in this case the jaw, or of course if the defences of the body weren't good enough, it finished you off and you died." He continues a learned study of the cartilege and bone-growth procedure in a non-adult which I do not reprint, except to say that bone-formation was not complete and the cartilege, later to be turned into bone, was naturally missing, as it would not survive. The technical details are not necessary here. I will, however, quote page 5 of his typescript lecture:

"In Professor Wright's day particular attention was directed only to when these centres of ossification first appeared, and the time when the epiphysis joined onto the main shaft. They never bothered about the changes in bones, and it wasn't until a man called Professor Wingate Todd of Western Reserve University in Cleveland, Ohio, got the idea of going about this in a scientific way, that any fresh light was thrown on how to date bones.''

In 1926 Prof. Wingate Todd "began his great pioneer work on how bones develop and grow old ... So he and his associates started examining about a thousand babies from the year age nothing until they were twenty. They chose them from a good cross-section of American society, so that there would not be too much variation in their health and so on, in their size, so he could get a uniform result, and at regular intervals, every three months when they were babies, every six months until they were about thirteen or fourteen, and then every year until they were about eighteen or nineteen, he had them measured as to their height, and to their weight; a note was made of any disease they'd had during the course of the previous period when they'd not been seen, and they were X-rayed; in fact, every joint was X-rayed very, very carefully ... and then, before he could really publish his work, he died in 1938. But his successors carried on his work ...''

One of the things that emerged from this colossal experiment was that "there is a great deal of difference between the apparent age of a bone as seen on the X-ray plate and the real age", and "even in a homogeneous group of children ... selected from the better class parents, there was a big range of variation in the maturity of the bones''.

"Now we have to distinguish between chronological age and skeletal age, or maturity. Chronological age is the actual age that the child is; the skeletal age, or maturity, is the apparent age that the bones show. In other words, if a child develops very fast, its bones will appear to be the bones of a child older than its actual age. If it's slow in developing, then its bones will have the appearance of a younger child than it actually is. And he was able to show that there was a big difference in perfectly normal children as to the actual maturity of the bones or the apparent age of the child. And this is an endeavour to show what I'm saying. These were children who were four years old, these were children who were six years old, these were children who were eight years old. And yet they are all exactly the same. The maturity of them all is that of a six year old boy ... So it at once disposes of any attempt at accurately assessing the age of a skeleton from the appearance of the bones. All you can do is say that this skeleton has an apparent age of eight years, ten years, or twelve years, but it could easily be two years older or two years younger. Well that I think deals a rather strong blow against Professor Wright's coming down so definitely about the ages of the children, or the bones of the children, in the Tower.''

He goes into the matter of diet in the middle ages, and the lack of Vitamins A and D which accelerate bone-growth in our own time: "the times at which ossification centres appear are now only used to really indicate how much Vitamin D the child has been taking in its diet; no attention is paid to them as regards dating the age of the child, they merely indicate its state of health.'' Medieval children, in fact, were well behind modern children in development for this reason. "So if we applied modern standards to these old bones we are going to be out, apart from this big swing of uncertainty, by about a year to a year and a half from a poor diet, and in the case of the elder child, probably by a further year or a year and a half, which means that if we accept Professor Wright's estimation of the apparent age of Edward — we'll call him Edward — at between twelve and thirteen, then he would really be between fourteen and sixteen.'' It was, nevertheless, on the teeth that the Tanner-Wright conclusions most solidly rested, and on this, too, Dr. Lyne-Pirkis suggests, in the light of modern knowledge, the deductions are totally without certain foundation.

On dentition, too, the prolonged and exhaustive American survey came to the conclusion that "it was quite impossible to arrive at the age of a child from the time the teeth erupted, because there were such enormous variations even in normal children. So that shattered at one blow the long held belief that you could date bones from either the time when the teeth came out, or from the time when ossification centres appeared, or when epiphyses like this joined onto the main shaft here in the femur and in the tibia..''

He adds: "There is no method of dating bones, over a matter of several hundreds of years, to a greater accuracy than plus or minus about a hundred years, so quite obviously, if we used radio-carbon dating, which is the one I'm referring to, we are only going to get an answer which would say 1370 to 1570 ...And, incidentally, it would destroy most of the bones, for you need quite a large quantity of bones to get enough radio-carbon out .... it really reduces these bones to the sort of circumstantial evidence that one reads about in thrillers and detective stories. And here are a set of bones which belong to children — there's no argument about that — because of the absence of the epihyses, and the ends of the bone; they belong to children of different ages, and we assume that their age lies roughly between, shall we say, the age of probably about seven or eight and fifteen or sixteen. And that's really as far as anybody could go, even if they examined the bones again today .... because all the work that has been done, and the more work that is being done, increasingly shows this big variation in the normal and the impossibility of being able to pin down the real age of a skeleton.''

He concludes: "So I'm afraid that the conclusion at the end of this lecture is not that we can be more accurate than Professor Wright. We are quite certain that we cannot be anything near as accurate as he thought he was. We cannot date bones nearer than plus or minus two years in a good society, and if we have a mixed society, with some people getting good diets and some people getting poor diets, then it's more likely to be plus or minus three years. So that it would still be possible under those considerations for the Princes to have been alive when Richard III died on Bosworth Field''.

Professor Morgan also, on recent advances in forensic study, dismisses the assumption of "evidence of consanguinity" made by Prof. Wright regarding the teeth, and like other modern experts totally rejects the "extensive stain" on the facial bones as having anything whatever to do with death by suffocation, as the original examiners claimed. With regard to the "chronic disease affecting the lower jaw and teeth" in the elder child, he is inclined to accept this as "possibly valid", but adds "apparent evidence of disease might on the other hand be a result of decomposition". Most authorities agree that this disease, if it existed, could have resulted in death from natural causes.

The most one can say, I think, on all this evidence is that it is significant that bones of children were found in the Tower in the vicinity of what was once the royal apartments; but analysis of them gives absolutely no indication, on modern systems of examination, as to when these children died, what they died of, or what their ages were within a margin of several years. It cannot, therefore, be ascertained if they died in the reign of Richard III or Henry VII, given the assumption that they died between 1483 and 1485; and this assumption on the evidence cannot be made in any case within a period of at least one hundred years in either direction.

It is perhaps necessary to add that apart from Buck's reference (writing about 1619) to bones "lately" found in a turret of the Tower, and rumoured to be those of the princes but possibly those of an ape escaped from the Tower menagerie, it was claimed in an account published by L.A. de Maurier in 1680, from a MS translation from the Delaval papers, that Maurice de Nassau, Prince of Orange (1567-1625), had told of the discovery "in Queen Elizabeth's time" of the "skeletons of King Edward V and the Duke of York, his brother" in a walled-up chamber, which "the prudent Princess, not willing to revive the memory of such an action", ordered to be re-sealed. There is an apparent repetition of the same story on the flyleaf of an edition of More and recorded in 1647, connecting this discovery of children's skeletons on "a Table" (the de Maurier account had indicated a bed) in a walled-up room with the date of imprisonment of Sir Walter Raleigh and Lord Grey of Wilton in the Tower. A plan of the "Little roome" (close to the Guard chamber and passage to the King's Lodgings) was appended. As Grey and Raleigh were first imprisoned in 1603 (Grey's execution was commuted and he stayed there some years longer), this story may be linked with that of Buck. Though learnedly discussed,[4] these stories must probably be relegated to the realms of fantasy, or muddled reporting. In any case their discovery would seem to be in the early part of the reign of James I, not Queen Elizabeth. As John Morgan writes: "What possible motive could there be for suppressing the discovery?" The behaviour of King Charles II in at once feeling they should be given royal burial (even although the Warrant for making of the urn cautiously uses the phrase "supposed bodies of ye two princes") is surely the natural one. And in this case at least there were definitely some human bones to bury. It is nevertheless not uninteresting, as Morgan points out, that the sites indicated in respect of the two tales of skeletons should be fairly close.

In any system of detection, therefore, the matter of the bones has to remain open: nothing can be produced as "proof". But the 1674 discovery at least has, like so much else in this baffling case, to be seriously noted.

XII — *The Bones in Westminster Abbey*

1 *Have the Princes' Bones been found in the Tower?* "An annotated summary of contemporary accounts of bones discovered in the Tower of London and alleged to be those of Edward IV's two sons. It is based on a correspondence in *Notes and Queries* (1889-90) and an article by L.E. Tanner: *Recent Investigations regarding the fate of the Princes in the tower* (1934). The material has been rearranged and augmented from other sources to present a comparative survey of the reported discoveries."

2 *Recent Investigations regarding the Fate of the Princes in the Tower* — Communicated to the Society of Antiquaries by Lawrence E. Tanner, Esq., M.V.O., M.A., F.S.A., and Professor William Wright, F.R.C.S., F.S.A., Oxford, 1935.

3 Dr. Richard Lyne-Pirkis: Typescript of lecture: *Regarding the Bones found in the Tower,* given to Richard III Society, 1963.

4 J. Robinson: *Notes and Queries,* 7 Series. Vol. VIII (1889), p.361. John Morgan: *Have the Princes' Bones been found in the Tower?*

Epilogue

What, I think, emerges from the material I have produced, some of it not known or compared before, is that the mystery of the princes remains a mystery, whatever historians of a firmly traditionalist point of view may say to the contrary. The ascription of the murder of the princes to Richard III is totally without any factual evidence whatever that would be accepted in any Court of Law. Yet it is continually presented as fact, and this reflects no credit whatsoever on the academic processes by which history is presented. If our standards of historical deduction are to be raised, this fact must be accepted, and considered.

To some extent, notwithstanding the medieval historians, it has been accepted by bodies such as the I.L.E.A. (Inner London Education Authority), who have encouraged students of history to listen to a taped trial of Richard III as a part of their campaign to teach a more serious questioning of historical material, and the processes of political propoganda. For this is, without question, the major period of history on which the most debatable of historical methods have been based. It is the outstanding example of *assumption,* largely based on political propaganda, presented as *fact;* although as it happens there are a number of other historical assumptions that have been more revealingly analysed, because they belong to later periods more copiously documented, such as the eighteenth century.

Here historians such as Professor E.P. Thompson (*The Making of the English Working Class*), Professor E.J. Hobsbawm (*The Age of Revolution*) and Professor George Rudé (*Paris and London in the Eighteenth Century*) have revolutionised our ways of thinking about the people of England and France as opposed to the mere history of their kings and military leaders. Dr. Christopher Hill, Master of Balliol College, Oxford, has similarly turned seventeenth century historical thought to a more penetrating analysis of the importance and lasting influence of the Levellers and other subsidiary political groups. The whole controversial subject of the French Revolution has been vigorously illuminated not only by the late J.M. Thompson and George Rudé in this country, but in France itself by the historians Georges Lefebvre and Albert Soboul, the present Professor of the History of the French Revolution at the Sorbonne.

Unfortunately we are, as a whole, still a conservative nation and in the medieval period at least wedded to almost total acceptance of the validity of chronicles which on all the evidence, internal and external, are nothing more than journalism as partisan, or frankly inaccurate, as a great deal of journalism today. Even where, in times close to the Middle Ages, writers such as Thomas More, frankly dramatising their subject, still accept doubts, many later historians have eliminated the doubts on no conclusive evidence at all. The tentacles of the propaganda octopus stretch wide and few people seem born with questioning or sceptical minds. Until medieval historians emerge of the outstanding quality and originality of those I have mentioned on other periods, the Richard III "tradition" will remain without serious sceptical evaluation of the kind I have attempted to give it in this book.

One reason for this has been the unfortunate fact that the Middle Ages are considered to have ended with the reign of Richard III and modern history begun with that of Henry VII. History itself has no such clear-cut dividing lines, but one of the results has been the cutting off of so-called students and historians of medieval history from equal study of the reigns of Richard's supplanter, Henry VII, and his son. It is partly because of this, as I have said, that double standards have arisen about the nature of the "tyranny" of Richard III in comparison with that of his immediate successors. (S.B. Chrimes, writing on Lancastrian and Yorkist policies as well as on the reign of Henry VII, reveals a more balanced picture.) History cannot thus arbitrarily be lopped off in sections, like the branches of a tree. It is a continuous process. And this, too, the modern habit of academic "specialisation" has tended to obscure. The whole process of historical evaluation is overdue for reasoned and less rigid systems of dating. And most of all it needs more profound consideration of the human and psychological factors involved.

For illumination of this, let us only study a passage of James Gairdner in his *History of the Life and Reign of Richard III* (p.250): "Edward's widow, although reluctantly, gave one of her two sons into his keeping, *and even after the murder of both,* was persuaded again to be reconciled *and zealously to befriend him"* (italics mine).

This is what I mean by the "human factor". One occasionally has an odd feeling that male historians are not human beings at all, but have drifted here from outer space, where there are no mothers and no children in our sense of the terms. Perhaps this is why, in the case of Richard III, it is non-academic historians and even amateur lovers of history who have been instrumental in raising doubts on the whole issue. In the end they have beaten down a lot of prejudice about the nature of other aspects of his reign; but there is still much to do.

There is no evidence whatsoever that Richard III, a man conspicuous for his loyalty to his brother Edward in a power-hungry age, murdered that brother's children, totally unnecessarily, to gain a throne from which they were in any case legally barred. Moreover, he never announced their deaths, so what could he have hoped to gain by them? There is every possible form of evidence that for Henry VII to assert his claim to the throne, ballasted by marrying the boys' sister, those princes should be dead or not available. This Richard III undoubtedly knew, and surely Henry Tudor must have known it too. Beyond that I state categorically no historian of real integrity can go, without admitting that anything further is pure speculation.

It is because so many historians have refused to admit their theories are supposition that the whole apparatus of analysis and investigation of historical evidence has been called into question. I suggest the investigation in this book, made on as wide a scale as possible and with careful juxtaposition of evidence and recent material, must and should be seriously considered, even if on some points rejected, by all historians of this period and this subject. There are still possible sources open to investigation, as I have indicated, and they are beyond my present resources. I would like to think of this book as a starting point for new and deeper research into the subject, both in this country and abroad. To the new young historian, who will long survive me, the field is still wide open.

In the meantime, it is the minds of practising politicians that we really need on this subject. For this is basically a political story, concerning the governance of the realm, as well as the forces that drive men in that capacity. The urge to govern well may be at times a destructive as well as a constructive force; it depends on the obstacles in the way. But the obstacles in Richard's case were the children of the brother to whose memory his loyalties seemed always to remain constant, in death as they had in life; and to dispose of them when the state needed a mature guiding hand, by means acceptable by medieval standards of law, was a very different thing to disposing of them yet again, and quite unnecessarily, by their secret deaths, which was certainly no more acceptable then than now.

It is this aspect of the traditional history, given Richard's character as a welder of family unity as well as a lawgiver and human being of moderate and generous tendencies, that has given rise to so many doubts from long before Horace Walpole's time to our own. It is a crime which does not make sense; a crime, in fact, far more necessary to Richard's supplanter and the new dynasty, as is shown by the steady elimination of Yorkist heirs who had remained free and alive under Richard III. Politically, it cannot be explained any more than it can be explained psychologically: which is why people close to the political scene, like Buck and Walpole, have been the most urgent questioners.

We know a good deal more now than either Buck or Walpole, yet the question, I am the first to admit, still remains. Indeed, it has always been there; as some of my contemporary and near-contemporary material shows. If the bones are not conclusive, it is not only because, as now proved by exhaustive modern medical research, the ages could belong to the time of either Richard III or Henry VII; it is because the position in which they were found, deep under the stonework, suggests these could be much older remains, going back possibly to before the White Tower and royal apartments were built. The Romans long had a fortress on or close to this site, and they too had children (sometimes by the native population) and buried them. An archaeologist whose speciality is Roman Britain, only a few days after I finished the previous chapter, pointed out to me that the Romans did not even scruple at times to execute children in a rebellious country, and this might well be a spot where it could happen. Even nearer to, as well as during, Richard's time, the Tower community must have included many children belonging to the several hundred people employed and living there. Epidemics could have raged among this community, and been brought in from outside, like the "sweating sickness" that devastated England and the City of London, killing three mayors and three sheriffs in quick succession during the year 1484. It cannot be totally ruled out that the princes might have succumbed to such a disease, especially as the elder prince, given that the discovered bones are those of the royal children, was suffering from a serious jaw disease which would have weakened his resistance. Richard's dilemma in reporting their deaths would remain, and they would be heaven-sent for Henry.

It is still, however, on the presence of the bones that the supposition of the death of both princes, rather than the escape of at least one of them, mainly rests. Advances in radio-carbon dating since Dr. Lyne-Pirkis' 1963 lecture now indicate this form of examination can be done without so much damage to the few bones in this case available. If these could be dated to belong to the medieval period, within say a hundred years of 1483, we would at least know that they are still viable evidence. If they are considerably older, then that would dispose of the matter.

In any case, even if it could conclusively be proved that the two children whose bones were found died in 1483 or 1484, it still would not confirm Richard's own complicity. One of the most interesting things to emerge, to my mind, from this enquiry is the early date at which the Duke of Buckingham was named as the murderer. The Divisie Chronicle of c.1500, and Commines writing probably even earlier, both give this as an alternative to Richard's having had them killed, and neither suggests that Buckingham did it on Richard's behalf. How was it this story was spread so soon on the continent, and are there any even earlier references? And from what source did the story spring? Once again, one wonders about Morton, his flight from Brecknock before the Buckingham rebellion got under way, and his eventual two-year stay on the continent. What did Buckingham reveal to him?

Assuming his wife and her family had no influence on Buckingham's actions or ambitions, there is another possibly significant but overlooked factor, apart from his access to the

Tower as Constable and his apparent request for custody of Morton. Let the Croyland Third Continuator (p.487) speak:

"In a few days after this, the before-named dukes [Gloucester and Buckingham] escorted the new king to London, there to be received with regal pomp; and, having placed him in the bishop's palace at Saint Paul's, compelled all the lords spiritual and temporal, and the mayor and aldermen of the city of London to take the oath of fealty to the king. This, as being a most encouraging presage of future prosperity, was done by all with the greatest pleasure and delight. A council being now held for several days, a discussion took place in Parliament (*sic*) about removing the king to some place where fewer restrictions should be imposed upon him. Some mentioned the Hospital of Saint John, and some Westminster, *but the duke of Buckingham suggested the Tower of London;* which was at last agreed to by all, even those who had been originally opposed thereto." (Italics mine).

In other words, it was Buckingham, at least according to the Croyland account, who had originally suggested that the young king should be placed in the Tower. Was his mind already working along regal lines, his own claim of inheritance, and the accessibility of the king, Edward V, for murder? If so, and his wife suspected or realised it, there may have been a special reason for her request to Richard to join her sister, the ex-Queen, in sanctuary, after her husband's execution. Had she a tragic revelation or suspicion to convey? It would certainly explain Elizabeth Woodville's new attitude to Richard so soon afterwards. For Richard the dilemma would remain. How many would believe his lack of complicity, if the Duke of Buckingham were accused on suspicion, without proof?

Was Morton himself involved in a scheme to get rid of the princes, either with or without Buckingham? He certainly seemed to be tempting Buckingham to think along the lines of his own claim to the throne, at the point where More so abruptly broke off his narrative. In any case, the rumour of their disappearance or murder suited Henry Tudor's plans, as it would have suited Buckingham's, and this would be so even if they were only concealed by someone supporting those plans.

It is curious that Mancini, the recipient of the rumour, knew Dr Argentine, physician to the elder prince. Argentine was later indubitably and rewardingly attached to the Court of King Henry

VII. Can it be totally ruled out that Argentine was an agent of Henry Tudor already, and used means of his own to hasten the death of at least the elder prince, whom he alone claimed was expecting his death at the hands of his uncle? Argentine as a doctor would have known if death from natural causes was near, in any case, and could have realised the help to Henry of suggesting it was due to a more sinister cause. We come back again to the apparent assumption, everywhere, that Edward V, if not the younger boy, was dead.

It is also strange that it is only in Holland and France, Morton and Cato territory, that these murders are so persistently recorded. Why did not Richard's visitor from *Germany,* Nicolas Von Poppelau, a man of considerable political standing and writing at about the same time, after Richard's death, even seem aware of the rumour, let alone record the fact?

It is from other sources that we must expect our only possibility of genuine elucidation. It is very difficult to believe that further research to discover letters and historical documents, here and abroad, will not one day provide a key. It is in the hands of the large body of young historians now trained by our proliferating universities. One hopes some of them at least will recognise the challenge, and meet it with all the resources of grants now available to them.

The enquiring minds among human beings are always there, whatever the generation. It is the questioners who have built and sometimes reformed our society, and from history we can always learn lessons.

Bibliography of Principal Sources Used

Contemporary and Tudor

André (or Andreas), Bernard: *Life of Henry VII* (Cotton MSS, Dom. A. xviii). (Poet Laureate under Henry and tutor to Prince Arthur. History begun c.1505)

Calendar of Close Rolls (Henry VI, Edward IV, Edward V, Richard III)

Calendar of Patent Rolls (Henry VI, Edward IV, Edward V, Richard III)

Calendar of State Papers & MSS, Milan.

Calendar of State Papers & MSS relating to English Affairs, Venice.

Carmeliano, Pietro: Poems (BL Royal MS 12A xxix; BL Add. MS.33736; Bodleian Library MS, Laud 501.)

Chronicle of Calais (ed. J.G. Nicholas, Camden Society, 1846)

Chronicles of London (ed. Kingsford, 1905. Facsimile ed. Alan Sutton, 1977)

Commines, Philip de: *Memoirs* (2 vols. ed. Andrew R. Scoble, 1855)

Cotton MSS (British Library)

Croyland Chronicle (Third and Fourth Continuator: Ingulph's History of the Abbey of Croyland, trans. & ed. Henry T. Riley, 1854)

Divisie Chronicle (Holland), c.1500.

Drake: *Eboracum* or *History and Antiquities of York*.

England Under the Yorkists, 1460-1485. (Contemporary documents, ed. Isobel D. Thornley, M.A. Preface by A.F. Pollard, 1921.)

Excerpta Historica (collection made 1831)

Fabyan, Robert: *The New Chronicles of England and France* (A City of London Alderman and Lancastrian, writing in the times of Henry VII, but apparently present in London during reign of Richard III)

Great Chronicle of London (c.1498)

Fortescue, John: *Commendation of the Laws of England.* Harl. MSS, 433, 293 (British Library)

Historie of the Arrivall of Edward IV (also known as the Fleetwood Chronicle) (Camden Society, 1838)

Leland, J: *Collectanea* (ed. Hearne, 1770)

Letters and Papers of Richard III and Henry VII (RS — Harl. MS. 433, f.1596)

Mancini, Dominic: *The Usurpation of Richard III* (ed., trans. and Introduction by C.A.J. Armstrong, 2nd ed., 1969)

More, Thomas: *The History of King Richard III* and Selections from the English and Latin Poems (ed. Richard S. Sylvester, 1976)

Municipal Records of the City of York in the XVth Century (ed. Robert Davies)

Paston Letters, The, 1422-1509.

Plumpton Correspondence, The (Camden Society, 1839)

Privy Purse Expenses of Elizabeth of York (ed. Sir Harris Nicolas, 1830)

Rotuli Parliamentorum, Vol. VI (Rolls of Parliament)

Rous, John ("the Monk of Warwick"):*Historia de Regibus Anglie* (Cotton MSS) and the Rous Roll.

Rymer, T. Add. MSS. 4616.

Rymer, T. *Foedera*

Stonor Letters, The

Stow: *The Survey of London. Annals.* (Stow was born 1525)

Vergil, Polydore: *Historia Anglica* (Camden Society, 1844) (Vergil came to London in 1502 and worked under the patronage of Henry VIII as his official historian)

Warkworth Chronicle (Camden Society, 1839)

Wyrcester, William   (b.1415, d.1490): *Annals.*

Secondary — Printed Books

Buck, Sir George: *The History of the Life and Reigne of Richard III* (Published with alterations by his great-nephew 1647. Buck died 1622. Facsimile ed. with Introduction by A.R. Myers, E.P. Publishing Ltd., 1973)

Campbell, Lord: *Lives of the Lord Chancellors*

Chambers, R.W.: *Thomas More* (1935: Paperback ed. Cape, 1976)

Chastelain, Jean-Didier: *L'Imposture de Perkin Warbeck*
(Brussels, 1952)

Cheetham, Anthony: *The Life and Times of Richard III* (illustrated
biography. Introduction by Antonia Fraser, 1972)

Chrimes, S.B.: *Henry VII* (1972)

Chrimes, S.B.: *Lancastrians, Yorkists, and Henry VII* (1967)

Clive, Mary: *This Sun of York* (1973)

Cooper: *Annals of Cambridge*

Edmondson: *Constables of England*

Ellis: *Original Letters* (Harl. MS.433)

Gairdner, James: *History of the Life and Reign of Richard the
Third,* including *The Story of Perkin Warbeck* (3rd ed.1898)

Gutch: *History of Oxford* (1792)

Habington, William: *Edward IV* (1640)

Halsted, Caroline A.: *Richard III* (1844, 2 vols. Facsimile ed. Alan
Sutton, 1977)

Hanham, Alison: *Richard III and his early historians, 1483-1535*
(1975)

Harvey, John: *The Plantagenets* (1948)

Hume, David: *History of England,* Vol. III (Notes K - O)

Jenkins: *History of Exeter*

Kendall, Paul Murray: *Richard III* (1955)

Kingsford, C.L. *English Historical Literature in the Fifteenth
Century* (1913)

Lamb, V.B.: *The Betrayal of Richard III* (1959)

Lindsay, Philip: *King Richard III* (1933)

Lingard, John: *History of England,* Vol. IV (1854)

MacGibbon, David: *Elizabeth Woodville* (1938)

Markham, C.R. *Richard III: His Life and Character* (1906)

Ross, Charles: *Edward IV* (1974)

Sandford: *Genealogical History*

Scofield, Cora L.: *Life and Reign of Edward IV* (2 vols. 1923)

Surtees, Robert: *History of Durham*

Tudor-Craig, Pamela: *Richard III* (Catalogue of National
Portrait Gallery Exhibition, 27 June - 7 October 1973)

Turner, Sharon: *History of England during the Middle Ages*
(1825)

Walpole: Horace: *Complete Works,* Vol. 5, including *Supplement to the Historic Doubts;A Reply to the Observations of the Rev. Dr. Milles on the Wardrobe Accounts of 1483, etc.;* and *Remarks of the Rev. Mr. Masters on the Historic Doubts.*

Walpole, Horace: *Historic Doubts on the Life and Reign of Richard III* (1768. Facsimile ed. E.P. Publishing Ltd., 1974)

Woodhouse, R.I.: *The Life of John Morton* (1895)

Secondary — Papers, Lectures, Articles and Booklets

Archbold, W.A.J.: *Sir William Stanley and Perkin Warbeck* (Eng. Hist. Review XIV, 1899)

Archbold, W.A.J.: Entry on James Tyrell in *Dictionary of National Biography*

Bindoff, S.T. Lecture on John Howard, Duke of Norfolk, as murderer of the princes. National Portrait Gallery. Also Report, Folger Library, Vol. 10, No. 1, 22 April 1961.

Budden, John: *Biographical Sketch of Cardinal Morton* (from a MS c.1610). Ed.Prof. Buckman, GFS, FLS. Proceedings of the Dorset and Natural History and Antiquarian Field Club, Vol. III, 1879.

Desiderata Curiosa, Lib. VII, 1735. Number VIII. Thos. Brett, LL.D, to William Warren, LL.D: containing an account of Richard Plantaganet

Hammond, P.W. *Edward of Middleham, Prince of Wales* (Glos. Group Publications, 2nd ed. 1973)

Hammond, P.W., Shearring, H.G., and Wheeler G.: *Battle of Tewkesbury,* 4 May 1471 (pub. by Tewkesbury Festival 1971 Committee)

Hanbury, H.C. *The Legislation of Richard III.* American Journal of Legal History, Vol. 6, 1962.

Hastie, Tom (I.L.E.A. History Teachers Centre): *History — A Preparation for Life?* Lecture given to National Museum of Labour History and South Place Ethical Society. *The Ethical Record,* Vol 83, No. 4, April 1978.

Kelly, H.A. *Canonical Implications of Richard III's Plan to Marry his Niece* (Traditio xxiii, 1967)

Kincaid, Arthur Noel: *The Dramatic Structure of Sir Thomas More's "History of King Richard III"* (Studies in English Literature, 1500-1900, Vol. 12, 1972. British Library, Boston Spa, Wetherby).

Kirke, Henry: *Sir Henry Vernon of Haddon*. Derbyshire Archaeological and Nat. Hist. Society, Vol. 41, 1919.

Lee, Sidney: Entry on Thomas More in *Dictionary of National Biography*

Lyne-Pirkis, Dr. Richard: *Regarding the Bones Found in the Tower* (unpub. lecture given to the Richard III Society, 1963)

Masters, Robert: *Some Remarks on Mr Walpole's "Historic Doubts on the Life and Reign of Richard III"* (read at Society of Antiquaries, Jan. 7 and 14 1771: *Archaeologia* Vol. 2 1771)

Milles, Rev. Doctor: *Observations on the Wardrobe Account for the year 1483* (read at Society of Antiquaries, 8 March 1770: *Archaeologia* Vol. I, 1770)

Morgan, John: *Have the Princes' Bones been found in the Tower?* "An annotated summary of contemporary accounts of bones discovered in the Tower of London and alleged to be those of Edward IV's two sons". Lecture given to Australian branch of Richard III Society.

Myers, A.R.: *The Character of Richard III. History Today* Vol. 4, No. 8, August 1954. Also: Correspondence on this article and subject (Audrey Williamson and Isolde Wigram) No. 10, October 1954

Pollard, A.F.: *The Making of Sir Thomas More's Richard III.* (From "Historical Essays in Honour of James Tait", ed. J.G. Edwards, V.H. Galbraith and E.F. Jacob, 1933)

Pollard, A.J.: *The tyranny of Richard III* (Journal of Medieval History 3, 1977)

Pugh, T.B.: *The Marcher Lords of Glamorgan and Morgannwg,* 1317-1485 (Glam. County History, Vol. III, The Middle Ages, ed. Pugh, Cardiff, 1971)

Ricardian, The. Journal of the Richard III Society. Quarterly, December 1972 to March 1978. (Individual contributions are listed in my Notes and References, at the end of each chapter)

Roth, Cecil: *Sir Edward Brampton, alias Duarte Brandão, Governor of Guernsey,* 1482-1485 (*La Société Guernesiaise:* Report and Transactions for the year 1956. Vol. XVI, Part II.)

Sewell, Rev. W.H.: *Memoirs of Sir James Tyrell* (Proceedings of the Suffolk Institute of Archaeology, Vol. V, 1886)

Tanner, Lawrence E. and Prof. William Wright: *Recent Investigations regarding the Fate of the Princes in the Tower* (Society of Antiquaries, Oxford, 1935: from *Archaeologia,* Vol. LXXXIV)

Williamson, Audrey: *The Mystery of the Princes* (Sunday Times Magazine, 11 March 1973)

Wills of Sir James Tyrell, 31 May 1475 (HA79:T276/3): Sir Thomas Tyrell, 17 October 1550 (incomplete) and 12 June 1551 (HA79: T276/12 and 16): and Sir John Tyrell, 28 July 1548 "in his sickness" and 20 June 1573 (HA79: T276/9 and 21). (Suffolk Record Office, Ipswich Branch)

Index

DATE DUE		
NOV 2 1 1996		